Playhouse and Cosmos

Playhouse and Cosmos

Shakespearean Theater as Metaphor

Kent T. van den Berg

Newark: University of Delaware Press
London and Toronto: Associated University Presses

Associated University Presses
440 Forsgate Drive
Cranbury, NJ 08512

Associated University Presses
25 Sicilian Avenue
London WC1A 2QH, England

Associated University Presses
2133 Royal Windsor Drive
Unit 1
Mississauga, Ontario
Canada L5J 1K5

Library of Congress Cataloging in Publication Data

van den Berg, Kent.
  Playhouse and cosmos.

  Bibliography: p.
  Includes index.
  1. Shakespeare, William, 1564–1616—Knowledge—
Performing arts.   2. Theater in literature.   I. Title.
PR3034.V36   1984   822.3'3   82-49308
ISBN 0-87413-244-4

Printed in the United States of America

For my Mother and Father
and for Sara and David

Contents

Acknowledgments

My first efforts to develop the argument presented here were inspired and assisted by Maynard Mack and Harry Berger, Jr., when I was their student in undergraduate and graduate courses at Yale University. Professor Mack supervised my 1970 doctoral dissertation on Shakespearean theater and has encouraged my efforts ever since. To Professors Berger and Mack and to my colleagues and students for assisting and sharing my explorations of Shakespearean drama over the past twenty years I am deeply grateful.

I was fortunate to have the opportunity of presenting preliminary sketches of this book at the annual conventions of professional associations and at the Folger Shakespeare Library. I owe much to my hosts and to my audiences. The papers read were: *Edward III* and *Henry V*," at the Northeast Modern Language Association Annual Convention, Boston, March 1973; "The Elizabethan Theater as Metaphor," at the Shakespeare Association of America, Annual Meeting, Pasadena, March 1974; "The Poetics of Theatrical Space," Conference on Language and Style, at the City University of New York Graduate Center, New York, April 1977; "Playhouse and Cosmos," at The Folger Shakespeare Library, Washington, D.C., August 1977; "Toward a Theory of Shakespearean Representation," at the Shakespeare Association of America, Annual Meeting, Boston, April 1980.

A version of chapter 4 appeared in *PMLA,* vol. 90 (1975), pages 885–93; I wish to thank the Modern Language Association of America for permission to reprint. The illustrations are reproduced courtesy of the Beinecke Rare Book and Manuscript Library, Yale University and the Newberry Library. I am grateful to the editorial board of the University of Delaware Press, to its anonymous reader, and to the staff of Associated University Presses for their assistance and forbearance.

Portions of this work were supported by a Regents Fellowship from the University of California, and by research grants from The Ohio

State University. To the staff of the Huntington Library I owe all that a scholar could wish and more: an unsurpassed renaissance library; the best garden in the world; hospitality, encouragement, and friendship. The book was completed at Ohio State where I taught in the Division of Comparative Studies in the Humanities. The challenges of interdisciplinary teaching were a valuable stimulus. I thank Robert C. Jones and Rolf Soellner for reading the manuscript, and especially Tom Woodson, Richard Bjornson, Lowanne Jones, Sara van den Berg, and Gisela Vitt, my colleagues in Comparative Studies, for the intellectual and moral support I needed to write it.

To Sara I am grateful for all manner of things. She has lightened my prose when it was ponderous and my thoughts when they were obscure. She made me believe (when no one else could) that this project was worth completing, and that I could do it. The book is somewhat less wooden for her efforts—and for her sake.

Seattle
June 11, 1984

Introduction

Shakespeare used his theater not only as a vehicle for dramatic poetry, but also as a metaphor of reality. His text abounds in rhetorical variations of the commonplace that "all the world's a stage" and "life's but . . . a poor player";[1] what is more, his characters often become actors or spectators, staging plays within the play, so that relationships of life and theater are embedded in the dramatic action itself.[2] In *As You Like It,* for example, Rosalind is "a busy actor" long before she calls herself one (III.iv.54); her verbal metaphor merely points to an analogy more concretely established in her disguise as Ganymede. In disguise, she becomes her own actor and dramatizes herself for Orlando, just as the actor plays Rosalind (playing Rosalind) for the audience. While Rosalind's disguise gives self-conscious emphasis to theatrical artifice, it also functions as a metaphor of her response to love, disclosing in the outward form of theatrical counterfeiting the inner reality of her character. Role-playing reveals in Rosalind a mixture of evasiveness and self-display, and in Orlando a mixture of self-absorption and self-deception, that motivate the drama of courtship. The game of love helps Rosalind and Orlando to recognize, play out, and overcome these obstacles to a relationship, so that for them, as for the spectators, theatrical artifice is a means to truth.

This book offers a comprehensive and systematic description of Shakespearean theater as metaphor by examining the social, intellectual, and architectural contexts within which Shakespeare's idea of the theater took shape, and by distinguishing the different ways in which he related play and reality. The theory of Shakespearean theater as metaphor offered here will bring together topics that have been separately treated in other studies: (1) Shakespeare's theatrical metaphors as instances of a traditional *topos,* as indications of his concept of drama and his world view, and as a means of influencing the audience's response; (2) performance as an extended, nonverbal

11

metaphor that concretely embodies the idea of life as theater; (3) metaphor (in this extended sense) as a process of representation, a dynamic interrelating of play and reality that is objectified in different ways by dramatic structure; (4) the metaphoric process as a model of the process of individuation by which the self is constituted in its relation to the world.

The value of my theory resides in its relation to the last and most general of these topics: the nature of artistic representation as a model of our own being. Whatever its ostensible object of representation, the mimetic work of art ultimately objectifies human nature. The human significance of art was recognized in Renaissance theory, where it emerges as a corollary to the humanist and neoplatonic confidence in our ability to master fate and transform our nature "with freedom of choice and with honor, as though the maker and molder" of ourselves, as Pico della Mirandola says in his famous *Oration on Human Dignity*.[3] The artist's godlike power of creation seemed to offer an ideal model of our freedom to shape the inner world of our own being. In his *Apologie for Poetrie*, Philip Sidney proposes that God made man in "his own likenes" as a maker of worlds, and that man exhibits this likeness most of all in poetry, "when with the force of a diuine breath he bringeth things forth far surpassing [Nature's] dooings."[4] Sidney's idealism finds its natural contrary in the fear that the creative power displayed through the mimetic impulse makes human nature unstable and reduces an apparently meaningful cosmos to mere raw material for the human will. Our plenty makes us poor. Nature's world seems "brasen" because the poet's "golden" world is so much better. Human nature, since Adam's fall, is likewise sundered into golden and brazen worlds: "our erected wit maketh vs know what perfection is, and yet our infected will keepeth vs from reaching vnto it."[5] Poetry prompts us to reach for perfection by emulating its ideal images of virtuous action, but this mimetic desire has its dark contraries in the global ambitions of a Tamburlaine or the envious emulation of a Richard Crookback. Shakespeare, in particular, dramatized the mimetic impulse through the whole range of human nature, from erected wit to infected will. Yet we cannot hope to understand Shakespearean mimesis merely by seeking analogies of it in the role-playing or play-making activities of the characters, however illuminating such analogies may be. We must begin with at least a rudimentary theory of mimesis grounded in the actual conditions of representation in the Elizabethan playhouse.

A mimetic work's internal coherence as an artifact and its relation to the reality it "imitates" embody our problematic *presence* to ourselves and to others. Of the many modern approaches to this topic, the one most immediately relevant to literary interpretation seeks the dimensions of human presence in the duality of language as spoken and written discourse. Oral communication is a social act that confirms our need and capacity to know other minds and (more generally) our openness to reality beyond the self. While speaking and listening presuppose our presence to each other, reading and writing suspend presence and thrust us back into ourselves. It is a commonplace among anthropologists that literacy weakens the cohesiveness of the preliterate tribal communities and fosters individualism. At the personal level, the acquisition of literacy destroys the unity of naive experience, separating the individual from the community and forcing him to distinguish (in himself and in others) the inner self from the outward character. As Walter Ong puts it: "With writing, the earlier [oral] noetic state undergoes a kind of cleavage, separating the knower from the external universe and then from himself . . . splitting up the original unity of consciousness and in this sense alienating man from himself and his original lifeworld."[6] To put this in a more directly Hegelian way, through literacy we leave the path of mere natural unreflective being and sunder ourselves apart through the process of self-realization. But Hegel adds that "this position of severed life has in its turn to be suppressed"; moreover, "the hand that inflicts the wound . . . [must] heal it."[7] The cleavage of naive experience by writing and especially by print engenders the impulse to master and possess the world as the object of thought, manipulation, and control; literacy inspires the knowledge that is power. Walter Ong proposes that printing, by fixing the spontaneous temporal flow of oral discourse into regularized, consistent, and reproducible spatial forms, offers a symbol and an effective instrument of order that allows creative responses to the social and psychological complexities caused by literacy.[8] This spatial ordering—with the hierarchies, logics, and technologies that follow from it—is one way in which literacy heals the wound it makes.

Literary—and especially dramatic—mimesis is another way of coming to terms with the consequences of literacy. By representing reality, a literary work both confirms and compensates for the suspension of presence inherent in literacy. Literature's representation of the world for the mind's eye is almost always attended by its recreation of speech for the mind's ear. As Philip Sidney said, poetry is "a speaking picture."[9] The capacity of writing to render speech may be the model and instigation of its capacity to imitate reality. For the notion of reality derives in large part from the experience of our presence to another person, and that experience is most vivid in the activity of speaking and listening. A literary work directly embodies the relation of speech to presence when it conveys and mediates its image of reality through fictive storytellers, dialogue, or narrative patterns derived from oral communication. This is not to say that literature must presuppose the priority of speech to writing and commit itself to a "metaphysics of presence"; it may instead suggest that our presence to the world, no less than its literary image, is a subjective fiction.

The ambivalent coexistence of oral and written modes of discourse in literature and drama, and the relation of this ambivalence to our own being as presence, are implicit in the topics and terminology of criticism. The capacity of a work to imitate nature, to disclose a reality beyond itself, to instruct, edify, motivate, and civilize its auditors— these are the familiar topics of traditional mimetic and rhetorical criticism, and they reflect a tacit understanding of literature as speech. The autonomy of a work, its internal coherence, its power to reconcile divergent themes and elements in the *discordia concors* of aesthetic harmony, its integrity as an artifact, its reflexive concern with its own being as art—these are the familiar topics of formalist or intrinsic criticism, and they reflect the independence, the inwardness, "the self-sufficing power of Solitude" that literature confers upon the mind during the act of writing, reading, and interpreting.[10]

These different perspectives characterize two approaches to Shakespearean drama that occupy opposite ends of a critical spectrum: "theatrical" criticism, which treats plays as performances, and "metadramatic" criticism, which treats them as reflexive examinations of their own nature as dramatic art.

At its polemical extreme, theatrical criticism holds that Shakespeare's plays are mere scripts for performance, that they exist and can be properly apprehended only in the theater, and that the private, subjective, and purely imaginative experience of the reader is irrelevant and misleading.[11] However useful as a corrective, this position denies the most obvious and most important fact about Shakespeare: the unsurpassed *literary* excellence of his "scripts." While Shakespeare never prepared any of his dramatic texts for readers, his earliest critics (including his fellow actors, Heminge and Condell) praised his work as literature: "Read him, therefore; and againe, and againe."[12] Reading Shakespeare is not only immensely satisfying in itself, but also illuminates aspects of the text that ought to be important in performance. Elizabethan performance, especially as Shakespeare used it, was an intensely literary experience. Dramatic speech gained from writing a preternatural capacity to articulate thoughts

and feelings; Shakespearean techniques of scene setting and impersonation embodied dimensions of inwardness that distinguish the literary from the oral frame of mind; the playhouse itself defined the
place of performance as a subjective world, corresponding to the
Renaissance concept of the poem as a second nature created in the
mind. This concept, superimposed on the traditional rhetorical
understanding of poetry as a kind of oratory ("a speaking picture"),
reflects a new view of poetry derived from reading and writing: a view
of the poem as a thing or place, an enclosure or interior containing
fictive experiences, a theater of the mind. One purpose of this book is
to reaffirm, even within the context of "theatrical" criticism, the literary nature and value of Shakespearean drama.

Metacriticism stands at the opposite extreme from theatrical criticism. Even when the metaplay is considered as a text for performance, it is perceived as a closed system that converts its relations to
actors and audience, as well as to its ostensible subjects and themes,
into aspects of its reflexive relation to itself. The metacritic typically
emphasizes the moments of scepticism, iconoclasm, or misunder-
standing in a play's action, as if to suggest that the play itself is metadramatic by default: it refers to itself because it cannot refer to
anything else. Richard Fly, for example, proposes that *Troilus and
Cressida* is "the work of a dramatist no longer in serene control of his
craft and, indeed, perilously close to capitulating before a medium
that appears to have grown hostile and intransigent to his creative
efforts."[13] He concludes that this and other "troublesome plays" have
as their metadramatic subject "the artist's inability to create a meaningful order out of hostile and intractable materials."[14] The assumption underlying this and most other metacritical efforts is stated by
Howard Felperin when he calls for "a philosophical study of Renaissance drama" based on "the knowledge that 'reality' by the semiotic
nature of language, the medium of theater, is always unavailable."
The plays themselves metadramatically enact the process of dis-
covering this critical assumption: "Surely it is the search for this missing referent [viz. "reality"] that moves the dramatists of the
Renaissance, and their characters, to mount play within play within
play in the desperate hope of finding it and leaves us and them with
the sad knowledge that it remains unfound."[15] This assumption is
held by most critics who discuss the relationship of play and reality.[16]

The assumption is false. The value of Shakespearean drama consists largely in its ability to accommodate and then transcend radical
scepticism and metadramatic self-consciousness, in order to restore a
more stable sense of reality beyond self and theater. Shakespearean

drama preserves the sense of presence by differentiating subjective and objective realities, and allowing each to retain its separate and independent character in and through the other. In chapter 4, I shall have more to say about metacriticism; my readings of *As You Like It*, *Henry V*, and *Macbeth* will show in detail three different ways that Shakespeare places moments of metadramatic self-consciousness in a larger structure of mimetic reference. But the basic question of "reality" as the referent of "play" must be dealt with here.

The distinction between play and reality seems, at first, self-evident. Johan Huizinga states flatly that "play is not 'ordinary' or 'real' life. It is rather a stepping out of 'real' life into a temporary sphere of activity with a disposition all of its own."[17] But from another point of view, "play" and "reality" appear to be concepts abstracted from and then imposed on experience as a whole. Jacques Ehrmann, in his critique of Huizinga, argues that "play cannot be defined by isolating it on the basis of its relationship to an *a priori* reality and culture; to define play is *at the same time* and *in the same movement* to define reality and to define culture. . . . For—we need not insist on it—there is no 'reality' (ordinary or extraordinary!) outside of or prior to the manifestations of the culture that expresses it." Ehrmann concludes from this that "play, reality, culture are synonymous and interchangeable."[18]

Even if there is no a priori distinction between play and reality, such a distinction can be made as one way of organizing experience within play itself. Play and reality are not positive but dialectical terms: they are defined by their relation to each other. A concept or mode of play will both reflect and influence a correlative concept of reality. The distinction between these terms and their relationship are not a given of Shakespearean drama, but one of its most characteristic achievements. And this achievement metaphorically expresses the experiences and accomplishments of a play's main characters.

The dialectical relationship of play and reality is complicated by what, for convenience, I shall call the principle of replication. When play is distinguished from reality, the distinction is reproduced both within play and within reality. Reality, as that which is distinct from play, must be further distinguished from appearance and illusion; it becomes problematic or inaccessible, lying within or beyond the surface of life. What Jonas Barish calls "antitheatrical prejudice" bears witness to the problematic sense of reality that emerges as a contrary of play. Tertullian, Prynne, and Rousseau condemn the "ontological subversiveness" of play and would abolish the theater in order to restore the unity of life.[19] As Ehrmann insists, "the status of 'ordinary life,' of 'reality,' is . . . thrown in question *in the very movement of thought given over to play.*"[20] It is no accident that the disunity of experience, its sundering into "appearance and reality," is the most pervasive Shakespearean theme, and that this theme is set forth in theatrical terms: disguise, role-playing, mistaken identity. The theme reflects in dramatic fiction the division within the real for which theater itself is, if not the cause, at least a metaphor.

The duality of play and reality is also replicated within play. This replication affects both the ludic and the mimetic dimensions of drama. Most forms of playing (sport as well as drama) are structured by binary oppositions—competing teams, protagonist and antagonist—analogous to the opposition of the play-event as a whole to ordinary life. When the opposition is played out or resolved, the play-event itself terminates, and the participants return to reality. In the third chapter of this book, I shall propose that the major oppositions in Shakespearean drama—for example, that between the "normal world" and the "green world"—are replications of this kind, subsuming within the play its relation to reality beyond the theater. Drama reflects its relation to reality in another, more obvious way: it represents reality. As mimesis, drama creates an image of reality from which as play it is independent. The mimetic and ludic dimensions are complementary. Huizinga points out that mimesis can be a means of affirming the independence of play; by impersonating a character, the actor discards his own identity; the audience, by accepting the imitation, can enter another world.[21] Play, in turn, by its very autonomy, encourages mimesis because it provides a viewpoint that is (or presumes to be) outside the real. From such a viewpoint, reality can be treated as an object of thought, concern, and representation.

Through replication, representation ceases to be a one-to-one correspondence of image and reality and becomes a complex analogy of relationships—an extended metaphor. The actor imitates human reality not because he mimics life directly but because his relation to his role resembles the internal relations that constitute human personality in general; as the actor is to his role, so the inner self is to whatever character it assumes on the stage of the world. Relationship by analogy allows each term greater independence than is possible when the representation is treated as a mere reflection, subordinated to reality. If the stage represents the world, and "all the world's a stage," then the two terms are separate, independent, and equivalent; we respond to each through the other, attending to their interrelationships. As E. H. Gombrich says: "All artistic discoveries are discoveries not of likenesses but of equivalences which enable us to see reality in terms of an image and an image in terms of reality. And this equivalence never rests on the likeness of elements so much as on the identity of responses to certain relationships."[22] The reciprocity of image and reality is a central feature of Shakespearean mimesis. It is evident in the several kinds of thematic and affective "complementarity" or equilibrium toward which the play's action progresses.[23]

In Shakespearean drama, the "play world" and "real world" are both elements of dramatic fiction. These elements are related within a play in a manner that prompts in us a feeling that the play as a whole is likewise related to a reality beyond the theater. The content of that reality and the play's relation to it cannot have been specified by the dramatist, but are established in our own interpretive response. Yet that response is guided by relations of "play" and "reality" that the dramatist does establish inside the theater and within dramatic fiction. This understanding of Shakespearean mimesis preserves Huizinga's commonsense distinction of play and reality while avoiding the naive assertion that reality can be directly known and imitated as it is in itself, and that a work, to be understood as imitation, must be compared to something outside itself that it supposedly resembles. Instead, its correspondence to external reality will be studied in terms of its own substance and structure.

The principle of replication complicates the nature and the analysis of mimesis by multiplying the referents of "play" and "reality." The "play world" in Shakespearean drama is the fictive world of the play as a whole (for example, the world of *Hamlet*); the imaginary, festive, or metamorphic realm within a play—Oberon's moonlit wood, Falstaff's tavern, Lear's stormy heath; and the playhouse, the actual locus of playing, imagination, and metamorphosis. The "real world" is the world of normal life outside the playhouse; the image of life, ordinary or fantastic, that the play presents as real; and the particular setting within the play that the characters accept as real—Theseus' Athens, Bolingbroke's court, the dukedom in Italy to which Prospero returns from the magic isle. A major objective of this book is to show how these different oppositions of "play" and "reality" are distributed and combined in the structure of Shakespearean drama.

A brief summary of my conclusions will be useful as an introduction to the first three chapters of this book. The architecture of Elizabethan theaters, which was most clearly articulated in the large open-air playhouses, distinguishes and relates play and reality in ways that help to define dramatic structure. Play and reality are related at three different levels: (1) the theatrical event as a whole is held apart from reality beyond the playhouse walls; (2) within the playhouse, the immediate activity of playing and pretending shared by actors and spectators is metaphorically related to the play's image of life; (3) within that dramatic image, the characters distinguish and relate worlds presented as "play" and "reality": country and city, tavern and court, holiday and every day, green world and normal world. The first two levels are defined in spatial terms by the architecture of the playhouse; the third is established in the temporal dimension of dramatic action through the pattern of withdrawal and return. These three levels, though distinct, are analogous and reinforce one another, so that the theatrical occasion is deeply implicated in the imaginary world of the play. Thus, for example, the characters' journey from their normal world to the forest in *As You Like It* recapitulates the spectators' journey to the playhouse. The "green world" of the forest provides a stage on which Rosalind disguises herself and becomes her own actor. The characters' return from the forest to the normal world is only anticipated as the play concludes, but it is virtually acted out by the spectators when they return from the playhouse to their normal world.

Chapters 1 and 2 of this book primarily concern the first two levels, especially the manner in which these are defined by the Elizabethan playhouse. My analysis will emphasize two basic spatial relationships established by playhouse architecture: the relation of the theatrical event as a whole to the world outside, and the relationship inside the playhouse between the stage and the auditorium. The first relationship objectifies the imaginative autonomy of the theatrical event; the second facilitates the metaphoric interplay between theatrical performance and the play's image of reality. These two spatial relationships juxtapose play and reality in tangible ways that lend substance to the metaphoric relations of play and reality established by Shakespeare at the third level in dramatic fiction. These metaphoric relations, described in chapter 3, are temporal as well as spatial; play and reality are distinguished and related through the pattern of withdrawal and return that structures the experience of both characters and spectators. Chapters 4, 5, and 6 examine in detail the different uses of this pattern as a metaphor in *As You Like It, Henry V,* and *Macbeth.* That these three plays represent the major Shakespearean genres has mostly negative value in preventing a theory of Shakespearean theater from reducing itself to a theory of Shakespearean comedy, history, or tragedy. The positive value of these plays inheres in the fact that they present progressively more complex and comprehensive extensions of the theatrical occasion as a metaphor of reality. I have not attempted to compare Shakespeare's use of this metaphor with that of his contemporaries or to trace its development through his career. My more limited subject is sufficiently complex to warrant separate treatment.

This book conforms to the nature of its subject. The first three chapters set the stage for the interpretations that follow and have the same kind of value as an actual stage might have for the plays themselves. This value is both limited and fulfilled by the fact that Shakespearean drama subsumes theatricality as a metaphoric embodiment of its meanings. Because they convert theater to metaphor, the plays are largely independent of the theater itself and can be well understood and thoroughly enjoyed by readers. For the same reason, my analyses of *As You Like It, Henry V,* and *Macbeth* could be read (although they could not have been written) without the preceding account of the Elizabethan theater. But just as the reader benefits from seeing the plays performed or from reading them with Shakespeare's theater in mind, so my account of the theater assists interpretation by disclosing the potential metaphoric values from which Shakespeare produced the infinite variety of his meanings. Briefly, these values are: the autonomy objectified by the playhouse and the theatrical enterprise as a self-sustaining commercial venture; the freedom, actualized in the shared experience of actors and spectators, to withdraw from ordinary life and transform both self and world from within; and the capacity, embodied in the mimetic power of performance, to return from the inner world to the outer and either reconcile their rival claims or preserve personal integrity in the face of their unreconciled opposition. In this book, I hope to show how the Elizabethan theater defined these values and how Shakespeare appropriated them in three of his plays.

Playhouse and Cosmos

1

Playhouse Architecture
and the Poetics of Theatrical Space

The Importance of the Playhouse

For Shakespeare, the world of the play was, first of all, the playhouse that contained the theatrical event. The concept of drama as fiction independent of reality, the idea of the world as a theater, the treatment of performance as a metaphor, and even dramatic structure as a pattern of withdrawal and return have their physical foundation in spatial relations defined by the playhouse. Rudolf Arnheim, in *The Dynamics of Architectural Form,* shows that "the design of a building is the spatial organization of thoughts about its functions. . . . Since all human thoughts must be worked out in the medium of perceptual space, architecture, wittingly or not, presents embodiments of thought when it invents and builds shapes."[1] The architecture of the playhouse objectifies in its basic spatial relationships the metaphoric relations of play and reality that Shakespeare establishes in dramatic fiction. It also embodies a complex world view that juxtaposes different metaphoric perceptions of the cosmos as a theater. It is, finally, an embodiment not only of particular thoughts, but also of thought itself, insofar as thought turns away from the experiential world, recreates its image in the mind, and projects possible (or impossible) outcomes for human existence.

In proposing that the playhouse is an embodiment of thought, I do not assume that its builders followed a sophisticated architectural program, or even that they unified the building by means of a coherent, preestablished design. To the contrary, I shall need to emphasize at a later stage of this argument that the playhouse was a discordant combination of two different structures, joined together for commercial, not aesthetic reasons. Nor does my proposal rest on elaborate conjectures about upper and inner stages, discovery spaces, lofts, and traps.

23

We know very little about the stage furnishings and even less about how they were actually employed in the *mise en scène*. I have therefore taken Alvin Kernan's advice that "it might be enough to accept a general 'type' of theater and then spend our effort on trying to recover its symbolic values."[2] This procedure is justified insofar as the symbolic values inhere in the basic spatial relations that we know something about, rather than in details about which we can only guess.

There is reason to believe that the architectural form with which this book is concerned did not differ greatly from one playhouse to another. None of these structures was designed by an architect; they were all built by carpenters, like James Burbage, Peter Street, or Gilbert Katherens, who knew from workshop traditions, rules of thumb, and available precedents the one right way to build any given structure; for them originality of design was no virtue.[3] (The first playhouse *was* original and innovative, but only because it combined two familiar structures for a novel purpose.) The builder's contract for the Fortune (1600) specifies many important features merely by referring to their counterparts at the Globe, which had just been built from the timbers of the old Theater; the builder's contract for the Hope (1613) makes similar reference to the Swan. The cohesiveness of this tradition is visible in several panoramic maps and views, in which the bankside theaters and gamehouses look virtually identical and are, in their roundness, conspicuously different from all other buildings in the city.[4]

Some degree of uniformity in the design of the stage, its furnishings, and the tiring-house façade was assured not only by the conservative nature of builders' traditions but also by the requirements of the players. Because they could not always perform in their own houses, but had to mount their plays on short notice in other places (most of them indoors), they built in the playhouse the stage that had taken shape in the Tudor hall (itself a standardized structure): a platform erected in front of a partition (the "screen") with two doors and a gallery above.[5] The players could count on finding this basic acting area wherever they performed. In all Elizabethan playing places that we know of, the stage was thrust out into the auditorium, which surrounded it on three sides. As often as this arrangement is referred to in the prologues of plays, the auditorium is spoken of as "round," even when the hall was in fact rectangular.[6] The round or polygonal shape of the outdoor theaters merely made more explicit the spatial relation of actors to audiences in all Elizabethan playing places. This is one indication that the playhouse differed from other Elizabethan theaters in articulating more clearly an architectural form that was common to them all.

The distinction important to this book is not between indoor and outdoor, or temporary and permanent theaters, but between two different kinds of event, both of which might be described as modes of play in the largest sense of the term: (1) social events, like festivals, royal entries and progresses, tournaments, banquets, that are in some way "staged" or that include theatrical performance as one of their elements, and (2) the theatrical event as an occasion in itself, socially, economically, and architecturally independent and self-sustaining. Within the theatrical event, the festive and ceremonial elements of Elizabethan society could be recreated and their expressive functions, their relation to reality, explored. C. L. Barber has shown that Shakespeare's plays "provided a 'theater' where the failures of ceremony could be looked at in a place apart and understood. . . . In making drama out of rituals of state, Shakespeare makes clear their meaning as social and psychological conflict, as history. So too with the rituals of pleasure, of misrule, as against rule; his comedy presents holiday magic as imagination, games as expressive gestures."[7] Shakespearean drama translates "social into artistic form," as Barber says, by reversing the original relation of part to whole: the play dramatizes social activities that contain elements of play, so that both play and reality become parts of the dramatic image itself. G. K. Hunter's comparison of Shakespearean comedy to earlier court comedies by John Lyly further illustrates this development. Lyly refers to his court audience as "real," his plays as "unreal," approaching reality by mirroring in art the virtues of the audience. What for Lyly had been a relationship between the play and its audience becomes for Shakespeare a relationship within the play itself: "If Shakespeare is going to talk about the 'unreality' of his play he must oppose it to a 'reality' which is also presented in the play, as part of *its* world. . . . It follows that the theme of Appearance and Reality involves for Shakespeare, as it need not do for Lyly, the problem of interconnecting his levels of reality, of making his action complete in itself and convincing, though fictional."[8] This achievement required a twofold independence of drama; drama had to be distinct as play from ordinary life and as mimetic fiction from the actual occasion of performance. The importance of playhouse architecture to Elizabethan drama lies in the fact that it defined both of these distinctions—in the same way as but more clearly than other playing places of the time.

The Playhouse as Heterocosm

Just enough work has been done in the phenomenology of architectural form to make it possible to establish the inherent symbolic values of the spaces defined by the playhouse. The playhouse can readily be described in the very general categories of current theory because its function is rudimentary and evident in its form. It had to accommodate only a single event, the performance, that involved all of its inhabitants at the same time, instead of the disparate, independent, and sometimes conflicting activities that most buildings contain. Not only is performance a single event, but it is also, in terms of its spatial requirements, unusually simple: a large number of people enter the structure and assume more or less stationary positions to watch a smaller group perform in the separate space provided; when the performance is over, everyone leaves. Finally, the playhouses were freestanding, self-enclosing structures that were not, and did not need to be, integrated with the environment of neighboring buildings. For these reasons, the playhouse was freer than most structures to conform to shapes that are (apparently) inherent in the nature of architectural interiors as such.

At the most general level of phenomenological description, any building is a bounded, coherent place, to which one withdraws from the surrounding world, usually with a specific purpose in view. The building, itself a "structure," exists to accommodate a more structured activity than would be possible or convenient without it. On this basis, David Burrows considers interior space as "a covering metaphor for ritual, art and games because it suggests a common pattern of withdrawal and restructuring within the field of symbolic action. Most interiors are surrounded by some sort of . . . wall that defines their boundaries. . . . The insider is always more or less aware of what lies outside . . . as an alien, perhaps disorderly or even threatening nonpresence. The content of interiors is in one way or another stylized by comparison with the content of the outside. Its pattern has an overall tendency to gravitate inward and its activities to interconnect."[9] A number of phenomenologists agree that any interior tends to "gravitate inward," and that interiority as such is naturally or ideally *round*. In the words of Karl Jaspers, "every being seems in itself round"[10]—as if shaped by surface tension, like Marvell's drop of dew (a symbol of the soul), which

> Shed from the Bosom of the Morn
> Into the blowing Roses,
> . . . .

> Round in itself incloses:
> And in its little Globes Extent,
> Frames as it can its native Element.[11]

Gaston Bachelard, writing on "the phenomenology of roundness" in *The Poetics of Space,* develops the implications of Jaspers' idea:

> When a thing becomes isolated, it becomes round, assumes a figure of being that is concentrated upon itself. . . . Images of full round-ness help us to collect ourselves, permit us to confer an initial con-stitution on ourselves, and to confirm our being intimately, inside. For when it is experienced from the inside, devoid of all exterior features, being cannot be otherwise than round.[12]

This whole line of thought becomes less impressionistic and more credible in Arnheim's study of architectural form. He compares a building seen from the outside—a solid, that displaces space and ex-pands radially from its center—to an interior, that is a "closed world of its own." "An interior reveals its typical character most clearly when its walls or ceilings, or both, are concavely rounded," he argues, be-cause "concave boundaries define the hollow of the room as the domi-nant volume." He goes on to propose that an interior can represent man, its occupant, "because he constitutes a focal center from which vectors issue radially and fill the empty space with his presence. The hollow volume is perceived as an amplification and extension of the human focus."[13]

Arnheim's generalizations are especially pertinent to the playhouse. It was designed to focus attention on the actor, who, from the center of the "wooden O," filled the auditorium with his voice (which, if the acoustics were effective, was amplified) and with his presence. As John Webster wrote in 1615,

> By a full and significant action of body, [the actor] charmes our attention: sit in a full Theater, and you will thinke you see so many lines drawne from the circumference of so many eares, whiles the *Actor* is the *Center.*[14]

The statements I have quoted from Burrows, Jaspers, Bachelard, and Arnheim imply an analogy between the interior of a building and the internal world of the self. In most buildings, there is little to reinforce such an analogy or make it meaningful; we are more aware of the particular character and function of the building than of its universal or archetypal quality as an interior. But buildings like churches, museums, or theaters are exceptions to this rule, because their particular functions conform more closely to the general significance of the interior "as a covering metaphor for ritual, art, and games" and as a spatial objectification of mind. A theater is an "embodiment of thought" in a more exact sense than other buildings, because it is an architectural model of the interior world we inhabit in thought, fantasy, or dream. While most buildings mediate a relationship with their environment through entrances and windows that have symbolic as well as instrumental value, a theater merely shuts out the external world and focuses attention on the stage, which contains an image of life that acts out possibilities, impulses, or aspirations seldom fully realized, or even clearly envisaged, in actuality. The circular shape of the playhouse emphasizes the subjective, inner-directed quality of any theatrical space; the spectators were seated, or stood, with their backs to the circumference, facing the center of the interior. The self-enclosing shape of the playhouse auditorium embodies the self-sufficiency established in subjective experience when a person exercises the "power of . . . withdrawing himself from the world and taking his stand inside himself."[15]

This admittedly impressionistic phenomenological view of the playhouse brings together, and is in turn substantiated by, more familiar findings of theatrical, intellectual, and literary history. A brief look at this material will further clarify the nature of the playhouse as an autonomous world and as an architectural model of the interior world of subjective experience.

Any building used as a theater puts a physical boundary between the performance and the world outside, but the playhouse establishes this boundary in a striking way that dramatizes the independence of the theatrical event. The large, freestanding, circular auditorium—a cylinder 80 to 100 feet across, nearly 40 feet high, open at the top—emphasizes the playhouse's function as an enclosure that isolates the theatrical event and secures its autonomy.[16] (Isolation was further emphasized by the location of playhouses outside the city limits, so that spectators had to cross the Thames or venture beyond the city walls to attend.) In the playhouse, the professional theater became for the first time a fully self-supporting venture, socially, imaginatively, and economically independent. William Ringler has demonstrated that the construction of the first playhouses, the Theater and Curtain in 1576 and 1577, quickly transformed the profession of playing "from a small private enterprise . . . to a big business."[17] By enclosing the stage, the players could charge admission, commission their own plays, offer a repertoire of regular performances, and thereby develop their art. While they often performed in the provinces, in London inns, at court, and elsewhere, the playhouse provided their chief source of income and the most conspicuous advertisement of their new status and proficiency; it both assisted and symbolized the disengagement of Elizabethan drama from the religious, social, and civic events that had occasioned most medieval and Tudor plays.[18] In his *Apology for Actors* (1612), Thomas Heywood says nothing of performances in "private" indoor theaters or at court; he repeatedly associates the actors with the playhouse and affirms its real importance in his extravagant claims for its "Ancient Dignity" as an English revival of the Roman amphitheater.[19]

The players did not, of course, gain full independence all at once in 1576, despite the commercial success of the first playhouses. Their profession was securely established only at the end of the century, and then only for two companies, only one of which—Shakespeare's—entirely financed and controlled its own theater building.[20] Nevertheless, the playhouse, from the very first, made drama appear to be a bold and controversial innovation, however much it may in fact have owed to medieval and Tudor antecedents. Ringler has demonstrated that the construction of the first playhouses provoked vehement opposition to playing that persisted until the theaters were closed in 1642: "The antistage treatises themselves show unmistakably that the opening of these large public theaters, 'those places . . . whiche are made uppe and builded for such plays and enterludes, as the Theater and Curtaine is'—'the sumptuous Theatre houses, a continuall monument of Londons prodigalitie and folly'—was the cause of the initial attack."[21]

Ironically, the same reputed Roman ancestor of the playhouse that indicated to actors its ancient dignity reminded their enemies of the pagan and diabolical origins of drama decried by the Fathers of the Church. John Stockwood preached in 1578, "I know not how I might with the godly learned especially more discommende the gorgeous Playing place erected in the Fieldes, then to term it, as they please to haue it called, a Theatre, that is, euen after the manner of the old heathnish Theatre at Rome, a shew place of all beastly and filthie matters."[22] Stephen Gosson extended Stockwood's attack by leveling Patristic denunciations of the Roman theater against Elizabethan players: "That Stage Playes are the doctrine and inuention of the Deuill, may bee gathered by *Tertullian*, who noteth verie well that the Deuill foreseeinge the ruine of his kingdome, both inuented these shewes, and inspired men with deuises to set them out the better thereby to enlarge his dominion and pull vs from God."[23] The horrific (and often repeated) description of the playhouse as "Satan's Synagogue" must have added fuel to the hellfire that awaits Faustus at the conclusion of Marlowe's play. It was rumored that the actor of Faustus, Edward Alleyn, decided to retire from the stage after a performance of the play during which a *real* devil had appeared among the counterfeit ones and threatened to fetch off his soul.[24] Faustus's bargain with the devil was one that Gosson felt every actor and spectator made in presuming to step outside of the divinely ordained order and enter the heathenish playhouse.

This sudden and vehement opposition surely emphasized for actors, playwrights, and their audiences that the playhouse had defined drama as an activity boldly new and different in its total separation from ordinary life. In this context of controversy, no dramatist as thoroughly involved in the theatrical enterprise as Shakespeare was could have avoided acute self-consciousness about the moral and philosophical implications of his medium. Nor was the antistage controversy limited to the professional theater, for it prompted a renewed interest in the old Platonic and Patristic debate about the nature and value of artistic representation as such. "That debate," as C. S. Lewis writes, "is simply the difficult process by which Europe became conscious of fiction as an activity distinct from history on the one hand and from lying on the other."[25] While the question properly applies to all modes of fiction, it is most often raised by, and discussed in terms of, dramatic fiction as presented in theaters, because theatrical performance is a physical displacement of reality by make-believe. It is relatively harmless to tell a story about a prince, but quite a different matter to put on royal garb and ask your auditors to pretend that you are a prince. Gosson urged that "in Stage Playes for a boy to put on the attyre, the gesture, the passions of a woman; for a meane person to take upon him the title of a Prince with counterfeit porte and traine, is by outwarde signes to shewe them selues otherwise then they are, and so with in the compasse of a lye, which by *Aristotles* iudgement is naught of it selfe and to be fledde."[26]

Gosson made the mistake of dedicating his first two antitheatrical tracts to Philip Sidney, who was at the time better known as a champion of Protestant piety than of poetry. Ringler surmises that Gosson probably did not learn of his error until the publication of the Spenser-Harvey correspondence in 1582, in which Spenser revealed that Gosson was "for hys labor scorned" by Sidney, "if at leaste it be in the goodnesse of that nature to scorne."[27] Further evidence of Sidney's response can be gathered from his *Apologie for Poetrie* (ca. 1580–83), in which he explains that, having "slipt into the title of a Poet," he was "prouoked to say somthing . . . in the defence of that . . . vocation . . .

which from almost the highest estimation of learning is fallen to be the laughing-stocke of children."[28]

Sidney speaks rather harshly of the popular drama ("not without cause cried out against" [196]) and offers no defense of the common players who had been Gosson's principal targets; nothing they had offered by the early 1580s was worthy of his respect. But Gosson's tracts would have aroused his interest even without their provocative dedications because the theater, as a metaphor, embodied what he most valued in poetry: its affective power and its imaginative independence. Sidney often refers to poems like the *Iliad, Odyssey,* or *Aeneid* not as texts that we read or hear, but as actions that we see performed in the theater of the mind. The poet's ideas of good and evil are embodied in exemplary characters:

> *Tullie* taketh much paynes, and many times not without poeticall helpes, to make vs knowe the force loue of our Countrey hath in vs. Let vs but heare old *Anchises* speaking in the middest of Troyes flames, or see *Vlisses* in the fulnes of all *Calipso's* delights bewayle his absence from barraine and beggerly *Ithaca*. . . . See whether wisdome and temperance in *Vlisses* and *Diomedes*, valure in *Achilles*, friendship in *Nisus* and *Eurialus* euen to an ignoraunt man carry not an apparent shyning. (165)

For Sidney, a poem, as "a speaking picture" (158), has the immediacy and impact of theatrical performance.

To the charge that poets are liars, Sidney replies that the truest poetry is the most feigning, and he refers at once to the theater: "Now, for the Poet, he nothing affirmes, and therefore neuer lyeth. . . . though he recount things not true, yet because hee telleth them not for true, he lyeth not. . . . What childe is there that, comming to a Play, and seeing *Thebes* written in great Letters vpon an olde doore, doth beleeue that it is *Thebes?*" (184, 185). Sidney distinguishes fiction from history and lying by locating it in a second world held apart from real life. The poet, "not inclosed within the narrow warrant of [Nature's] guifts," can range freely "within the Zodiack of his owne wit. . . . Her world is brasen, the Poets only deliuer a golden" (156). As Meyer Abrams says, the distinctively new element in Renaissance poetics was "the replacement of the metaphor of the poem as imitation, 'a mirror of nature,' by that of the poem as heterocosm, 'a second nature,' created by the poet in an act analogous to God's creation of the world.[29] The playhouse offered dramatists, actors, and spectators a heterocosm in a palpable architectural form.

From the *Theatrum Mundi* to the Globe

The definition of poem or play as a heterocosm requires a new attitude toward traditional metaphors that describe the world, or God, in terms of more familiar human attributes, and requires as well a new way of establishing metaphoric reference. In medieval theology, God is compared to a poet and the world to a poem, but always with the reservation that God's creating *ex nihilo* is essentially different from human making: "the creature cannot create," Augustine declares.[30] The medieval analogy moves in one direction only, from man to God, and emphasizes their differences. This asymmetrical mode of reference is also evident in the medieval concepts of poetry as a reflection of reality, as the veil of truth, as ornament or rhetoric—concepts inherited and revised by Renaissance theorists. The Renaissance analogy of God and poet moves in both directions and emphasizes similarities. This is evident in the opening sentences of Puttenham's *Arte of English Poesie* (1589):

> A Poet is as much to say as a maker . . . such as (by way of resemblance and reuerently) we may say of God: who without any trauell to his diuine imagination, made all the world of nought. . . . Euen so the very Poet makes and contriues out of his owne braine, both the verse and matter of his poeme, and not by any foreine copie or example. . . . The premises considered, it giueth to the name and profession [of poet] no smal dignitie and preheminence, aboue all other artificers, Scientificke or Mechanicall.[31]

The new concepts of the poet as creator and the poem as heterocosm emerge together with, and are described by means of, a new metaphoric mode of reference that establishes its two terms as equivalents and invites us to view each in terms of the other—God as poet, poet as God.

All of this has a direct bearing on a familiar but little understood topic: the Elizabethan concept of the playhouse as a "theater of the world." While there is some disagreement among scholars about the precise meaning of the analogy, all assume that its purpose was to define the playhouse as an architectural emblem of the cosmos. But this assumption (to which I shall return in the next chapter) is only half true, and we will not appreciate its full significance until we grasp the other half of the phenomenon: the use of the *theatrum mundi* analogy to define the playhouse as a heterocosm. The distinction I am making here is illustrated by a poem that Thomas Heywood prefixed to his *Apology for Actors*. Heywood begins with a conventional description of the *theatrum mundi:* "The world's a Theater, the earth a Stage, / Which God, and nature doth with Actors fill." But his real purpose is to defend the playhouse, not to describe the cosmos, so he concludes by reversing the terms of the analogy:

> If then the world a Theater present,
> As by the roundnesse it appeares most fit,
> Built with a starre-galleries of hye ascent,
> In which *Iehoue* doth as spectator sit,
>
> . . . .
> He that denyes then Theaters should be,
> He may as well deny a world to me.[32]

When Shakespeare's company named their new playhouse the Globe and gave it the motto *Totus mundus agit histrionem,* they suggested not only that the world is a theater, but also that their theater is a world in itself. For them, as for Heywood, the theatrical metaphor was an expression of professional pride; it gave to the name and profession of player "no smal dignitie and preheminence."

It is likely that the *theatrum mundi* analogy had been associated with the original playhouse, the Theater, and that the name of its successor, the Globe, was chosen to perpetuate this association. A passage in Dekker's *Guls Hornbook* (1609) implies as much in alluding to the dismantling of the Theater and its reconstruction as the Globe:

> How wonderfully is the world altered! and no maruell, for it has lyen sicke almost fiue thousand yeares; So that it is no more like the old *Theater du munde* then old *Paris* garden is like the Kings garden at *Paris.*
>
> What an excellent workeman therefore were he that could cast the Globe of it into a new mould: And not to make it looke like *Mullineux* his Globe with a rownd face sleekt and washt ouer with whites of egges; but to have it in *Plano,* as it was at first, with all the ancient circles, lines, paralels and figures. . . .[33]

Surely Dekker was not the first to describe the old building as a theater of the world; its impressive size and round shape would have suggested the analogy from the beginning. In 1576 the word "theater" was seldom used to name a playing place but appeared often on the title pages of anthologies and compendia, where the word clearly had a cosmic meaning—examples include Theodor Zwinger's *Theatrum vitae humanae* (1565, 1571, 1576, 1586–87, [1596?], 1604), Boaistuau's *Theatrum mundi. The Theater or rule of the world* (ca. 1566, 1574, 1581, etc.), or van der Noodt's *Theatre [of]* . . . *voluptuous Worldlings* (1569).

The best known and most impressive book to use the world-theater concept in its title was an atlas published by Abraham Ortelius in 1570, *Theatrum Orbis Terrarum,* which went through forty-one editions in Shakespeare's lifetime.[34] This book could by itself have suggested the name of the first playhouse. To present a theater of the whole world, an epitome of life, is—more than anything else—the distinguishing feature of Elizabethan drama.[35]

The change in name from Theater to Globe shifts the emphasis within the *theatrum mundi* idea from the world itself to a man-made model or equivalent of the world. Dekker associates Shakespeare's Globe with the terrestrial globe made by Emery Molyneux in 1592. This globe, and a companion celestial globe, were widely admired and much talked of, being twice as large (in area) as Mercator's globes of 1541.[36] Hakluyt gave Molyneux's terrestrial globe prominent advance notice in the preface to his *Principal Navigations, Voyages and Discoveries of the English Nation* (1589), saying that it would display "the newest, secretest, and latest discoueries" made by English explorers, and show the courses followed by the English circumnavigators, Drake and Cavendish.[37] Thomas Hood and Robert Hues published treatises on the Molyneux globes in 1594, and Thomas Blundeville mentioned them in his *Exercises* of the same year.[38] These authors commend the globe as an instrument in navigation, useful for charting courses over very long distances. No doubt the globe had another kind of value—symbolizing and instilling in English sailors the imperial confidence, so important to the later history of Great Britain, that the entire world could be brought under the dominion of human will.

The title page of Mercator's great atlas of 1595 presents the globe as the product and symbol of newly realized human powers. It pictures Atlas as a cosmographer who has set down the earth at his feet in order to inscribe its features on a blank globe, making (as Donne would say) "On a round ball / . . . That, which was nothing, *All.*"[39] The full title captions the emblem: *Atlas sive cosmographicae meditationes de fabrica mundi et fabricati fugura* ("Atlas, or the meditations of a cosmographer on the making of the world and the shape in which it was made"). The mediation itself describes the spherical shape of the cosmos not as a symbol of the Creator's perfection or of eternity—which is what we might expect[40]—but as a shape that answers to the mind's desire for total knowledge. Mercator, in effect, appeals to the "phenomenology of roundness":

> This universall Globe, which is rather an object of the secret conceptions of humane understanding, than of the sharp-sightednes of our eyes, in regard of the perfect clearenes, and absolute puritie, is

called by the Grecians κόσμος, which name Pithagoras gave it first, the Latines *Mundus*. Plinie in his second Booke, and the first Chapter of his naturall Historie, saith, it is that, *in the compasse whereof all things are enfoulded*. . . . Now that the forme of the world is round, as a most absolute, and a perfect Globe, the latine name chiefely & the consent of those, who call it so, & decipher it round, prooveth it evidentlie: but also many other naturall reasons, make us beleeve, that it is so: . . . because this figure is most capable, & most simple, & that all the parts fall into themselves, & that it supporteth it selfe, & is comprehended & enclosed in its selfe: having no neede of any tye or joincture, not sensible of beginning or ending in any of the parts thereof. . . .[41]

This same emphasis on the aesthetic or imaginative appeal of the globe—as if its beauty warranted its truth—is even more evident in Robert Hues's treatise on the Molyneux globes:

A Globe is of a figure most proper and apt to express the fashion of the Heavens and earth as being most agreeable to nature, easiest to be understood, and also very beautifull to behold. . . . [It] is of the most convenient forme; and therefore more aptly accomodated for the understanding and fancy (not to speake any of the beauty and gracefulnesse of it), for it representeth the things themselves in proper genuine figures.[42]

A map or diagram of the cosmos refers beyond itself to relationships that (presumably) exist in the actual world; a globe reproduces the world itself in miniature. A globe is thus a different mode of representation, at once more objective ("it representeth the things themselves") and more subjective, being "more aptly accommodated for the understanding and fancy." In both its objective and subjective dimensions the globe exemplifies a confidence in human mastery, a faith in mind over matter, that unites the cartographers and merchant adventurers of the Renaissance with the more abstruse minds of the neoplatonic academies.

The globe epitomizes an important moment in the history of consciousness: the separation of the mind as subject from the world as object.[43] The development of Renaissance cartography and especially the new interest in globe making reflect not only new knowledge but also a new confidence in the human ability to stand outside of the entire macrocosm and comprehend the totality of existence as the reflection of subjective wholeness and self-sufficiency." In this respect, Giovanni Pico della Mirandola's *Oration on Human Dignity* was as important to cartography as the discoveries of Magellan and Copernicus, for, as P. O. Kristeller shows, Pico's man is capable of detaching himself from the world and regarding it as an object: "Man is no longer a definite element in the hierarchical series, not even its privileged center: he is entirely detached from the hierarchy and can move upward and downward according to his free will. Thus the hierarchy is no longer all-inclusive, while man, because of his possession of freedom, seems to be set apart from the order of objective reality."[44] Ernst Cassirer argues that this subjective freedom releases the creative energies and *libido dominandi* that Burckhardt found characteristic of the Renaissance; "For all true creativity implies more than mere action upon the world. It presupposes that the actor distinguish himself from that which is acted upon, i.e. that the subject consciously stands opposed to the object."[45] The globe, as a human artifact, manifests human freedom not only to stand outside the world, but also to regard the microcosm as being equivalent or superior to the macrocosm. This is evident in a familiar passage from Sir Thomas Browne's *Religio Medici*, written about 1636 and published, ironically, in 1642, the year Shakespeare's Globe and the other playhouses were closed for good:

> The world that I regard is my selfe, it is the Microcosme of mine owne frame that I cast mine eye on; for the other, I use it but like my Globe, and turne it round sometimes for my recreation. Men that looke upon my outside, perusing onely my condition, and fortunes, do erre in my altitude; for I am above *Atlas* his shoulders, and though I seeme on earth to stand, on tiptoe in Heaven. . . . whilst I study to finde how I am a Microcosme or little world, I finde my self something more than the great.[46]

All of this lends credence and new significance to the old conjecture that the Globe playhouse had as its emblem a picture of Hercules holding the world. Ernest Schanzer, who has carefully reviewed the evidence, is inclined to doubt that the Globe had such an emblem because he finds no correspondence between the picture and the motto *Totus mundus agit histrionem,* and because "a picture of Hercules carrying the terrestrial globe offends against both mythology and common sense."[47] But the "offense," the paradox of holding up the world while standing on it, is precisely what makes the emblem expressive. By picturing a literal impossibility, it invites interpretation as a symbol and application as a metaphor. While its range of significance is large, all of its meanings are related to the new mode of subjective freedom implicit in the Renaissance concepts of the poem as heterocosm, man as actor, and the world as stage. The emblem pictures our capacity to contain in thought the world that actually contains us, reversing the usual relation of microcosm to macrocosm.

It may also picture our presumption to exist independently of the world and appropriate it as the object of our thought, manipulation, and control.

In a moralistic context, the emblem readily acquires negative meanings, expressing the perverse and self-defeating nature of selfishness and pride. In Whitney's *Choice of Emblemes* (1586), a man is pictured carrying a large globe on his back to demonstrate graphically that worldly greed is contrary to the true nature of things, and that is ambition is ultimately impossible. The motto is *Nemo potest duobus dominis seruire* ("Nobody is able to serve two masters [God and Mammon]"), and the poem concludes: "Those that first their worldlie wishe do serue, / Their gaine, is losse, and seeke their soules to sterue."[48] Behind this conventional moral we may hear, as Spenser did, the despairing cry of Narcissus: *inopem me copia fecit.*[49] Spenser applies this phrase not only to the lover in the *Amoretti* (sonnets 35 and 83) but also to Avarice in *The Faerie Queene*, "Whose wealth was want, whose plenty made him pore."[50] Indeed, the new subjectivity threatens the mind with a Narcissus-like impasse, insofar as it locates the source of all meaning and value within the self, and thereby reduces the world to a mirror that merely reflects human preferences, a neutral object upon which any value can be imposed.

Mercator offers a more affirmative, heroic interpretation of the emblem in his "Preface Vpon Atlas": Atlas is pictured lifting the world because he is the founder of astronomy and cartography and the first maker of globes.[51] Allusions to this Euhemerist tradition are common in atlases and treatises of cosmography. A woodcut in William Cuningham's *Cosmographical Glasse* (1599) shows Atlas kneeling in a terrestrial landscape holding a globe encased in a large armillary sphere. On the frontispiece of Ralegh's *History of the World* (1614), History (given her Ciceronian sobriquet "Magistra Vitae") holds up the globe while trampling Death and Oblivion underfoot.[52] Schanzer himself cites the title page of Lafreri's atlas (ca. 1570), which shows Atlas holding the earth, and two statuettes (dated ca. 1590 and 1631) of Hercules supporting a terrestrial globe.[53] Atlas, Hercules, or Magistra Vitae hold up the globe to symbolize the works of cosmography, cartography, or history as heroic achievements.

The few references that seem to associate Hercules or Atlas with the Globe playhouse suggest the same kind of metaphoric application. Hamlet asks Rosencrantz whether the boy actors have triumphed in London and forced all of the adult companies to go on tour: "Do the boys carry it away?" Rosencrantz replies, "Aye, that they do, my lord—Hercules and his load too" (II.ii.353–54). Ejner Jensen detects a similar allusion in *Antonio and Mellida,* a play written for the boys by John Marston in 1601.[54] In the induction, the "little eyases" discuss the adult roles they are about to play, confident that they can "frame [their] exterior shape / To haughty form of elate majesty." One says: "Who cannot be proud, stroke up the hair, and strut?" The other replies:

> Truth; such rank custom is grown popular;
> And now the vulgar fashion strides as wide,
> And stalks as proud upon the weakest stilts
> Of the slight'st fortunes, as if Hercules
> Or burly Atlas shoulder'd up their state.

Finally, there are the well-known lines in an elegy on Richard Burbage:

> And you his sad Companions to whome Lent
> Becomes more Lenton by this Accident,
> Hence forth your wauing flagg, no more hang out
> Play now no more att all, when round about
> Wee looke and miss the *Atlas* of your sphere.[55]

If Shakespeare's theater had this emblem—I have not, of course, *proved* that it did—the globe carried by its Hercules or Atlas is the theater itself. The emblem symbolizes the achievement of the players in sustaining their own theatrical realm and holding it up as an equivalent of the real world. The motto—for it *is* appropriate—proclaims this equivalence: *Totus mundus agit histrionem.*

Such a motto would not have been so appropriate if the Globe playhouse had built in the countryside. As a heterocom, it was, in particular, an equivalent of the urban world, offering a clarified image of the new modes of consciousness and behavior developed in response to the special needs of life in the city. As Fernand Braudel insists, the European city—and preeminently London—was itself a heterocosm: "Towns were marked by an unparalleled freedom. They had developed as autonomous worlds and according to their own propensities. They had outwitted the territorial state. . . . They ruled their fields autocratically. . . . They pursued an economic policy of their own (and created) protective privileges. . . . The formula so often used to describe this strong and privileged urban body can be repeated without misgivings: 'The town is a world in itself.' "[56]

The city imposed its autonomous and self-isolating character on its citizens, and required of them new and more complex modes of interpersonal relationship. Urban society is not a community of the traditional sort. A community—whether household, feudal manor, village guild, or congregation—is an organic whole, united by a single purpose in common bonds of reciprocal and cooperative effort. To such a group the metaphor of the body and its several organs, a metaphor developed by Aristotle, Plutarch, and Saint Paul, is entirely appropriate. While this metaphor was frequently invoked in Shakespeare's time (once, memorably, by Shakespeare himself), it did not express the actual nature of urban life, at least in London.[57] As Richard Sennett has shown, London was not an organic body but "a gathering of strangers."[58] Its population doubled in Shakespeare's lifetime, largely through immigration from rural communities. Most of the immigrants were young and single. Most came alone, usually from a distance of more than fifty miles—as Shakespeare did, from Stratford.[59] Most entered the city as separate and autonomous individuals, cut off from the connections to family and common labor that defined and limited the self in the rural community.

The difference between rural community and urban society corresponds to, and helps to establish, different phases of cognitive development in the individual. According to Jean Piaget, "the crucial step in a child's cognitive development is the change from concrete operations to formal or abstract operations. Until this transformation, the child makes no distinction between reality and the symbols used to describe reality. . . . He cannot step outside himself, so to speak, and see himself thinking about a category."[60] Communal cultures do not encourage this independence. Studying children in the Wolof tribe of Senegal, Jerome Bruner and Patricia Greenfield observed that a child's action is valued and rewarded only in relation to tribal needs: "a child is not treated as a person who may grow to have functions separate from others . . . and the personal desires and intentions which would isolate him from the group are also discouraged." As the child grows older, he becomes "less and less an individual and more and more a member of a collectivity."[61] By contrast, the urban social environment induces subjectivity and self-consciousness. In complex societies, it is important that a person learn to manipulate concepts and words, and to abstract ideas from immediate experience, even as he must learn to abstract himself from the group. Only then can he join the city on his own terms: "The power of abstraction allows him . . . to observe himself participating in nature rather than [be] simply buffeted by it."[62]

The capacity to distinguish concepts and words from their referents, and to realize their power to distort or transform the outer world, is attended by a theatrical sense of the self as an actor in life's

drama. This theatrical sense, as Sennett has demonstrated, is especially important in urban life. In the city, people must meet and
communicate as strangers, without recourse to the richly circumstantial context of familial and communal ties that define and substantiate
persons who live together in smaller groups and know one another
intimately. In order to supply the missing context of communal life,
Sennett argues, urban society provides a repertoire of fashions, man-
ners, and conventional roles, and offers them as a medium of communication. He compares the problem of the urban citizen to that of
the actor in a theater; both must find a way "to arouse belief in one's
appearance among a milieu of strangers": "Social expression will be
conceived of *as presentation* to other people of feelings which signify in
and of themselves, *rather than as representation* of feelings present and
real to each self."[63] Social roles, like dramatic roles, must have
significance and value apart from the unknowable inner feelings of
the strangers who are actors and audience in the urban theater.

Inevitably this ideal of public life begets its natural contrary: both in
the city and in the theater, the concept of the private self emerges to
challenge and complicate conventional public roles defined by and for
others. Shakespeare provides a paradigm of this development in
Hamlet, when the Prince protests that he knows not "seems" but then
defines his inner reality negatively as the contrary of the seeming he
repudiates (I.ii.76–86). No "forms, moods, shapes of grief" (82) can
denote him truly:

> These indeed seem,
> For they are actions that a man might play,
> But I have that within which passeth show—
> These but the trappings and the suits of woe.
>
> (83–86)

Hamlet changes his attitude toward seeming when he puts on his
antic disposition, when he uses a play to expose Claudius's secret
crime, and when he urges his mother to seem virtuous until the pretense becomes a habit, and so a reality: "Assume a virtue, if you have it
not. . . . For use almost can change the stamp of nature" (III.iv.161,
169). In *Hamlet,* and in his other plays, Shakespeare uses his theatrical
medium as a metaphor to explore the new self-consciousness that was
emerging in the urban heterocosm. The actor in the character embodied the duality of inner self and public role; the stage and fictive
setting illustrated the difference between reality and the symbols used
to describe reality; and the playhouse itself offered an architectural
emblem of the interlocking subjective and objective worlds within
which everyone must play his or her part.

ATLAS
SIVE
COSMOGRAPHICÆ
MEDITATIONES
DE
FABRICA MVNDI ET
FABRICATI FIGVRA.

Gerardo Mercatore Rupelmundano,
Illustriſſimi Ducis Iuliæ Cliviæ & Mõ:
tis &c. Coſmographo Autore.
Cum Privilegio.

DVISBVRGI CLIVORVM.

Gerardus Mercator, *Atlas,* 1595 (title page). (Courtesy of The Edward E.
Ayer Collection, The Newberry Library, Chicago.)

To M. K N E W S T V B *Preacher.*

H E R E, man who firſt ſhould heauenlie thinges attaine,
And then, to world his ſences ſhould incline :
Firſt , vndergoes the worlde with might, and maine,
And then , at foote doth drawe the lawes deuine.
    Thus G o d hee beares, and Mammon in his minde:
    But Mammon firſt, and G o d doth come behinde.

Matth. 6.
Non poteſtis deo
ſeruire & Mam-
monæ.

Oh worldlinges fonde, that ioyne theſe two ſo ill,
The league is nought, throwe doune the world which ſpeede:
Take vp the lawe , according to his will.
Firſt ſeeke for heauen, and then for wordly neede.
    But thoſe that firſt their wordlie wiſhe doe ſerue,
    Their gaine, is loſſe, and ſeeke their ſoules to ſterue.

*Primùm quærite
regnum dei, &c.
Ibidem.*

Sic

**Geffrey Whitney, *A Choice of Emblemes and Other Devises*, 1586. (Courtesy of
The Beinecke Rare Book and Manuscript Library, Yale University.)**

THE FIRST BOOKE OF THE

William Cuningham, *The Cosmographic Glasse*, 1559. (Courtesy of The Beinecke Rare Book and Manuscript Library, Yale University.)

Sir Walter Ralegh, *History of the World*, 1614 (frontispiece). (Courtesy of The Beinecke Rare Book and Manuscript Library, Yale University.)

2

Reality in Play
Playhouse as Emblem, Performance as
Metaphor

When the theater is defined as a second world, the primary distinction of play and reality is replicated both within play and within reality. The architecture of the playhouse embodies the principle of
replication by defining the stage as a separate and independent space
within the larger circle of the auditorium. This architectural duality
distinguishes in spatial terms the mimetic dimension of drama as an
image of life from the ludic dimension of drama as autonomous play
in "a temporary sphere of activity with a disposition all of its own."
This duality within drama is a metaphor of a corresponding duality
within the real itself.

Stage and Auditorium as Cosmic Emblems

The playhouse as an architectural emblem of the cosmos symbolizes
the dual nature of reality. The most elaborate description of this
emblematic architecture, from which I must distinguish my own view,
is provided by Frances Yates:

> The Theatre of the World [is] the "Idea" of the Globe Theatre. To
> the cosmic meanings of the ancient theatre, with its plan based on
> the triangulations within the zodiac, was added the religious mean-
> ings of the theatre as temple, and the related religious and cosmic
> meanings of the Renaissance church. . . . His theatre would have
> been for Shakespeare the pattern of the universe, the idea of the
> Macrocosm, the world stage on which the Microcosm acted his
> parts. All the world's a stage. The words are in a real sense the clue
> to the Globe Theatre.[1]

45

The basic architectural elements of the playhouse were its circular auditorium and its rectangular platform stage. It is probably a mere coincidence that these two elements, the circle and the square, were brought together by Italian Renaissance architects for the centrally planned church. The synthesis had two purposes: (1) to provide a basis for an austere geometric design that would emphasize the organic unity of the building as a whole—"a rational integration of the proportions of all the parts of a building in such a way that . . . nothing could be added or taken away without destroying the harmony of the whole";[2] and (2) to objectify a complex neo-Pythagorean symbolism of harmonic ratios that expressed "the mathematical sympathy between the microcosm and the macrocosm."[3] There is no evidence that either purpose was achieved or even attempted by the builders of English playhouses, despite Miss Yates's intriguing suggestion to the contrary. Even if the playhouse had been built as a geometric symbol on the Vitruvian principles developed for the Renaissance church, such symbolism could hardly have affected the building's actual function as a theater, and would have had only ornamental value.

I shall argue that the English playhouse was *occasionally construed* as an architectural emblem of the cosmos—which is not to say (as Miss Yates and others have) that it was designed and built with such meanings in mind. References to the playhouse as a cosmic emblem are usually brief, often casual, sometimes jocular; Dekker, we have seen, mocked the pretensions of Shakespeare's company in calling their houses "Theater" and "Globe." These references do suggest that both the stage and the auditorium were sometimes associated with familiar images of the cosmos, but this iconography gained no support (and needed none) from the sophisticated geometrical symbolism of the Italian architects. I shall argue that the cosmic emblems seen in the stage and auditorium coincide with and rationalize the inherent symbolic values of the spaces defined by playhouse architecture, and that these spaces influenced the presentation and perception of theatrical performance as a metaphor of reality. Descriptions of the playhouse as a *theatrum mundi* are valuable insofar as they translate into a familiar idiom intuitions about the phenomenology of theatrical space that are otherwise difficult to grasp.

The real flaw in Miss Yates's thesis is her assumption that the playhouse was distinguished by architectural unity. Theater historians have shown that it was, to the contrary, a discordant combination of two different structures—as fine an example of "complexity and contradiction in architecture"[4] as one could wish. In this respect, the first

Italian theater, designed by Andrea Palladio in the 1580s, offers an instructive contrast to the first English playhouse, built by James Burbage in 1576. The *Teatro Olimpico* is a self-conscious and ostentatious attempt, commissioned by an academy of literati, to unify theatrical space by Vitruvian principles. Licisco Magagnato emphasizes the importance of an architect's intervention into the evolution of theatrical space:

> Before Palladio the rearrangement of the hall to serve the needs of a theatre had never been envisaged as requiring organic structural transformation. . . . It is only in the *Olimpico* that an attempt is made to confront the true problem of the theatre—and the problems of the theatre all turn on this central question of the relation of actors to spectators—as architectural problems, and to find an organic and unitary solution to them in the terms proper to this art and to no other.[5]

James Burbage was no architect but a carpenter-turned-actor who merely copied existing structures—an animal-baiting arena and a Tudor hall stage—that he jammed together without regard for architectural coherence. The stage and tiring-house unit was independent in design, construction, and use from the auditorium that framed it. The two structures, writes Glynne Wickham, "were linked together for commercial expediency rather than conceived in the first instance as a single entity, functional and aesthetic."[6] Wickham suggests that there was a social as well as architectural incongruity in the playhouse; it offered, in effect, a private indoor stage within a public open-air auditorium: "Into the game-houses familiar to all sections of society and open to everyone, regardless of rank, who possessed the penny needed to gain admission, the actors brought the scaffold, the screen and the 'houses' of their master's private hall."[7] The result was the awkward arrangement depicted by de Witt in his famous drawing of the Swan playhouse. "The drawing," as Walter Hodges says, "shows a large rectangular stage set out in a round arena, a square peg in a round hole. If we could come fresh to this arrangement, surely it would strike us at once as a rather clumsy and uncomfortable feature."[8]

Palladio's "organic and unitary solution" may have been well suited to the academic revivals of Greek and Roman tragedy—the first play performed there was Orsato Guistiniani's version of Sophocles' *Oedipus Rex*—but it would hardly have been appropriate to the aesthetic demands of Elizabethan drama. The playhouse, in all its heterogeneity, can better present the "multiple unity" or *discordia concors* of Elizabethan dramatic fictions, precisely because the architectural components are not subordinated to a single organic form but remain separate and relatively independent.[9] This remarkable independence of elements within the playhouse defines the spatial and imaginative relationships in Elizabethan theatrical experience.

The multiple unity of playhouse architecture enriches and complicates its significance as a cosmic emblem in ways not fully anticipated by Frances Yates. She argues that the playhouse was "a bold and original adaptation of the ancient [Roman] theatre" that offered a cosmic emblem "expressive of a Renaissance rather than a medieval outlook on man and his world."[10] Her own argument is a bold and original revision of the more orthodox view that the playhouse was (as Alvin Kernan puts it) "obviously a model in plaster and wood of the conservative world view of the late Middle Ages . . . a fixed cosmos of earth and heaven and hell."[11] There is warrant for both interpretations. Miss Yates finds her Renaissance cosmic emblem primarily in the circular auditorium, while Kernan finds his medieval cosmic emblem in the stage, with its hell in the cellarage beneath and its heavens painted on the canopy above. Elizabethans occasionally construed both the stage and the auditorium as cosmic emblems. Each emblem belongs to a different iconographical tradition and suggests a different concept of man's place and power in the world.

The relationship of these emblems in the playhouse expresses in familiar, conventional language the inherent symbolic values of existential space. The nature of these values is suggested in very general terms by Christian Norberg-Schulz in his synthesis of current architectural theory:

> The simplest model of man's existential space is . . . a horizontal plane pierced by a vertical axis. . . . The vertical direction expresses a rising up or falling down and has since remote times been . . . considered the sacred dimension of space. It represents a "path" towards a reality which may be "higher" or "lower" than daily life. . . . The *axis mundi* is thus more than the centre of the world, it represents a connection between the three cosmic realms. . . . The horizontal directions represent man's concrete world of action. In a certain sense, all horizontal directions are equal and form a plane of infinite extension. . . . For its definition, therefore, the place needs a pronounced limit or border. The place is experienced as an "inside" in contrast to the surrounding "outside." . . . A place, therefore, is basically "round."[12]

Few buildings in the history of architecture have objectified this archetype as completely as the playhouse, which, like a sculptor's mold, shaped the imaginative world of Shakespearean drama.

The vertical configuration of cellarage, stage, and canopy conforms to the medieval emblem of the Christian cosmos that envisages earth, placed between heaven and hell, as a stage on which men are tested and judged. On occasion, Shakespeare's characters look beyond their local circumstances to the universal dimensions of this world theater: "This goodly frame the earth . . . this most excellent canopy, the air, look you, this brave o'erhanging firmament, this majestical roof fretted with golden fire." (II.ii.295–98), as Hamlet says. This theatrical setting holds the God-made world over against all the "shaping fantasies" that distort subjective experience, making the goodly earth seem to Hamlet a "sterile promontory" (295–96) and the heavens "a foul and pestilent congregation of vapors" (299). Most of Shakespeare's references to the traditional world stage place man in a cosmic setting that dwarfs his pretensions to freedom and power. This is the world in which, as Isabella warns Angelo,

> proud man,
> Dressed in a little brief authority,
>
> Plays such fantastic tricks before high heaven
> As makes the angels weep.
>
> (*MM*, II.ii.117–18, 121–22)

a world in which heroic self-assertion dwindles to the empty histrionic postures of Macbeth's "poor player, / That struts and frets his hour upon the stage" (V.iv.24–25).

The medieval cosmic emblem amplifies symbolic values that are inherent in the stage space. Any highly articulated rectangular space tends to impose its structure on everything it contains; in such a space we are *placed* in relation to a set of coordinates—up-down, side-to-side, front-to-back—that easily take on symbolic value. Francis Berry points out that Shakespeare often uses the horizontal axis to suggest opposition or conflict, as when Richard III pitches his tent on one side of the stage and Richmond his on the other, and the vertical axis to suggest relationships of power and subordination, as when Richard II appears upon the battlements at Flint Castle and then comes down to "the base court" and yields to the usurper.[13] The cosmic framework of heaven, earth, hell is merely the largest and most important of several lines of force within the rectangular space of the stage.

The circular auditorium offered a different cosmic emblem. While the stage may have descended from the medieval scaffold (by way of the Tudor hall), the auditorium was frequently described as a descendant of the Roman amphitheater. In 1576 this Roman ancestor was claimed for the first playhouse, proudly named The Theater; some twenty years later de Witt made his drawing of the Swan because he thought it resembled the Roman structure; in Jacobean times Heywood asserted this resemblance with great enthusiasm in his *Apology for Actors*.[14] As an edifice of imperial Rome, the amphitheater is a more impressive monument to man's creative power than the medieval scaffold, and thus it is more appropriate as an emblem of the world man asserts himself in, conquers, and shapes to the pattern of his own ideals. The playhouse as amphitheater embodies what Marlowe calls "the wondrous architecture of the world" that moves the aspiring mind of Tamburlaine to conquest; this is the world-theater filled and transfigured by Cleopatra's Antony:

> His face was as the heav'ns, and therein stuck
> A sun and moon, which kept their course and lighted
> The little O, th' earth.
> His legs bestrid the ocean: his reared arm
> Crested the world.
>
> (*AC*, V.ii.79–81, 82–83)

These lines suggest the Herculean figure of the actor filling the "wooden O" with his voice and presence. The circular auditorium evokes feelings of freedom and power as readily as the rectangular stage evokes feelings of order and limit. We recall Arnheim's suggestion that a circular interior "is perceived as an amplification and extension of the human focus." "Curved walls," he continues, "look as though they had acquired their passive shape by yielding to the invading possessor. . . . The occupant feels elevated and expanded as he reaches out to the confines of the room."[15] The concave boundary that yields to its beholder reinforces the exhilarating (or terrifying) sensation of a world that offers no resistance to imagination or will. In such a world personal identity itself becomes fluid—"I am Antony, / Yet cannot hold this visible shape" (IV.xiv.13–14)—and self-transformation seems a real possibility.

In his *Fable of Man*, the Spanish humanist Juan Luis Vives envisages the world as a theater in which Protean man achieves self-realization by acting out the full range of human potential, culminating in a perfect imitation of Jupiter himself. Vives's image of the world-theater is derived from the same ancestor claimed for the playhouse, the Roman amphitheater:

> At a command of almighty Jupiter, by whom all things are done, this whole world appeared, so large, so elaborate, so diversified, and beautiful in places, just as you see it. This was the amphithea-

ter: uppermost, to wit in the skies, were the stalls and seats of the divine spectators: nethermost—some say in the middle—the earth was placed as a stage for the appearance of the actors.[16]

The playhouse, with its galleries rising above and around the stage, duplicated the conventional features of this Renaissance world-theater, just as its cellarage, stage, and canopy delineated the medieval cosmos. The playhouse, like its drama, embraced both the traditional world picture and the new philosophy, and contained the medieval within the Renaissance world view.

When we turn from the playhouse and its iconography to the metaphoric values of theatrical performance, we will find that the terms "medieval" and "Renaissance" are too limited. What was at issue for the dramatist was not cultural history but two different ways of seeing and representing reality, both current and valid, yet neither quite complete without the other. One mode of vision sees an objective world, not of our own making, with which we must come to terms, confined in a self not of our own making, with all its natural imperfections, its need and fear of others. The other mode of vision sees a world subjectively real, plastic to the shaping power of imagination, a stage-world in which we may transform ourselves at will, or be transformed, like Bottom, by forces beyond our will. While these opposed realities are established differently in different plays, the contrast between them is a general feature of Shakespearean drama, and this contrast is obliquely figured forth by the different cosmic emblems embodied in the playhouse.

There is no evidence that these cosmic emblems could by themselves have predetermined the dramatist's meaning or the spectator's response. But they do express, in an indirect and symbolic way, the actual effect of theatrical space on the perception of dramatic action in the playhouse. Our imaginative response to drama is partly determined by our spatial relation to it. If we share the same space with the actors, we are likely to respond to their actions as a theatrical performance in which we, as spectators, are actually involved. But if they occupy a separate space, distinguished from ours by an architectural boundary, then we are more intensely aware of their actions as the representation of events that are taking place not in the theater but somewhere else.[17] The architecture of the playhouse combines these alternatives. The stage, raised up from the yard, backed by the tiring-house, and covered by the canopy (which was supported by two pillars rising from midstage), was a clearly defined rectangular space, a box with three of its four walls removed. Because this space was distinct from the larger circle of the surrounding auditorium, it could be readily identified with a reality distinct from the theatrical event.[18] But the acting area could also be perceived as part of the circular space defined by the auditorium. As John Webster says, "the *Actor* is the Center" and the audience is the circumference.[19] The actor who stood downstage center stood in the center of the auditorium as well; the playhouse located him simultaneously in two different, discontinuous spaces.

The effect of this ambivalence is to superimpose on the play's image of reality the immediate activity of performing and pretending shared by actors and spectators. If we are asked to accept the actors as characters and the stage as their world, we are also invited to interpret the characters as actors and their world as a stage. This superimposition of performance on the dramatic image combines the two modes of reality, man-made and God-made, creative and mimetic, that are symbolically represented by the stage and auditorium as cosmic emblems.

Theater and Metaphor

The contrasting realities defined by playhouse architecture are not merely juxtaposed or set in opposition to each other, face to face, for the auditorium encloses the stage. If this architectural form is an "embodiment of thought," it embodies the subjectivity of consciousness by which our perceptual and behavioral engagement with the external world is "internalized" and recreated within the self. In the playhouse, we turn our back on reality in order to contemplate its theatrical image, which is held apart from its referents in the outer world and placed within the heterocosm of imagination and play. This spatial relationship defines two intimately related features of Shakespearean drama: its use of performance as a metaphor of reality, and the subjective nature of that reality.

Any metaphor is a metaphor of mind, whatever its particular content, because it makes us aware that reality is transformed when it becomes an object in and for consciousness. The theatrical metaphor dramatizes this subjectivity. Unlike other basic metaphors (e.g. nautical, military, alimentary, corporal), its substance is provided by a human mimetic activity that already represents reality, even before being appropriated as the vehicle of a metaphor. The theatrical metaphor reverses the mimetic relationship and gives it a reflexive structure: the stage represents a world that resembles a stage; the actor impersonates a character who plays the actor.

Most proponents of the metacritical approach to Shakespeare assume that this reflexiveness embodies radical scepticism: a denial that there is any reality accessible to imitation. The very effort to represent reality reduces it to illusion, just as thought inevitably reduces experience to concepts and relationships with others to structures within the self. Lionel Abel, for example, asserts that "a gain for consciousness means a loss for the reality of its objects"; he concludes from this that "in the metaplay life must be a dream and the world must be a stage."[20] But this conclusion is only half true. The reflexive movement of metaphor, by being repeated, returns to reality; concepts can disclose new realms of experience; structures within the self can form the basis of relationships with others. If the world resembles a stage, then the stage can indeed represent the world; if everybody plays the actor, then the actor truly does epitomize humanity.

Efforts to preserve thought and metaphor from epistemological scepticism, from the collapse of otherness upon the self, generally rely on a dialectical process that begins with a withdrawal into subjectivity but culminates in a return to otherness. In the next chapter, I shall argue that the action of Shakespearean drama conforms to such a pattern of withdrawal and return, and that the mimetic function of Shakespearean theater as metaphor can be fully understood only in relation to this pattern. The present chapter is limited to the spatial structure of metaphor (within which the pattern unfolds); it therefore emphasizes the subjective dimensions of the theatrical metaphor while deferring to the next chapter consideration of the metaphor's mimetic capacity to restore within subjectivity itself a viable sense of objective reality.

As a metaphor, the theater discloses what becomes visible when life is regarded as if it were a play. What becomes visible is a theatricality within life itself that may call in question its pretense of being "real": "All the world's a stage, / And all the men and women *merely* players." As metaphors of self and world, the actor and stage disclose subjective reality within the apparently objective, other-directed activities of role-playing and perception. These theatrical metaphors subvert the naive or ordinary sense of the self as a being firmly located in a world of others to whom it can directly present itself by performing in a certain way. In the course of the action, the Shakespearean character often ceases to be himself and becomes not only the actor of himself but also the audience of his own performance; his role-playing embodies self-consciousness. The character's world becomes a stage not only when it is treated as the locus of his deliberate performances for others, but also—and especially in Shakespeare—when it stimulates imaginative projections that make the outer world reflect the inner.

The World as Stage: Subjectivity in Perception

It is hazardous to base speculations about Shakespearean mimesis on assumptions about the position of the characters on stage and the *mise en scène*. Evidence about Elizabethan stagecraft is scanty, and the little we have suggests that the players availed themselves of a bewildering (and by modern standards inconsistent) variety of options. Many Elizabethan dramatic episodes have no determinate setting at all; it is enough that the actors are present to each other and to the audience. The large platform stage, which did not have to be set, readily accommodated such encounters. At the opposite extreme, the upstage area and tiring-house façade, if they resembled the interior of a Tudor hall, could have represented such an interior realistically. Between these extremes are a variety of partial realizations of the play's world, assisted by properties (throne, bed, city walls and gate, banquet table), symbolic groupings of characters, or simply by the general structure of the stage as an architectural emblem of the cosmos.

More than any other English Renaissance dramatist, Shakespeare resorted to another, curiously undramatic procedure: poetic descriptions of the characters' world. It is a mistake to assume that he had to do so because of the inadequate scenic resources of the Elizabethan stage.[21] The dramatist seldom needs a particular setting; most of Shakespeare's poetic scenes—for example, those provided by the Chorus in *Henry V*—are quite gratuitous. When we must know where the characters are, the briefest reference will suffice: "Well, this is the Forest of Arden" (*AYL*, II.iv.13), "This is Illyria, lady" (*TN*, I.ii.2). Yet some of the most magnificent lines in Shakespeare are given over to lavish descriptions of settings that no stage—nor nature itself—could equal:

> Now entertain conjecture of a time
> When creeping murmur and the poring dark
> Fills the wide vessel of the universe.
> From camp to camp, through the foul womb of night,
> The hum of either army stilly sounds
>
> Fire answers fire, and through their paly flames
> Each battle sees the other's umbered face.
> Steed threatens steed, in high and boastful neighs
> Piercing the night's dull ear. . . .
>
> (*H5*, IV.Chor. 1–5, 8–11)

Other familiar passages have the same effect: the flowery moonlit landscapes of *A Midsummer Night's Dream,* the "dreadful summit of the cliff / That beetles o'er his base into the sea" where Hamlet might lose his sovereignty of reason; the "temple-haunting martlets" that build their "pendent bed and procreant cradle" in the eaves of Macbeth's castle; the barge that Cleopatra sat in, like a burnished throne, with poop of beaten gold, silver oars, and purple sails that made the wind lovesick with perfume.

Francis Berry explains the convention of verbal scenery "where the imagined spectacle is at odds with the actual spectacle" by pointing out that it allows the dramatist his "only escape . . . from the compulsion of having to show the now, the objective, present-tense, interpersonal world of dramatic actions." The narrated scene is, by contrast, subjective and imaginative.[22] Berry inexplicably dismisses as an irrelevant distraction the discrepancy between what the spectators actually see on the stage and what they are asked to imagine. He thinks it would be better for them to shut their eyes while listening to Enobarbus describing Cleopatra in her barge or to the Chorus in *Henry V.*[23] To the contrary, the fact that the narrated scene must be imagined and exists on a different level of realization from the characters and stage is essential to its value. The poetic power of Enobarbus's speech to create a compelling image of Cleopatra and to capture entirely the attention of his listeners corresponds to the seductive power of the Egyptian queen herself:

> For her own person,
> It beggared all description; she did lie
> In her pavilion, cloth-of-gold of tissue,
> O'erpicturing that Venus where we see
> The fancy outwork nature.
>
> From the barge
> A strange invisible perfume hits the sense
> Of the adjacent wharfs. The city cast
> Her people out upon her; and Antony
> Enthroned i' th'market place, did sit alone,
> Whistling to th'air; which, but for vacancy,
> Had gone to gaze on Cleopatra too,
> And made a gap in nature.
>
> (II.ii.198–202, 212–19)

The speech concretely embodies the effect it describes; Enobarbus makes a gap in the play's action and displaces the actual stage image with an imagined scene. In so doing, he has the same kind of effect on

his Roman audience (and on Shakespeare's audience) that Cleopatra
had on Antony.

Shakespeare uses verbal scenery to dramatize the subjective element in our relation to the world that is implicit in our capacity for
fiction and play. To Elizabethan enemies of the stage, this subjectivity
was as dangerous an enchantment as Cleopatra herself; Gosson,
Prynne, and others believed that poets and players, by inventing
imaginary worlds, "threaten God's primacy as creator . . . and in-
sinuate that the original creation left something to be desired."[24] In
defending poetry, Philip Sidney could not refute this charge. What he
claims for the poet, he must deny to Nature: "Her world is brasen, the
Poets onely deliuer a golden."[25] The poet, in "making things either
better than nature bringeth forth, or, quite a newe, formes such as
neuer were in Nature" (156), may convey a feeling that reality is
"brazen," inchoate, or otherwise inadequate to the human spirit.
Francis Bacon is more explicit. Poetry, he explains, "by submitting the
shows of things to the desires of the mind . . . [gives] some shadow of
satisfaction to the mind of man in those points wherein the nature of
things doth deny it, the world being in proportion inferior to the
soul."[26]

Shakespeare's stage objectifies this new sense of reality by offering a
split image of the play's world: the characters are physically present
and visually overdetermined by elaborate, emblematic costumes,[27]
while the particular setting of the action, in the absence of realistic
scenery, can be made visible only to the mind's eye by verbal description. Thus the characters are more substantially real than their environment, which exists only as they define it; for them the world is
indeed inferior to the soul and easily shaped by the desires—or the
fears—of the mind.

Shakespeare's poetic scene setting was ideally suited to dramatize
the way in which our perception of the world is distorted or transformed by our state of mind. The lovers in A Midsummer Night's Dream
see "Helen's beauty in a brow of Egypt" (V.i.11) and give "to airy
nothing / A local habitation and a name" (16–17), because love looks
"not with the eyes but with the mind" and transposes "Things base
and vile . . . to form and dignity" (see I.i.232–35). Macbeth, obsessed
with murder, finds that "present fears / Are less than horrible imaginings" (i.iii.137–38); in his world, as on the stage, "nothing is, but what
is not" (141–42). Prospero's "bare island" is not at all the same place
for Antonio and Sebastian that it is for Gonzalo and Adrian; the
difference in their perceptions reflects differences in their characters:

Adrian.	The air breathes upon us here most sweetly.
Sebastian.	As if it had lungs, and rotten ones.
Antonio.	Or as 'twere perfumed by a fen.
Gonzalo.	Here is everything advantageous to life.
Antonio.	True; save means to live.
Sebastian.	Of that there's none, or little.
Gonzalo.	How lush and lusty the grass looks! how green!
Antonio.	The ground indeed is tawny.
Sebastian.	With an eye of green in 't.

(Tmp., II.i.46–54)

A realistically set stage would settle these differences in favor of one or the other contending parties by providing either a verdant or desert landscape, but a bare stage leaves the question open and draws the spectators into it. Which island shall we imagine, Antonio's or Gonzalo's? The point is not to resolve the debate, or even to recognize the character of each disputant, but to realize the mysteriously indeterminate quality of their world. In *The Tempest,* as in *A Midsummer Night's Dream* and *Macbeth,* the unlocalized stage conveys a sense that the world's stage has lost its substance and objectivity, and become such stuff as dreams are made on.

Over against these subjective perceptions of the world stood the traditional architectural emblem, representing the fixed cosmos of earth and heaven and hell. Alvin Kernan proposes that the overarching presence of this emblem "constantly, though silently, said that the soaring poetry and brave sound of the human voice which dominated the stage and claimed the theater were ultimately contained by an enduring reality."[28] He says further that the characters' subjective perceptions of reality, and dramatic fiction itself, are not only placed or framed but also refuted by the cosmic emblem: "Imagination usually falters and fails in this drama," he writes, "shattering against the prior reality of the world represented by . . . the platform stage . . . as if the playwrights could not themselves finally believe in the power of their own make-believe to transform the world."[29] Hamlet's reference to the cosmic stage, quoted above, suggests a different conclusion. His subjective perception of the world as a "sterile promontory" does not shatter against the prior reality of the "goodly frame." Instead, each vision of reality remains to mock the other. If anything, the fixed cosmos gives way too easily to the pressure of the mind, like the cloud "that's almost in the shape of a camel," or "like a weasel," or "very like a whale" (III.ii.361 ff.). When the medieval cosmic emblem is enclosed by a playhouse auditorium and made the locus of fictions, its status as a true reflection of cosmic order may come into question and that

order seem no less a fabrication than the stage itself. So it seemed to
Francis Bacon, who dismissed traditional world views as "Idols of the
Theater": "In my judgment all the received systems are but so many
stage-plays, representing worlds of [the philosophers'] own creation
after an unreal and scenic fashion."[30] In Shakespearean drama, the
failure of imagination to transform reality is of less consequence that
the failure of reality to limit and fulfill the imagination. And for
Shakespeare the only reality that is not inferior to the inner self is the
complex reality of another self.

Character as Actor: Subjectivity and Role-playing

As a metaphor, the actor virtually personified the significance of
the poetic or architectural heterocosm as a model of human subjectivity. The concept of the poet as creator of a heterocosm emerges in
Renaissance literary theory as a corollary to a new confidence in man's
self-transforming power.[31] This new philosophy was developed in its
most radical form by the Florentine Academy and extravagantly
affirmed in Giovanni Pico della Mirandola's *Oration on Human Dignity*.
The *Oration* begins by proposing that God "took man as a creature of
indeterminate nature," and allowed him to choose his own place in
the cosmos, where, like an actor, he could give shape to his own being
"on this stage of the world": "We have made thee neither of heaven
nor of earth, neither mortal nor immortal, so that with freedom of
choice and with honor, as though the maker and molder of thyself,
thou mayest fashion thyself in whatever shape thou shalt prefer."[32]
Pico's protean man is the actor of himself.

Pico presupposes a cause-and-effect relation between cosmic mobil-
ity and self-transforming power; when we are removed from "a fixed
abode" we are able to fashion ourselves in whatever shape we prefer.
The *Oration* thus suggests a connection between two important aspects of Renaissance poetics and Shakespearean theater: the freedom
of the participants to step out of ordinary life into a temporary sphere
of activity, and their experience of role-playing and pretending
within the play world. Sidney makes this connection when he relates
the imaginative independence of the poem as heterocosm to its affective power to shape human nature. He brings Pico's concept of man to
his defense of poetry when he argues that God "made man to his
owne likenes" as a maker of worlds and "set him beyond and ouer all
the workes" of Nature, "which in nothing hee sheweth so much as in
Poetrie, when with the force of a diuine breath he bringeth things
forth far surpassing [Nature's] dooings" (157). The poet's ability to

create a second world manifests man's protean capacity to fashion freely the little world of his own being, and the poem encourages this capacity in the reader, who will be moved to emulate its exemplars of virtuous action: "Who readeth *Aeneas* carrying olde *Anchises* on his back, that wisheth not it were his fortune to perfourme so excellent an acte?" (173).[33]

Gosson's philosophy of human nature is the obverse of Pico's. Man is the only created thing in the universe that has no natural place in its its order:

> Fire and Ayre mount vpwards, Earth and Water sinke downe, & euery insensible body else, neuer rests, til it bring it self to his owne home. But we which haue both sense, reason, wit, and vnderstanding, are euer ouerlashing, passing our boundes, going beyonde our limites, neuer keeping our selues within compasse, nor once looking after the place from whence we came, and whither we muste in spight of our hartes.[34]

In Gosson's view, the release of emotion is reprehensible because it threatens man with internal anarchy. Reason alone cannot ensure the stability of mental life merely by repressing emotions; the mind must seek in its consciousness of the outer world the effective limit of its scope and the necessary curb of all its energies, whether passionate or rational. To "let the world slip" by watching a comedy (as Christopher Sly does in *The Taming of the Shrew*) is to risk forfeiting one's identity (as Sly does): a preacher of 1577 warns, "Thou losest thy selfe that hauntest those scholes of vice, dennes of theeues, and Theatres of all leudnesse."[35]

For Gosson, as for Sidney, the metamorphic power of fiction is epitomized by the actor. Gosson argues that the actor exploits and intensifies what all modes of fiction manifest and encourage—the radical instability of human nature and the refusal to accept one's place in the divinely established order of things:

> If we grudge at the wisedome of our maker, and disdaine the calling he hath placed vs in, aspyring somewhat higher then we should (as in the body; when . . . the flesh would be spirit, this confusion of order weakens the head): So in a commonweale, if priuat men be suffered to forsake theire calling because they desire to walk gentlemenlike in sattine & veluet, with a buckler at theire heeles, proportion is so broken vnitie dissolued, harmony confounded, that the whole body must be dismembred and the prince or the heade can not chuse but sicken.[36]

All poems, but especially plays, "are the Cuppes of *Circes,* that turne reasonable Creatures into Brute Beastes."[37] Fiction usurps the sovereignty of reason.

The figure of the usurper as actor is common in Elizabethan drama; its exemplar is Shakespeare's Richard of Gloucester, who wets his cheeks with artificial tears, frames his face to all occasions, adds colors to the chameleon, changes shapes with Proteus, and uses these talents to seize the crown (see *3H6*, III.ii.182–95). But politics provides only one perspective on "usurpation." When characters in Renaissance fiction disguise themselves and play roles or are more deeply changed by the passions of love or madness, they objectify the metamorphic power that was claimed for fiction itself by both its defenders and its detractors. Shakespeare's theater actualized the central concepts of Renaissance poetics: just as the playhouse objectifies fiction's independence as a heterocosm, the actor embodies the related idea of man's self-transforming power.

Shakespeare's insights into the nature of subjectivity and role-playing may have grown from his response to the requirements of theatrical performance. While the actors attempted to submerge themselves as completely in their characters as the conditions of theatrical production allowed, the dramatists were attempting to disengage the characters from the two-dimensional types they inherited from literary and dramatic tradition. Shakespeare made these two efforts complement each other. He met his fellow actors half way by creating characters who are, in different ways, inherently theatrical. Many of his characters disguise themselves and consciously play roles, while others undergo self-transformation at a deeper level of psychic change in response to the metamorphic pressures of love, ambition, guilt, rage, or madness. The actor could be readily identified with such a character despite his prominence as an actor, because there is an aspect of the character that his own activity in impersonation embodied. And the character, by the same procedure, was freed from the confines of its conventional type, because the type became a role for the character as well as for the actor.[38]

The duality of actor and role, while prominent in medieval drama, functions as a metaphor of character only in Elizabethan drama. What makes the difference is the principle of replication: the medieval tension between the festive occasion of performance and the reality represented in the play becomes in Elizabethan drama a duality within the represented reality itself. This replication, objectified and facilitated by playhouse architecture, combines actor and role to embody the subjective reality of character.

The distinction between a mere juxtaposition of actor and role and their metaphoric relationship in a fictive character can be illustrated by a comparison of two similar dramatic roles: Herod of the mystery plays and Shakespeare's Macbeth.[39] The duality of actor and role is evident in these lines from Herod's part:

> A-nothur way? owt! owt! owtt!
> Hath those fawls traytvrs done me this ded?
> I stamp! I stare! I loke all abowtt!
> Myght I them take, I schuld them bren at a glede!
> I rent! I raw! And now run I wode!
> A! thatt these velen trayturs hath mard this my mode!
> The shalbe hangid yf I ma cum them to!
> *Here Erod ragis in the pagond and in the strete also.*[40]

The actor seems actually to intrude into the text to tell the spectators what Herod feels and does. His lines do not allow him to "identify with the character" or "immerse himself entirely within the fictive personality and recreate it as his own," in the sense these phrases have when applied to modern naturalistic acting. Clearly the style of performance evident in Herod's lines was one way to derive maximum theatrical intensity from an amateur actor who could not be expected to possess much skill in impersonation, but who might, for all that, take on his assignment with Bottom's enthusiasm: "I will move storms; I will condole in some measure. To the rest. Yet my chief humor is for a tyrant. I could play Ercles rarely, or a part to tear a cat in, to make all split" (*MND*, I.ii.29–32). The lines themselves encourage the actor's extravagance and serve the deliberate end of burlesque. As Robert Weimann indicates, the medieval Herod no less than the Shakespearean character allows a multi-consciousness of actor and role, and gives this duality an important dramatic function: to create the image and control the threat of tyranny:

> As [Herod] mingles with the audience and rages in the open street, he forfeits the reverence and the menace of his station and almost surrenders the representational dimension of his role. At the same time, the audience is drawn into the play and given the role of frightened subjects. . . . Terror, playfully experienced, acts as a charm against real terror. . . . The comic version of tyranny has a liberating effect: exaggerated authority becomes laughable.[41]

The immediate social reality of performance—the festive occasion and the plebeian actor who "out-herods Herod"—counteracts the represented reality of tyranny.

Shakespeare retains this duality of actor and role in figures like Richard of Gloucester and Macbeth but internalizes it to express the subjectivity of the characters. Both his debt to the tradition and his modification of it are evident when Herod's lines are compared to Macbeth's first soliloquy:

> Macbeth. [*Aside*]   Two truths are told,
> As happy prologues to the swelling act
> Of the imperial theme.—I thank you, gentlemen.—
>   [*Aside*]
> This supernatural soliciting
> Cannot be ill, cannot be good. If ill,
> Why hath it given me earnest of success,
> Commencing in a truth? I am Thane of Cawdor.
> If good, why do I yield to that suggestion
> Whose horrid image doth unfix my hair
> And make my seated heart knock at my ribs
> Against the use of nature? Present fears
> Are less than horrible imaginings.
> My thought, whose murder yet is but fantastical,
> Shakes so my single state of man that function
> Is smothered in surmise and nothing is
> But what is not.
> Banquo.   Look how our partner's rapt.
>
> (I.iii.127–42)

Macbeth is more "realistic" than Herod because his lines absorb the duality of actor and role, making room for it in the fictive personality of the character. Macbeth describes himself as an actor who is about to perform a role in "the swelling act / of the imperial theme," and the "paradox of acting"—the actor's simultaneous engagement in and detachment from his part—is fully relevant to the character. The vividness and "depth" of his character result from the combination of a painfully intense involvement that unfixes his hair and makes his heart knock at his ribs, and a detachment that places him beside himself and indicates the amazement and revulsion with which he recoils from his own horrible imaginings. In fact, half of him seems to share Banquo's (and the audience's) perspective, as he observes how completely the other half of him is rapt. This dualism, inherent both in acting and in self-consciousness, has a direct and circumstantial bearing on his emotional and moral condition: "thought" both un-nerves him and sunders his integrity; it "Shakes so [his] single state of man that function / Is smothered," just as the action of the play is suspended by this "aside."

Playhouse architecture assisted this development of the Elizabethan dramatic character by defining one boundary between the theatrical event and the world outside and another more flexible boundary between actors and spectators. Before these boundaries were established, impersonation retained the duality of mimicry and performance evident in the Herod of the mystery plays. *As mimic,* the medieval actor imitated a fixed, preestablished role that remained as an external reference point, an element of reality that was unaltered by the imitation, even though the performance itself might be creative or even subversive, as in the plebian actor's burlesque of Herod. *As performer,* the actor remained in contact with the audience and did not presume to ignore its presence. He kept in touch with it by addressing it directly, by communicating private feelings in an overtly demonstrative style, or by supplying spoken stage directions for actions that could be understood without them ("I stamp! I stare! I loke all abowtt!"). Even passages of dialogue often had an exemplary or homiletic quality that made obvious an intention to communicate with the audience indirectly:

Everyman. Alas, I haue the[e] loud, and had grete pleasure
All my lyfe-dayes on good and treasure.
Goodes. That is to thy damnacyon, without lesynge,
For my loue is contrary to the loue euerlastynge
But yf thou had me loued moderately durynge,
As to the poore gyue part of me,
Than shouldest thou not in this dolour be,
Nor in this grete sorowe and care.
Everyman. Lo, now was I deceyued or I was ware;
And all I may wyte my spendynge of tyme.[42]

By defining a boundary between the theatrical event and the world outside, the playhouse encouraged dramatists, actors, and spectators to think of characters not as imitations but as theatrical equivalents of real people. Thus while the biblical Herod was the object of representation in the mystery plays, Holinshed's Macbeth was for Shakespeare merely raw material for dramatic invention. In the playhouse, the dramatist could reinterpret a conventional role, like the tyrant's familiar pattern of behavior, as an expression of personality. Even great historical figures like Julius Caesar or Henry V are recreated and interpreted in theatrical terms as actors who projected their larger-than-life roles into the historical imagination of future ages by playing their parts as though they knew that all the world's a stage.

Because the playhouse stage could be construed either as a part of the auditorium or as a separate space, it established an ambivalent barrier between actors and spectators. This ambivalence helped to define the duality within the subjective existence of the character that we have already encountered in Macbeth. For the actor, the audience was a stimulating, challenging presence that could not be ignored, while for the character the audience was not present at all. These would seem to be mutually exclusive perspectives, yet Shakespeare combines them. For the character-as-actor the audience objectifies the possibility of self-presence. Macbeth does not speak to the audience but rather speaks of himself as though he *were* the audience; he assimilates its presence as an aspect of his own consciousness in order to become aware of himself as the actor of himself.

Shakespeare's introspective soliloquies often have this distinctively theatrical quality. The character projects an image of himself onto the stage of his mind and then watches himself perform, often in an overtly or extravagantly theatrical way. A good example is the Bastard's first soliloquy in *King John,* just after he has given up his claim to be the legitimate son and heir of Sir Robert Faulconbridge and has been proclaimed instead Sir Richard Plantagenet, the bastard of Richard the Lionhearted. He comments sardonically on his new bastard-honor. Its ambivalence inspires his theatrical sense of "worshipful society," and he imagines the parts he will now be able to play:

> Well, now can I make any Joan a lady.
> "Good den, Sir Richard!"—"God-a-mercy, fellow"—
> And if his name be George, I'll call him Peter,
> For new-made honor doth forget men's names;
>
>   Now your traveller,
> He and his toothpick at my worship's mess,
> And when my knightly stomach is sufficed,
> Why then I suck my teeth and catechize
> My picked man of countries: "My dear sir"—
> Thus, leaning on mine elbow, I begin—
> "I shall beseech you"—that is question now;
> And then comes answer back like an Absey-book;
> "O sir," says answer, "at your best command,
> At your employment, at your service, sir":
> "No, sir," says question, "I, sweet sir, at yours."
>
>   (I.i.184–87, 189–99)

The Bastard uses the word "society" in almost its modern sense and provides an apt (if one-sided) definition of the concept in his picture of the world of "observation" and flattery, in which "Exterior form" conceals "the mounting spirit" of individualism.[43] As we have seen, what distinguishes modern urban society from the traditional community is this distinction between public role and private self, the accompanying sense of enhanced personal power, and the redefinition of the group as a gathering of strangers each playing a role and watching others play their parts.

Nowhere in Elizabethan England was the nature of urban society more evident than in the playhouse. The audience was conspicuously a gathering of strangers. At two or three thousand persons, the theater audience was the largest assembly that regularly formed in London. It was a more heterogeneous group than other large gatherings, since it had no corporate identity or common purpose, and required nothing from its members but the price of admission.[44] By virtue of its size and heterogeneity, the audience, like society, secured for its members a remarkable anonymity and freedom from the sense of responsibility that membership in a community usually entails.

The audience's anonymity is reflected in the convention on which dramatic fiction as such depends: that the audience, from the character's point of view, is not there at all. As an invisible and invulnerable presence, the audience is the image and guarantor of the character's subjective existence; it even becomes the silent partner of his personal aggressiveness and hypocrisy. It watches Othello strangle Desdemona without the slightest impulse to intervene and save her, even though it credits her innocence.[45]

The audience's contribution to characterization is especially clear in the convention of soliloquy. That soliloquy is a "convention" of drama should not explain away the surprising and paradoxical fact that the character's inmost thoughts—which he is often at pains to conceal from other characters—are spoken aloud in the hearing of a large group of people. Of course, the character's inner thoughts could not be directly revealed without the convention of soliloquy, but this truism conceals the more profound truth that his inwardness and subjectivity could not exist in the absence of such a society as the audience represents. The private self requires a public; the distinction between private and public, or inner and outer, is attenuated in a community but emphasized in a society. Subjective and private thoughts of whatever sort weaken community, and therefore the convention of soliloquy readily lends itself to such subversive meditations as are voiced by Richard of Gloucester, the Bastard, Brutus, Hamlet, Iago, and Macbeth.

In the community, where the division of a person into self and role is not encouraged, the "identification" or "empathy" by which we intuit the presence of a self within or behind the outward character is neither possible nor necessary. But in society and in the theater, persons acquire the third dimension of subjectivity precisely because the conditions of social life and theatrical performance impose distinctions between private self and public role, actor and character. Theatrical experience, as Helene Keyssar has shown, situates subjectivity in a world of others:

> A purpose of theater is to increase our consciousness of our specific individuality, while in the presence of others. When the world on the stage is maintained as separate from the world of the audience, we can be reminded fully of our separateness from the lives of others while simultaneously being confronted with the knowledge that we exist with others. . . . Theater allows the spectator to face himself privately but not alone.[46]

The social value of the theatrical occasion derives from its capacity to reconcile subjectivity and social existence, thus enabling the spectators to experience, in an intensified form, the new mode of being-together that life in the city, among its gathering of strangers, requires.

3

Reality and Play in Dramatic Fiction

The Pattern of Withdrawal and Return

The structure of Shakespearean drama distinguishes and relates subjective and objective dimensions of self and world. The theatrical occasion, as an experience of temporary withdrawal to a world of play, is a metaphor of dramatic structure, just as actor and stage are metaphors of character and setting. While actor and stage metaphors tend to identify reality with the artifice of the theater, the pattern of withdrawal and return accommodates but then subsumes this tendency by moving from reality to play and back, thereby placing the subjective and reflexive vision of life as theater in the larger context of the world beyond the playhouse to which the spectators inevitably return.

An instance of this pattern is evident in the contrasted settings noted by Northrop Frye in some of the pastoral comedies: their action begins in a normal world, then moves to a green world of disguise, imagination, and metamorphosis, and finally returns to the normal world.[1] While most clearly established in pastoral comedy, this pattern is also evident in other Shakespearean genres. The green world can appear in a history play as Falstaff's festive tavern, where Prince Hal temporarily assumes a "loose behavior" and plays many parts, or in a tragedy as Macbeth's world of black magic, where the equivocating fiend whets ambition with deceptive shows, until Nature herself rises against the usurper. The characters' experience of withdrawal and return replicates within the play the spectators' experience in withdrawing to the playhouse, which is the actual realm of disguise, festivity, and deceptive shows. The two experiences come together at the conclusion of plays like *As You Like It* or *The Tempest,* where the characters are about to leave the green world when the play concludes and the spectators leave the theater.

The pattern of withdrawal and return extends the principle of replication into the temporal dimension of dramatic action, establishing play and reality as opposed elements of the fictive world, and defining them dialectically in terms of their shifting relationship to each other. In one way or another, Shakespearean drama begins by preferring play to reality—characters seek the liberty of the green world, the protection of disguise, or the expressiveness of an "antic disposition"—but ends by preferring reality to play, whether in comedy's spirit of reconciliation—

> let us every one go home,
> And laugh this sport o'er by a country fire.
> (*Wives*, V.v.228–29)

in historical drama's spirit of qualified affirmation—

> Sound drums and trumpets! Farewell sour annoy!
> For here I hope begins our lasting joy.
> (*3H6*, V.vi.45–46)

or in tragedy's spirit of resignation—

> The weight of this sad time we must obey,
> Speak what we feel, not what we ought to say.
> (*Lear*, V.iii.324–25)

The pattern established when characters become actors and their world a stage is completed in the movement of return: the discarding of disguises, the renunciation of magic, the reaffirmation of social bonds, and whatever else is needed to restore characters and spectators alike to a world more real than the theater.

The pattern of withdrawal and return is by no means unique to drama; it can be found in all genres of Renaissance fiction. Don Cameron Allen sees its archetype in Renaissance interpretations of the wandering of Odysseus: "This is the way the topic begins: The hero crosses watery wastes impelled by power beyond his will; he arrives on islands or strands beyond the reach of the real; and there he finds a perfection of soul that makes actuality, when he returns to it, endurable."[2] But this basic movement is accompanied by theatrical metaphors even in works not written for the stage, as Walter R. Davis has shown:

The plot of pastoral romance consisted generally of the hero's mere experience of two worlds: his entrance . . . into "Arcady"; his experience of love and calm self-analysis in the inner pastoral circle; and his return to the outer world in harmony with himself. . . . Such a plot demands that the hero play the role of his ideal or possible self to the full; and this central aspect of the action is always made explicit by the disguise that the hero must assume before he can enter the pastoral land.[3]

It would be idle to propose that pastoral fiction is inherently theatrical or that the theater is a version of pastoral. Their common elements—the character as actor, the world as stage, the temporary sojourn in the inner circle—are based neither on the generic archetype of romance nor on the theatrical event but simply on the subjective dimension of human experience.

The common elements of Renaissance fiction and Shakespearean theater reflect the process of individuation by which the self comes to realization as a subject over against the world as object. This process is variously described in the Hegelian philosophy of mind, in developmental psychology, and in Toynbee's theory of the growth of civilizations;[4] a less specialized formulation is provided by José Ortega y Gasset in his essay "The Self and the Other":

There are . . . three different moments, which are repeated cyclically throughout the course of human history, in forms each time more complex and rich: (1) Man feels himself lost, shipwrecked upon things. . . ; (2) Man, by an energetic effort, retires into himself to form ideas about things and his possible dominance over them; this is taking a stand within the self. . . ; (3) Man again submerges himself in the world, to act in it according to a preconceived plan; this is action, *vita activa, praxis.*[5]

The act of withdrawal separates inner and outer worlds from the undifferentiated unity of natural, naive, or unself-conscious experience. Hegel likens the destruction of this unity to another fall of man, but the fall, of course, is fortunate: "The first reflection of awakened consciousness in men told them that they were naked. . . . The spiritual is distinguished from the natural . . . life, in the circumstance that it does not continue a mere stream of tendency, but sunders itself to self-realization. But this position of severed life has in its turn to be suppressed, and the spirit has by its own act to win its way to concord again."[6] The Renaissance concepts of protean man and fiction as an independent world, which were combined and objectified in the playhouse, are images of this sundering to self-realization. The self's return to others, its achievement of concord, is envisaged in different ways in manuals of courtesy and statescraft, arts of love, methods of oratory, and other techniques of intersubjectivity so often displayed on Renaissance stages.

A more basic, perhaps universal, expression of withdrawal and return is inherent in all representational art. Even in the visual arts, mimesis is a dynamic process unfolding within a spatial structure. The process has three phases, corresponding to the phases of individuation; mimesis, like the emerging self, moves from identity through difference to equivalence. When we look at a painting of a tree, we are initially more conscious of the tree than of the painting. All mimesis, however complex, is rooted in this element of mere recognition. This naive response, which lasts only for a moment, is prompted by the naivete inherent in perception.[7] We ordinarily look right through the senses at the world itself and can scarcely distinguish our sense impressions from the objects they represent to us. Prompted by this habitual response, we identify the painting with its object, looking right through the canvas at the tree. But the painting, as a representation, duplicates our perceptual relation to the world: we are looking at a way of looking at a tree. This duplication cancels the naive response and induces a self-conscious awareness of the painting as a mimetic artifact different from its object. Yet the awareness of difference tends to reintroduce the notion of an object "beyond" the painting. The object, of course, need not exist; what we are actually concerned with are two different ways of responding to the painting: as a thing in itself and as a representation of something else. These two responses form a reciprocal relationship: the artist, as Gombrich says, enables us "to see reality in terms of an image and an image in terms of reality."[8] Actual trees look different after we have seen their counterparts in the paintings of Constable or Van Gogh. Through the process of representation, image and reality become separate, independent, and equivalent.

Like Gombrich, W. K. Wimsatt proposes that the image is not a reflection but a metaphoric equivalent of reality: "A stone sculpture of a human head in a sense *means* a human head but in another sense *is* a carved mass of stone and a metaphor of a head. One would rather have one's head carved in stone than in cheese."[9] Philip Sidney expresses a similar idea of the mimetic process, but in didactic rather than cognitive terms. He argues that the poet's feigned images can influence our behavior in real life. For Sidney, as for Robert Frost, "the figure a poem makes . . . begins in delight and ends in wisdom."[10] The reader's progress from delight to wisdom resembles the hero's experience of withdrawal and return in pastoral romance. A poem's "charming sweetnes," its promise of pleasure, entices the reader to enter the poet's realm of fantasy: "with a tale forsooth he commeth vnto you, with a tale which holdeth children from play and old men from the chimney corner." "Pretending no more" than a tale, the poet "doth intend the winning of the mind from wickednesse to vertue" (172); in the end the poem returns the reader to reality, endowed with knowledge and a sense of purpose he did not possess before. The "tales of *Hercules, Achilles, Cyrus,* and *Aeneas*" embody "the right description of wisdom, valure, and iustice" (172) and offer the reader idealized images of virtuous action as roles to play in the theater of the world. Thus Xenophon's *Cyropaedia,* "an absolute heroicall poem" though in prose, "is not wholie imaginatiue, as we are wont to say by them that build Castles in the ayre," because actual rulers have emulated Xenophon's imaginary one: "so far substantially [the *Cyropaedia*] worketh, not onely to make a *Cyrus,* which had been but a particular excellencie, as Nature might haue done, but to bestow a *Cyrus* vpon the worlde, to make many *Cyrus's*" (157). A poem gains its relation to reality not only because it imitates nature but also because men imitate it.

This concept of mimesis, whether expressed in Sidney's terms, or in Gombrich's and Wimsatt's, involves a central paradox: the autonomy of the artifact enhances, instead of precluding, its relation to reality. Because mimesis as metaphor affirms both the integrity of a work and its power to disclose or influence a world beyond itself, it offers a model of "situated subjectivity,"[11] of the individual self tempered and fulfilled in its relation to others. This model has an important bearing not only on the Shakespearean character, but also on the relation of the Shakespearean play to its audience, reader, and interpreter.

As it passes from identity through difference to equivalence, the mimetic process combines three different modes of representation, any one of which can be sufficiently predominant to give a work its distinctive character: representation as a reflection of reality, as a self-referring object independent of reality, and as a metaphoric equivalent of reality. In Shakespearean drama, these three modes are unusually independent and are developed in succession, one after the other, in the beginning, middle, and end of dramatic action. Actor and stage are at first simply equated with character and world. Then their differences are affirmed and their relationships reversed, so that the character can be interpreted as an actor and the world as a stage. This process finally reaches an equilibrium of metaphoric equivalence: actor and character, stage and world, are seen in terms of each other as aspects of a more complex totality that includes both terms. Each of these modes can have metaphoric significance. Moreover, the mimetic process that establishes the sequence of modes becomes the basic unifying metaphor of a Shakespearean play; it relates the central imaginative experience of the characters to the experience of withdrawal and return that defines the theatrical event for the spectators.

Stage and Setting in Dramatic Structure

The shifting relation of the stage to the play's fictive setting (or settings) offers the most easily discernible dimension of the identity-difference-equivalence sequence. Stage and setting can be identified either by physical means—an emblematic or illusionistic set—or by the convention of verbal designation: "In Troy there lies the scene" (*Tro.* Prol. 1.). Most of Shakespeare's opening scenes either have indeterminate settings or else presuppose the interior of a great hall, which the acting area may have resembled; either kind of setting invites a simple, unself-conscious identification of stage with world.[12] Ordinarily, only the middle portions of a play contain settings remarkably different from the stage itself and therefore requiring imaginative visualization from the spectators—like the forests in the comedies, the battlefields in *Henry V,* or the stormy heath in *King Lear.* The final scenes often occur in the same setting (or the same kind of setting) as the opening scenes. The characters bring to that setting a new, balanced mode of perception and behavior that can accommodate the objective and subjective modes separated in the earlier scenes. Of course Shakespeare does not always employ this pattern of alternate settings and sometimes varies it. The first scene of *Hamlet* functions as an implicit prologue to the central imaginative experience of the play; the conventional expository opening is provided—rather self-consciously—by the second scene.[13] The last scene of *The Merchant of Venice* reverts to the green world of Belmont, thereby serving as a coda to the main action that concluded in the fourth act with Shylock's trial in Venice.

A Midsummer Night's Dream epitomizes the three-phase transformation of the setting and shows how each phase offers an appropriate metaphor for the corresponding phase of dramatic action. The action of the opening scene requires no specific setting; the location posited by most editors—"The Duke's Palace in Athens" or "A State-Room in Theseus's Palace"—may have been suggested to Elizabethan

audiences by the tiring-house façade, which resembled the screen
(with its doors and gallery) in the Tudor hall. In either case, locating
the first scene (and the last, which returns to the palace) demands no
unusual effort of imaginative visualization from the spectators. The
setting is simply "there". Its objectivity not only helps to meet the
requirements of exposition—the characters must be designated and
placed—but also has metaphoric bearing on the nature of the play's
normal world.

The action begins with the entrance of Egeus and the lovers, after
nineteen lines of implicit prologue spoken by Theseus and Hippolyta.
Egeus' complaint against Hermia and Lysander has the effect of
equating love with imaginative perception and making both appear
inimical to a world where place and person are objectively identified
in a manner that resists subjective transformations. Egeus' purpose
merges with the expository function of the scene: to identify the
principals and define their relationships:

> Full of vexation come I, with complaint
> Against my child, my daughter Hermia.
> Stand forth, Demetrius. My noble lord,
> This man hath my consent to marry her.
> Stand forth, Lysander. And my gracious Duke,
> This man hath bewitched the bosom of my child.
>
> (I.i.22–27)

The emphatic way he presents, labels, and differentiates the characters—" my child, my daughter Hermia," "Stand forth, Demetrius. . . .
Stand forth, Lysander"—relates his authority (and the Duke's, to
which he appeals) to the authority of exposition, which rests on the
apparently objective and inevitable quality of the perceptual world.
As Feste says, " 'That that is is'; so, I, being Master Parson, am Master
Parson; for what is 'that' but that, and 'is' but is?" (*TN* IV.ii.14–16).
Lysander rebels against this determinacy and subverts legal, parental,
and perceptual authority by winning Hermia:

> Thou hast by moonlight at her window sung
> With feigning voice verses of feigning love,
> And stol'n the impression of her fantasy.
>
> (30–32)

It is as if Lysander threatened the expository order of the play itself
by taking the part assigned to Demetrius.

Egeus's frustration will be echoed in the next scene, where Peter
Quince has difficulty persuading Bottom to stick to his part: "No, no,

you must play Pyramus; and Flute, you Thisby" (I.ii.50–51). This scene is a metadramatic parody of the expository elements in the opening scene: "First, good Peter Quince, say what the play treats on, then read the names of the actors, and so grow to a point" (8–10). Peter Quince announces the title of the play—"The most lamentable comedy and most cruel death of Pyramus and Thisby"—and then calls each player, "man by man, according to the scrip," to come forward and take his part, just as Egeus had made Demetrius and Lysander "Stand forth" and had attempted to impose parts on them. Presumably this scene, like the first, takes place in Athens; but the players, like the lovers, find the normal world too confining for the play of love: "if we meet in the city, we shall be dogged with company, and our devices known" (92–94). They resolve to meet in the woods, "by moonlight," to rehearse "most obscenely and courageously."

Lysander and Hermia have a similar idea. They hope to escape not only "the sharp Athenian law" (I.i.162) but also a mode of perception, inimical to love, that distinguishes so sharply between subject and object that even Athens is reduced to a "shady cloister" and the moon itself (so fecund in this play) made "cold" and "fruitless" (71–73). Lysander reveals their intention to elope in highly figurative language, the transforming power of which is projected into the setting he describes:

> To-morrow night, when Phoebe doth behold
> Her silver visage in the wat'ry glass,
> Decking with liquid pearl the bladed grass
> (A time that lovers' flights doth still conceal),
> Through Athens gates have we devised to steal.
>
> (209–13)

This setting is saturated with subjectivity. It is not perceived as a present reality but created in imagination; moreover, it reflects imagination's creative power to transform the real, decking with liquid pearl the bladed grass. It even reflects the tendency of imagination to seek its own reflection in the world it has transformed. The setting is finally subjective because it offers a symbol of the fulfillment Lysander seeks in leaving Athens and loving Hermia. That the love inspired by her beauty invites this marriage of imagination and nature is also understood (too well!) by Helena, her rival for the love of Demetrius:

> O happy fair!
> Your eyes are lodestars, and your tongue's sweet air
> More tuneable than lark to shepherd's ear
> When wheat is green when hawthorn buds appear.
>
> (182–85)

This erotic lyricism, with its impulse to "translate" both self and world into embodiments of desire, arises in the opening scene as a natural contrary not only to the repressive law of Athens but also to the objective mode of dramatic exposition.

Once the characters have been defined and placed, the dramatist can develop his theme by bringing the action to be represented into metaphoric relation with the subjective, imaginative means of representation. As the first scene closes, Helena anticipates the play's metaphoric and metadramatic development by speaking of love as poetic and theatrical transformation:

> Things base and vile, holding no quantity,
> Love can transpose to form and dignity.
> Love looks not with the eyes, but with the mind,
> And therefore is winged Cupid painted blind.
>
> (232–35)

In the forest scenes, the spectators must look with the eyes of the mind and transpose the stage into a luxuriant moonlit landscape. These scenes abound in elaborate panoramic descriptions that invite the audience to revel in imagination's power.[14] The spectator's creative inner sight is a concrete metaphor of love's transforming power, as John Russell Brown observes: "Our wavering acceptance of the illusion of drama is used as a kind of flesh-and-blood image of the acceptance which is appropriate to the strange and private 'truth' of those who enact the play of love."[15]

Within these general similarity of lovers and spectators, there is an important difference. What I. A. Richards says of metaphor in general applies to this case: "The disparities between tenor and vehicle are . . . as much operative as the similarities."[16] The spectators' response is not only less intense, but also more detached and balanced than that of the lovers. The forest scenes dramatize in the lovers not only the generosity of imagination that can transform and elevate another person but also the inability of such love to recognize the other for what she is in herself. Both Demetrius and Lysander see in Helena the beauty they had once found in Hermia, whom they now despise, Titania gazes on ass-pated Bottom and finds him as wise as he is beautiful. Throughout the play, the spectators' more balanced response is a norm against which the lovers' responses can be measured.

Shakespeare dramatizes the contraries balanced in this norm through the comic misunderstandings of the "rude mechanicals." The mechanicals, having no confidence in an audience's ability to imagine a fictive setting, will provide an actor to present "the person of Moonshine" and another to "present Wall" (III.i.53, 59). Yet they fear that dramatic illusion, if established at all, will be taken for actual fact: "To bring in (God shield us) a lion among ladies is a most dreadful thing. . . . half his face must be seen through the lion's neck, and he himself must speak through . . . and tell them plainly he is Snug the joiner" (28–29, 33–35, 40–41). Bottom calls attention to what he completely misunderstands in the nature of our response to drama: the distinctive "as if" quality that makes room between truth and falsehood for fiction. We gain through this quality a disinterestedness that is seldom ours on other occasions. Our ordinary response is either to assimilate or else to ignore whatever is present to us. Either way we negate the object's (or person's) presence. The aesthetic object seems luminous or revelatory because it remains ineluctably present longer than most other objects of our attention; it invites being intensely contemplated but resists being reduced to the forms of thought. (Hence the paradox that the representation of an object can have greater presence in the mind than the object itself.) Love develops a similar quality of disinterested attention.[17] The true lover tempers the impulse to possess his beloved as the object of desire with a countervailing respect for her independence; he grows from the condition of love as desire to love as a relationship of persons.

In *A Midsummer Night's Dream,* love's growth is understood as an unconscious process and therefore not fully dramatized but obliquely symbolized in the narrative and theatrical dimensions of the story. We are simply to accept the fact that the lovers somehow work through and overcome the blindness of desire during their long night in the wood. They awaken to each other's reality when they awaken from their "dream"; the harsh Athenian law is set aside, and they are married. That the lovers finally approach something like the spectators' balanced and disinterested response is suggested by the fact that they are spectators themselves in the last scene. The play they are watching, the mechanicals' production of "Pyramus and Thisby," gives them ample opportunity to exercise just that aspect of the spectators' response that they most need to balance their own lives: the detached, critical, consciously superior aspect. The warmer, imaginative aspect that can see Helen's beauty in a brow of Egypt and give local habitation to airy nothing is not repudiated, but converted from an instinctive reaction to a noble obligation "to give them thanks for nothing" (V.i.89): "If we imagine no worse of them than they of themselves, they may pass for excellent men" (213–14).

The treatment of the fictive setting in the final scene, which returns from the forest to Theseus's palace, objectifies the capacity for balanced and inclusive responsiveness that is the highest achievement of both love and theater. In the forest, the lovers had been unwitting actors in a "fond pageant" (III.ii.114), an implicit play within the play; theatrical performance functioned as a separate frame of reference in terms of which the audience could interpret the lovers' experience. But when the lovers sit down to watch "Pyramus and Thisby," the theater becomes part of their reality. What had formerly been a relationship between the play and its audience is gathered into the play's world. The discrepancy between stage and fictive setting that was so prominent in the forest scenes is recreated within the setting itself when Peter Quince's players attempt (this time without success) to convert the great hall back into a moonlit wood. This treatment of the setting provides a concrete model of the human capacity to contain subjective imagination within objective perception and relationships, just as the "strange and private truth" of the lovers is stabilized and publicly confirmed by their marriage.

Puck's epilogue, describing the play as a dream from which the audience has just awakened, is a nearly explicit statement of the analogy between the characters' and the spectators' experiences of withdrawal and return: as the moonlit wood is to Theseus' Athens, so the entire theatrical occasion is to our own normal world. In no other play does Shakespeare establish the analogy so emphatically. Such emphasis is not necessary to make the analogy effective, nor could such a confident and explicit discrimination of objective and subjective realms remain adequate to the growing complexity of Shakespeare's dramatic fictions.[18] We must recognize in particular that withdrawal and return are not always defined by means of contrasting places, even in the comedies. *The Comedy of Errors, Twelfth Night,* and *Measure for Measure,* for example, exhibit no rhythmic movement from normal world to green world and back.[19] Withdrawal can be purely psychological, accomplished by means of a disguise or antic disposition, or imposed by the confusions of mistaken identity that make a familiar world dreamlike. And this brings us from setting to character.

Actor and Character in Dramatic Structure

The indispensable requirement of withdrawal and return is a subjective treatment of world as stage and character as actor in the middle portion of a play. Bernard Beckerman points out that this subjectivity in Elizabethan drama subverts the usual subordination of inner self to outward character and of character to action that seemed to Aristotle natural requirements of the dramatic medium.

Elizabethan drama emphasizes not the growth of action but "the character's response to crisis," especially those responses that precede action and delay its achievement (as in Hamlet's revenge) or follow action and overshadow it (as in Lear's response to his daughters' ingratitude). Beckerman argues that this unwillingness to subordinate character to action results in "contradictory impulses" in the drama— to complete the story or instead to elaborate the effects of the action upon the characters.[20] These impulses combine to produce the distinctive curve of development in Elizabethan plays. The premises of the action are established in the opening scenes and the conflict resolved, sometimes hastily, in the final scenes, leaving a large middle portion of the play free for the dramatization of subjective responses.

The Comedy of Errors provides a rudimentary instance of this pattern. Egeon's narrative in the first scene gives us most of the story. He and one of his sons (Antipholus of Syracuse) were separated from his wife and their other son (Antipholus of Ephesus); Egeon now seeks the Syracusan Antipholus, who left him to seek his mother and twin brother. The action will be completed when this family is reunited— which happens suddenly near the end of the last scene. The bulk of the play is given over to the characters' responses to separation, confusion and loss. The Syracusan Antipholus, in particular, feels that he has lost himself in losing his family:

> I to the world am like a drop of water
> That in the ocean seeks another drop,
> Who falling there to find his fellow forth,
> Unseen, inquisitive, confounds himself.
> So I, to find a mother and a brother,
> In quest of them, unhappy, lose myself.
>
> (I.ii.35–40)

The feeling that identity is fluid and can be stabilized only through relationships is expressed in the action that follows through the stock device of mistaken identity.

In making this device express such an intensely subjective condition, Shakespeare differs significantly from his source, the *Menaechmi* of Plautus. The Roman comedy is much closer to the Aristotelian norm of dramatic objectivity than Shakespeare's. The Plautine characters retain an unshakable sense of themselves and a practical sense of their world as "a tickle place" where " 'tis best to be circumspect" (II.i).[21] They regard the errors to which they are subjected as insults (that provoke beatings), as deliberate deceptions (that alert wariness), or as inadvertent mistakes (that provide opportunities for

cozenage). They never ponder the larger implications of their situation, but remain constant to normal patterns of behavior in abnormal
circumstances. Resilient and predictable, the characters keep the play
focused on the action; they have little more personality than is necessary to motivate the incidents that make up the plot.[22] The action
retains the brisk pace congenial to farce, since there is no need to
interrupt it for moments of introspection.

The focus of Shakespeare's play lies elsewhere, on the characters'
responses to their situation. While preserving elements of Plautine
farce, he adds moments of lyric intensity and subjectivity that are
foreign to Roman comedy. Antipholus of Syracuse, so often mistaken
for his twin brother, begins to wonder if he really is the person he
thinks he is. When his brother's wife mistakes him for her husband,
he exclaims:

> What, was I married to her in my dream?
> Or sleep I now, and think I hear all this?
>
> . . . .
> Am I in earth, in heaven, or in hell?
> Sleeping or waking? mad or well-advised?
> Known unto these, and to myself disguised!
> (II.ii.181–82, 211–13)

In the corresponding scene in Plautus's play, Menaechmus expresses
more irritation than surprise: "Cylindrus or Coliendrus or what the
devil thou art, I know not, neither do I care to know" (II.i). He never
loses confidence in himself. When his servant warns him to suspect a
crafty courtesan's trick, Menaechmus just laughs: "Peace, foolish
knave, seest thou not what a sot she is? I shall cozen her, I warrant
thee" (II.i). But the abnormality of being mistaken for another stuns
Antipholus. It transforms his experience into a waking dream and
changes his world from the bustling commercial city of Ephesus into a
mysterious fairyland in which he fears being transformed by demonic
powers: "here we wander in illusions. / Some blessèd power deliver us
from hence!" (IV.iii.38–39).

Antipholus's fairy world, like the moonlit wood in *A Midsummer
Night's Dream,* is defined by its metaphoric relation to the theatrical
occasion. The spectators' awareness that Antipholus is an actor on a
stage, as well as a character in Ephesus, lends a kind of substance and
truth to his apprehension that he wanders in a world of illusions,
disguised to himself but known to others. He regains a measure of
composure in his bewildering situation only when his responses to it

are implicitly theatrical ones, as when he agrees to assume the role that others thrust upon him ("I'll say as they say, and persever so" [II.ii.214]) or adopts the more detached participation of the audience ("Until I know this sure uncertainty, / I'll entertain the offered fallacy" [184–85]).

At the conclusion of the play, the events of the plot are recapitulated and offered as a sufficient explanation of the confusions that attended them as they happened:

> I see we still did meet each other's man,
> And I was ta'en for him, and he for me,
> And thereupon these errors are arose.
>
> (V.i.388–90)

This explanation has the effect of retrospectively subordinating character to action. As the characters come to understand themselves in terms of the events that had earlier bewildered them, they regain a sense of their world as normal. They are, as Emelia suggests (V.i.402–8), reborn, delivered from their dream to reality. *The Comedy of Errors*, with its several Pauline homilies on the proper relations of masters and servants, husbands and wives, is an early Shakespearean exploration of the extent to which our sense of place and of our own reality depend upon our normative relations with others.[23]

The alternation from an objective emphasis on narrative to a subjective emphasis on character followed by completion of the narrative has a direct bearing on characterization that I want now to consider. This account of characterization, brief and schematic as it is, will be helpful as an introduction to the detailed analyses in the following chapters.

Characterization, like the mimetic process of which it is a part, moves from identity through difference to equivalence (or reciprocal relationship). This pattern in characterization is established by using the actor as a metaphor, just as the contrast of normal world and green world is established by using the stage as a metaphor.[24] The actor's relation to his role embodies the relationship of the objective and subjective dimensions of our being, our "fair and outward character" (*TN*, I.ii.51) and "that within which passeth show" (*Ham.*, I.ii.85). Personal identity is destroyed or transcended when the inner self is sundered from the outward character by disguise, dispossession, love, or madness—conditions often expressed through self-conscious role-playing. The ludic impulse is supplanted by a complementary mimetic impulse to reintegrate personality by reassuming one's given character as the outward expression of the self. In the end, character is not identical with self but becomes the medium through which the self is related to others. Each phase in this process gives the actor's relation to his role a different kind of metaphoric value. Moreover, the process as a whole focuses the large contrast of play and reality on the personal effort to maintain the freedom, integrity, and openness of human nature.

The initial phase of characterization reflects the mere identification of actor with character that results from the convention of representation and the requirements of exposition. We know that the actor is supposed to represent somebody, and we want at the outset to discover the identity and basic situation of that person. Therefore, in the initial phase, characters are generally defined objectively, from without, in terms of their appearance, status, sex, age, general disposition, and relation to other characters: Hamlet is Prince of Denmark, his father has recently died, his mother has married his father's brother, who has just succeeded to the throne.

The requirements of exposition become metaphorically expressive when the main characters are made aware of being objectively defined and protest that the definition is somehow inadequate. The actions that they might play, or must play, do not denote them truly; their full humanity is misunderstood or ignored. Often they are enervated or oppressed by the expectations of others. Portia, who must accept the husband designated by her father's bizarre trial, feels "aweary of this great world" (*MV*, I.ii.1–2). Rosalind is melancholy in "the envious court" (*AYL*, II. i.4) and must "show more mirth than [she is] mistress of" (I.ii.2–3), only to be banished by the distrustful duke because "the people praise her for her virtues" (I.ii.261). Hamlet, "the observed of all observers" (III.i.154), is "most dreadfully attended" (II.ii.266), oppressed by "the cheer and comfort of [Claudius'] eye" (I.ii.116)—"too much in the sun" (67). Such characters are readily motivated to seek liberty in banishment, or to disguise themselves to escape the demands of their society. Other characters, like Richard II, Othello, Lear, or Timon, who are initially quite certain of themselves and content with their relationships, are soon terribly disillusioned, forcibly dispossessed, or in some other way required to forfeit, and then to reconstruct, themselves.

The second phase of character development is "reflexive" for both the character and the audience. It dramatizes the character's response to a situation and (usually) his awareness of that response as a subjective condition that alienates him from others and prevents him from taking action in his usual way. Hamlet's melancholy, Lear's madness, and Othello's jealousy are obvious examples. Long before Othello recognizes his terrible mistake, and even before he has confirmed himself in jealousy, he realizes that his mere suspicions have destroyed his direct and confident way of life:

> O, now for ever
> Farewell the tranquil mind! farewell content!
> Farewell the plumed troop, and the big wars
> That make ambition virtue! O, farewell!
> . . . .
> Farewell! Othello's occupation's gone.
>
> (III.iii.347–50, 357)

The character's subjective response often takes an overtly theatrical form, as in the case of disguise or antic disposition. The audience therefore becomes more aware of the play as a play and of its own subjective involvement in the fiction, so that its self-consciousness mirrors the hero's. The effect is often a paradoxical one of simultaneous detachment and engagement.[25] Both the delusive nature of Othello's suspicions and their compelling reality for him are conveyed to the audience when he becomes audience to Iago's conversation with Cassio and misapplies Cassio's scurrilous remarks about Bianca to Desdemona. The same dual impression is intensified in the next scene (IV.ii) when Othello stages an encounter with Desdemona as a turn with a prostitute. His violence in forcing this degrading fiction on her offers a disturbing reflection of our own *libido speculandi*.

The reflexive phase of characterization not only divides the hero from others, but also separates inner self from outward character and sets them at odds: "I do entreat that we may sup together / You are welcome, sir, to Cyprus.—Goats and monkeys!" (IV.i.255–56). The third phase of character development reconciles the opposed emphases of the other two by restoring the self to others and by relating outward character and inner self as separate aspects of a fuller personality. The recognition scenes and marriages of the comedies and romances are obvious instances. In the tragedies, as in the comedies, self-recovery does not simply restore the initial identification of self with character; these two dimensions of personality remain distinct, even though they are related. Othello, in his final speech, attempts to recover himself by projecting a "character"—in the literal sense of the word as something "set down" in writing, "in your letters." This writing, like the playwright's script, prescribes speech:

> Then must you speak
> Of one that loved not wisely, but too well;
> Of one not easily jealous, but, being wrought,
> Perplexed in the extreme. . . .
>
> (V.ii.343–46)

His self-division is both confirmed and cancelled when "the noble Moor" kills the "dog" who murdered Desdemona:

> Set you down this.
> And say besides that in Aleppo once,
> Where a malignant and a turbaned Turk
> Beat a Venetian and traduced the state,
> I took by th' throat the circumcisèd dog
> And smote him—thus.
>
> (352–56)

"All that's spoke is marred," says Gratiano—marred by the mute action the playwright sets down: "*He stabs himself.*" Othello can no longer be fully identical with the outward character that has done the state some service, "that loved not wisely, but too well," and that smote the malignant Turk, except by killing the inner self that undermined that character. In this tragic context, the impulse toward absolute unity of being is suicidal.

The simplest form of resolution in the development of character is the removal of disguise. Yet even here the character that is revealed is not identical with, although it expresses, the inner self. The final scene of *Twelfth Night* offers an instructive instance. The scene hinges on the encounter of identical twins, who seem to occupy a single character: "one face, one voice, one habit, and two persons" (V.i.208). Viola, disguised in "masculine usurped attire" (V.i.242), has presented herself as Cesario; Sebastian has been mistaken for Cesario. They must be disengaged from their illusory union in this fictitious person before they can be restored to each other. When they meet, Sebastian momentarily mistakes Cesario for himself: "Do I stand there? I never had a brother" (218). Viola is more deeply astonished to see another person in her part. It can only be her brother's ghost, she thinks, for she fears him dead and has made Cesario his substitute ("him I imitate") [III.vi.363]):

> So went he suited to his watery tomb.
> If spirits can assume both form and suit,
> You come to fright us.
>
> (226–28)

Sebastian replies that he is not himself but the actor of himself; his identity is a duality:

> A spirit I am indeed,
> But am in that dimension grossly clad
> Which from the womb I did participate.
> Were you a woman, as the rest goes even,

> I should my tears let fall upon your cheek
> And say, "Thrice welcome, drowned Viola!"
>
> (228–33)

His response captures both halves of the Shakespearean character's dual nature: his inner freedom from all personal definition, and his confinement in and commitment to a body, sex, country, name, parentage, and all else that constitutes his "character." Character, however fully defined, is only a partial manifestation of the inner spirit; but, as Sebastian knows, the spirit is fulfilled only by assuming its character fully, "Else a great Prince in prison lies."[26]

A similar duality is affirmed in Viola. She goes on acting as Cesario, even after she has revealed her true identity. She postpones resuming her feminine self, claiming that her "woman's weeds" (V.i.265) are not available. At the moment of her reunion with Sebastian, she seems to hold herself at arm's length:

> If nothing lets to make us happy both
> But this my masculine usurped attire,
> Do not embrace me till each circumstance
> Of place, time, fortune do cohere and jump
> That I am Viola; which to confirm,
> I'll bring you to a captain in this town,
> Where lie my maiden weeds; by whose gentle help
> I was preserved to serve this noble Count.
> All the occurrence of my fortune since
> Hath been between this lady and this lord.
>
> (241–50)

She obliges Sebastian and the others to do what the audience has done all along: see and understand "Viola" in and through "Cesario." Orsino makes the final exit still referring to her as "Cesario" and a "man," as though she were completely at liberty to determine her character and even her sex. He has learned a great deal about respecting the independence, the "otherness," of the woman he loves.

The play itself, in a similar way, holds itself apart from the audience in order to elicit a deeper response to its truth. "Do not embrace me"—the phrase perfectly expresses the resistance this scene offers to the convention within which it unfolds. The audience is denied the gratification of the expected embrace; the long-anticipated reunion is only partly dramatized. Instead of embracing his sister, Sebastian addresses himself to the other characters and considers the consequence of the reunion for them. In doing so, he places the sentimental tone of the reunion within the encompassing comedy of errors. He turns to Olivia and remarks—the line always gets a laugh—"So comes it, lady, you have been mistook" (251). The subjective responses of the characters are placed within the objective reality of their relationships and thereby both limited and fulfilled: limited by being defined as subjective and partly erroneous, fulfilled by being answered through the corresponding responses of others. Viola's "imagination" that her brother lives proves true, and the disguise by which she had imitated him is shown to be false and deceptive. Orsino discovers the real nature of his feelings for Olivia and "Cesario." Olivia discovers both the fallibility and the naturalness of her sudden passion for—Sebastian, as it turns out.

The last scene of *Twelfth Night* appropriates the dual response that naturally attends the conclusion of any play. At the end, the play's design is complete, but this very perfection precludes our further involvement and obliges us to carry our memory of the performance back into our ordinary world. Thus at the very moment when the play is held apart as a completed dramatic artifact, it also enters the ongoing experience that we return to in leaving the theater. The conclusion of *Twelfth Night* reflects this dual response in characterization when it affirms the subjective autonomy of its main characters while likewise reestablishing their stable and enduring relationships with others.

Whether defined as a journey between contrasted settings, or as a process of character development, the pattern of withdrawal and return makes the theatrical occasion itself a metaphoric embodiment of the play's main theme. The plays examined in the following chapters illustrate three specific forms of this embodiment, while also exemplifying important general features of withdrawal and return. *As You Like It* is the clearest Shakespearean instance of the fact that contrasted settings and character development are complementary aspects of a single pattern that brings the theatrical event into dramatic fiction as a metaphor of reality: in this case, the reality of love as it develops in courtship from desire through imagination to relationship. *Henry V* demonstrates more clearly than any other Shakespearean play the affective dimension of withdrawal and return as a pattern that structures the audience's response; through this response the play's heroic ideal is defined in its complex relation to historical reality. *Macbeth* extends the pattern to opposite extremes, using it to disclose an intensely subjective experience in the main character, while also defining, in larger terms than Shakespeare uses anywhere else, the process by which modern societies emerge from archaic communities.

4

Theatrical Fiction and the Reality of Love in *As You Like It*

In chapter 3, I suggested that the reflexive quality of Shakespearean drama is only one element, though an important one, in the process of mimesis. A play reflects itself not to reveal the author's concept of drama, but to make theatrical artifice symbolize a reality beyond itself. I want now to illustrate this idea further by examining *As You Like It*.

Interpreters of the play have noted its reflexive quality. David Young shows how Shakespeare calls attention to "the theoretical and fictive aspects of his material" in order to make the play an examination of its medium, "exploring the implications of fiction, artifice, convention, genre, and of the impulses that give rise to art."[1] Albert Cirillo also insists that *As You Like It* is "self-reflective"—not only because its deliberate artifice sustains our awareness that we are watching a fiction even as we suspend disbelief, but also because the characters' experience in the play reflects our own experience of the play. The characters withdraw from their "working-day world" (I.iii.12) to the Forest of Arden and return with a new understanding of life. For us, the entire play is a second world that we enter temporarily and emerge from with a new understanding: "the play is our Arden."[2] Both Young and Cirillo assume that metadramatic self-consciousness is the play's primary value. Cirillo interprets it as "a self-reflective commentary on the unreality of the pastoral convention" (p. 26), and Young proposes that it is a "self-referring" exploration of "drama as literary expression and as theater" (p. 196).

In the following analysis of *As You Like It*, I shall develop and qualify this metacritical approach in two ways: first by showing the importance of theatrical performance to the play's reflection of itself, sec-

86

ond by demonstrating the mimetic function of this self-reflection. Theatrical artifice emerges in the course of the play, displacing the narrative artifice of the opening scenes; when the narrative mode is again prominent in the final scenes, Shakespeare sets a limit to his play's self-reflection and turns the spectator's attention to the world beyond the playhouse. This relationship of narrative and theatrical artifice is central to the play's mimetic function as a drama of courtship. Shakespeare emphasizes both modes of artifice in order to make their relationship a comprehensive metaphor of love.

Narrative and Theatrical Artifice

Fiction becomes doubly fictive in the theater: a play is plotted and written by the dramatist and presented on stage by the players. The fact that the dramatist writes *for* the stage does not obviate this distinction; it must have been much in Shakespeare's mind as he revised his source for *As You Like It,* Thomas Lodge's *Rosalynde,* to make the substance of that prose romance suitable for theatrical performance. If Shakespeare united the author's art and the actor's, he also distinguished narrative artifice from theatrical artifice and used the distinction to emphasize the contrast of normal world and green world.

In the opening scenes, Shakespeare stresses those contrivances that make characters function as narrators in establishing the premises of the action and as agents in developing the plot. So much of the first act is given over to exposition that we may come to feel, as Rosalind does, "news-crammed" (I.ii.88), while we attend to gratuitously elaborated passages of retrospective narration. Oliver, for example, summons Charles the wrestler to a plot against his younger brother Orlando, but first asks, "What's the new news at the new court?" (I.i.90–91). Charles replies, "There's no news at the court, sir, but the old news"—whereupon the beef-witted man is made to fill out the whole chronicle of Duke Senior's banishment and to embellish the tale with allusions to the legendary "Robin Hood of England" and the Arcadian "golden world." The wrestler's account, like Orlando's opening remarks about his upbringing, is deliberately flat and undramatic; we might say of the play's opening (as Celia says of Le Beau's pathetic story about the wrestler's victims), "I could match this beginning with an old tale" (I.ii.108). Of course, the old news does have some bearing on Oliver's hatred of Orlando, since the new court was established when "the old Duke [was] banished by his younger brother the new Duke," but while this parallel relates different strands of the plot to a common theme it has no dramatic function: Oliver's enmity is not thereby motivated or intensified, nor is its nature clarified for him or for any other character. The "tyrant Duke . . . [and] tyrant brother" (I.ii.269) remain storybook villains, who acknowledge both their own wickedness and the virtue of their intended victims. "I hope I shall see an end of him," says Oliver of Orlando, "for my soul, yet I know not why, hates nothing more than he. Yet he's gentle. . . ." (I.i.151–53). The usurping Duke, like Oliver, is helplessly compulsive in his malice. He capriciously banishes Rosalind on pain of death, his displeasure "Grounded upon no other argument / But that the people praise her for her virtues" (I.ii.260–61). These villains are permitted no greater freedom than those they oppress; they are crushed by the plot.

Every scene in the play requires both narrative and theatrical artifice, but the two modes are not given the same emphasis throughout. The conspicuous narrative artifice of the opening scenes is displaced by equally prominent theatrical artifice in the forest scenes, where characters become actors and spectators and invoke the theatrical situation as an image of real life: "All the world's a stage" (II.vii.139). Lodge's *Rosalynde* has the same contrast of normal world and green world that Cirillo claims is "self-reflective" in Shakespeare's play, but the prose romance could use only narrative resources to define the contrast. While we may speculate that the sojourn of Lodge's characters in their Forest of Arden reflects the reader's imaginative involvement in the fictive world of pastoral romance, in fact neither the reader's experience nor the outline of Lodge's plot is sufficiently well defined to make such an analogy effective. Shakespeare made it effective by adapting the prose romance for theatrical performance. To present Lodge's story on stage, he had to reduce its length by nearly half; as a result, the basic movement between court and forest is more pronounced. Moreover, the spectators' experience is more clearly articulated than the reader's as a journey to a fictive world, the playhouse, and thus offers a substantial counterpart of the characters' journey to the forest.

When Lodge first describes the forest, he envisages it as a theater, using this comparison to suggest the forest's self-enclosing and protected character, its isolation from the world of envy and strife from which the main characters have fled: his Arden is located in "a faire valley (compassed with mountaines, whereon grewe many pleasant shrubbs) . . . round about in the forme of an Amphitheater."[3] Walter R. Davis points out that this forest, unlike pastoral landscapes in romances by Sidney and Greene, is not entirely idealized but rather "an ambivalent place, redolent of amity but solitary as well, and therefore privative and unpleasant. . . . The positive value of the countryside consists for Lodge in the freedom of action that masks permit there."[4] In *As You Like It*, these attributes of the forest are objectified in the playhouse and in the artifice of theatrical performance.

Shakespeare's Arden, like Lodge's, is ambivalent. It appears alternately as an idyllic "golden world" and as a harsh "desert inaccessible," mirroring the disposition of the beholder. In the playhouse, this ambivalence finds its correlative in the indeterminate quality of the stage, set not by realistic scenery but by the subjective verbal responses of the characters.[5] The physical location of the opening scenes is only vaguely indicated and is not important to the characters, but the forest is repeatedly described, especially in Act II. In the forest scenes, the spectators are required to imagine a fictive landscape that is not physically present. Shakespeare's company may have employed emblematic tree properties, but these did not localize the stage as a forest and may even have intensified its indeterminacy. Werner Habicht has shown that tree properties had many different emblematic significances, including "deception, error, uncertainty, disguise, dueling, betrayal, mystery, dream, magic, or the goddess Fortune."[6] All these associations are appropriate in *As You Like It*. Moreover, it is likely that the tree properties, especially if they were large and elaborate, were placed on stage before the play began, so that they were visible during the opening scenes as well as during the forest scenes.[7] This circumstance must have emphasized the fact that the stage becomes a forest only in imagination, while making unnecessary the cumbersome scene changes that the script would seem to require. After the action moves to the forest in II.i, it returns to Oliver's orchard for one scene (II.iii) and to the ducal palace (or its grounds) for two (II.ii; III.i) before being relocated in the forest for the remainder of the play. These shifts in setting are not necessitated by the plot: II.ii–iii and III.i could easily follow I.iii; this sequence would require only one change of setting. The Shakespearean alternation of settings not only keeps the contrast of court and country before the audience but also requires from them a greater imaginative effort in establishing, then reestablishing, the stage as a forest.

The spectators' active participation in imagining the forest setting provides in their theatrical experience a concrete metaphor of the characters' experience in responding to the forest. Like the spectators, the characters imagine the setting, deliberately or unconsciously seeing what is not objectively there. In the first of the forest scenes, the banished Duke establishes the setting by proposing how he and his companions should respond to it:

> Now, my co-mates and brothers in exile,
> Hath not old custom made this life more sweet
> Than that of painted pomp? Are not these woods
> More free from peril than the envious court?
>
> (II.i.1–4)

Amiens' reply suggests that the values seen by the Duke in Arden are less the gift of nature than of imagination:

> Happy is your Grace
> That can translate the stubbornness of fortune
> Into so quiet and so sweet a style.
>
> (II.i.18–20)

The "old custom" of conventional pastoral sentiments offers the Duke a way to make a virtue of necessity. His description of the forest exemplifies a central strategy of the pastoral imagination—to accept as idyllic the security of a low and mean estate and to exchange the anguish of human malice for the more easily suffered harshness of the elements:

> Blow, blow, thou winter wind,
> Thou art not so unkind
> As man's ingratitude.
>
> (II.vii.174–76)

The forest, like the stage, offers little resistance to the imagination's transforming powers. While the genteel and optimistic Duke finds "tongues in trees, books in the running brooks, / Sermons in stones, and good in everything" (II.i.16–17), the melancholy Jaques as easily finds bad in everything, moralizing the spectacle of a wounded deer "into a thousand similes" (II.i.45), all of them indictments of man's inhumanity. When Orlando enters the forest, hungry, desperate, and dispossessed, he finds it "bleak," "uncouth," and "savage" (II.vi); but after he has joined the Duke's merry men, he sees, and would have everyone see, Rosalind's virtue "witnessed everywhere" (III.ii.8). The capacity of the forest to sustain the different poetic projections of its beholders is comically objectified when Orlando litters the stage with his poetry, hanging "odes upon hawthorns, and elegies on brambles; all, forsooth, deifying the name of Rosalind" (III.ii.341–42); he carves her name "on every tree" (III.ii.9).

In both *Rosalynde* and *As You Like It*, the heroine disguises as a page boy and, becoming her own actor, dramatizes herself for her lover. In Shakespeare's play, Rosalind's disguise translates the psychological "feigning" of courtship into the language of theatrical counterfeiting and thus invites the spectators to apprehend the fictive experience represented in the play in terms of their own actual experience of the play: just as Orlando pretends that Ganymede is Rosalind, so do the spectators pretend that another boy, the actor, is Rosalind. If she becomes her own actor, she is also a spectator at the encounter of Silvius and Phebe, which is presented to her as

> a pageant truly played
> Between the pale complexion of true love
> And the red glow of scorn and proud disdain.
>
> (III.iv.47–49)

Silvius's romantic longing and Phebe's *daunger* act out contrary impulses in Rosalind's love, just as the sudden union of Celia and Oliver reflects the giddiness of her passion and the reckless surrender it prompts in her. These mirroring relationships among the characters reflect the nature of the play itself as a mirror of love held up to the men and women in the audience;[8] reciprocally, the activity of playing, beholding, and pretending shared by actors and spectators lends its substance and immediacy to the fictive experience of the characters.

The Progress of Love

The forest, in short, is a reflection of the play as *theatrical* fiction. But the purpose of this analogy is not to make the experience of the characters a "self-reflective commentary" on the nature of the play as a theatrical event. Instead, the pattern of withdrawal and return objectifies in the action of the play and in the theatrical event the development of love in Rosalind and Orlando, as their courtship progresses from the impulsive reactions of love at first sight experienced in Duke Frederick's realm, through the subjective and imaginative responses to desire acted out in the forest, to love's fulfillment in the "world-without-end bargain" (*Love's Labor's Lost* V.ii.779) of marriage.

In *As You Like It*, Shakespeare presents a deft and surprisingly comprehensive synthesis of Renaissance attitudes toward love. Many of these attitudes are conveniently recorded in the first two of Spenser's *Fowre Hymnes: An Hymne in Honour of Love* and *An Hymne in Honour of Beautie*, which provide a compendium of erotic theories of the time, a love poet's commonplace book.[9] Especially significant for Shakespeare's play is a passage in the *Hymne of Beautie* (208–38) that traces love's progress from Petrarchan erotic frustration, through Platonic idealization and sublimation, to the respectful and mutually sustaining relationship of marriage. It is tempting to speculate that Shakespeare had this passage in mind as he wrote the play, although it deals in commonplaces he could have encountered elsewhere.

The passage begins by qualifying the old saw that Phebe, in *As You Like It,* quotes from Marlowe's *Hero and Leander,* "Who ever lov'd that lov'd not at first sight?" (III.v.82):

> . . . all that like the beautie which they see,
> Streight do not loue: for loue is not so light,
> As streight to burne at first beholders sight.
>
> (208–10)

The *Hymnes* of Love and Beauty acknowledge that love begins in the passions aroused "at first beholders sight" but must progress to a higher level. At the onset of desire, lovers are overwhelmed by passion and languish "like thrals forlorne" while the "tyrant Loue doest laugh and scorne / At their complaints" (*An Hymne of Love,* 134–36). The personification of Love as an imperious tyrant accords well with the lover's actual feeling that his passion afflicts him from without as an alien force that he cannot accept as an aspect of his own personality. The passions aroused by love at first sight are so intense that they frustrate their own fulfillment, reducing the lover to a Narcissus-like impasse, where his plenty makes him poor (see *An Hymne of Love,* 127–33, and *Amoretti,* Sonnet 35).

Rosalind and Orlando fall in love at first sight before they journey to the forest. While love's values are ultimately opposed to those of "the envious court" (II.i.4), love is initially as much an instinctive and tyrannical compulsion as are the irrational and wicked "humors" of Oliver and Duke Frederick. Oliver's plot to have Orlando killed by the wrestler dramatizes a treachery antithetical to love, but the wrestling is also treated as a metaphor of love's triumph over Rosalind and Orlando. "Sir, you have wrestled well," she says to him, "and overthrown / More than your enemies" (I.ii.254–55). In the next scene, when Celia urges her to recover herself, to wrestle with her affections, she replies, "O, they take the part of a better wrestler than myself" (I.iii.21–22). Orlando is overcome by desire quite as suddenly as Rosalind, and so completely that he cannot speak to her, even when she gives him a love token:

What passion hangs these weights upon my tongue?
I cannot speak to her, yet she urged conference.
O poor Orlando, thou art overthrown!
Or Charles or something weaker masters thee.

(I.ii.238–41)

His virtues "Are sanctified and holy traitors to [him]" (II.iii.13), betraying him not only to his envious brother but also to love, "that blind rascally boy that abuses every one's eyes because his own are out" (IV.i.197–98). Cupid's arrows and Fortune's blows fall together in Duke Frederick's court; both deities are blind and capricious. No sooner does Rosalind confess to Celia her love for Orlando than Frederick banishes her from court. The banishment externalizes love's inner tyranny by casting Rosalind into an unfamiliar and dangerous world where "Beauty provoketh thieves sooner than gold" (I.iii.106). Only a masculine disguise will permit her to accept both the forest and love on her own terms. When she resolves to disguise herself, Celia happily suggests that they go "content / To liberty, and not to banishment" (I.iii.133–34).

The narrative artifice of the opening scenes, which overtly subjects the characters to the requirements of the plot, expresses metaphorically the impersonal forces—love and fortune—that shape their lives from without and limit their freedom. The theatrical artifice of the forest scenes, on the other hand, affirms the characters' liberty to assert and transform themselves by deliberately playing roles and thereby translating the stubbornness of fortune into a variety of personal styles: the Duke's elegant pastoralism, Jaques's melancholy, Touchstone's dry cynicism, Corin's stolid rusticity.

For Rosalind and Orlando, the theatricality of the forest objectifies the second stage in love's progress toward fulfillment, in which desire becomes an internal and creative force expressing the imaginative energies of the self. In the *Hymne of Beautie*, Spenser's lover escapes the frustrations attending love at first sight by turning away from the overwhelming wealth of his mistress's physical beauty to create her image in his mind, "drawing out of the obiect of [his] eyes, / A more refyned forme" (213–14). The lover overcomes his excessive humility and self-abasement before the beloved by possessing her completely in imagination. He fashions her image "to his fancies will," cherishing it in "The mirrour of his owne thought" and embracing it "in his mind entyre": "He thereon fixeth all his fantasie, / And fully setteth his felicitie" (228–29). Passion is inwardly mastered by this exercise of imagination, so that it may enrich and express personality; the lover's mental image of his beloved conforms to "his spirits proportion" (1.227), so that he can respond actively to it as he could not to the woman herself. The Forest of Arden provides an appropriate stage for acting out this subjective response to desire, because it yields readily to the shaping power of imagination. In the forest, the once tongue-tied Orlando becomes poetical, "deifying the name of Rosalind" in odes and elegies and fashioning her "more refyned forme" as the epitome of feminine beauty and virtue. Rosalind's disguise is both a symbol of and a response to Orlando's poetic love; as Ganymede, she too feigns a Rosalind.

The development of the play's complex central relationship is clarified by the supporting characters—Touchstone and Audrey, Silvius and Phebe, Celia and Oliver—who exaggerate tendencies also present in Rosalind and Orlando. Touchstone joins Audrey where all the ladders start, in desire merely sexual. Like the other lovers, he is led to the altar in Nature's yoke, but he refuses (or is unable) to idealize his passion. Love remains for him a carnal restraint imposed on his otherwise free spirit: "As the ox hath his bow, sir, the horse his curb, and the falcon her bells, so man hath his desires" (III.iii.69–70). Touchstone is mordantly aware of the erotic and imaginative idealism that he does not experience inwardly; he dismisses it as self-delusion and hypocrisy. Thus, when Orlando begins a love poem, "From the east to western Inde, / No jewel is like Rosalinde" (III.ii.83–84), Touchstone instantly offers a parody that reduces Orlando's idealism to its foundation in sexual appetite: "If a hart do lack a hind, / Let him seek out Rosalinde" (III.ii.96–97). When Audrey asks Touchstone whether poetry is "a true thing . . . honest in deed and word," he replies: "No, truly; for the truest poetry is the most faining, and lovers are given to poetry, and what they swear in poetry may be said, as lovers, they do feign" (III.iii.16–18). His punning conflation of *fain* (to desire, or be apt to) and *feign* (to fashion, imagine, or dissemble) suggests how quickly desire stimulates imagination, and how inevitably imagination falsifies desire.[10] While the play as a whole does not ultimately support his sly indictment of love's and poetry's manifold dishonesty, the idealism of the lovers must be tested on the base metal of his cynicism to pass for true gold. Thus Celia warns Rosalind that "The oath of a lover is no stronger than the word of a tapster; they are both the confirmer of false reckonings" (III.iv.27–29); Phebe protests to Silvius, "O, for shame, for shame, / Lie not, to say mine eyes are murderers" (III.v.18–19); and Rosalind advises Orlando that romantic hyperboles "are all lies. Men have died from time to time, and worms have eaten them, but not for love" (IV.i.96). In the end, erotic idealism is granted qualified approval, and even Touchstone claims to have found a pearl of great price in his Audrey (V.iv.55–59). Lovers are fain to feign, but the artifice of love, like the artifice of theatrical fiction, is a means to truth.

Both kinds of artifice are epitomized by Rosalind's disguise. She assumes the disguise in the first instance to protect herself from sexual assault (see I.iii.108–22), then uses it to maintain the cautious approach to love that Celia had earlier recommended: "Love no man in good earnest, nor no further in sport neither than with safety of a pure blush thou mayst in honor come off again" (I.ii.27–29). This virginal impulse to protect feminine integrity from masculine desire assumes an extreme form in Phebe, and Rosalind affirms her more balanced personality when she condemns Phebe's perverse rejection of Silvius:

> . . . mistress, know yourself. Down on your knees,
> And thank heaven, fasting, for a good man's love;
> For I must tell you friendly in your ear,
> Sell when you can, you are not for all markets.
> Cry the man mercy, love him, take his offer.
>
> (III.v.57–61)

Rosalind's disguise allows her to control, by consciously indulging in game, both the impulse to resist the claims of love and the contrary impulse to yield too quickly—which Phebe cannot control at all once her excessively rigid defenses are broken down from an unexpected quarter by Ganymede.

Silvius exemplifies the Petrarchan lover's excessive humility and his deification of his mistress—tendencies also present in Orlando. In the fifth scene of Act Three, Phebe scornfully protests to Silvius that her disapproving looks could not possibly kill him, as he insists they will; Rosalind, who overhears this remark, must in turn assure Orlando in the next scene that her frown "will not kill a fly" (IV.i.101). What Rosalind would cure in Silvius and Orlando is not their idealism but their self-abasement that indicates that they are, in some measure, the victims of their passion. Their humility betrays their assumption that love's perfection requires only the lady's consenting, and, from Rosalind's feminine point of view, this assumption appears irresponsible. She would have Silvius recover his self-respect, so that he can play his part in the relationship he instinctively desires and can accept its consequences:

> You are a thousand times a properer man
> Than she a woman. 'Tis such fools as you

That makes the world full of ill-favored children.
'Tis not her glass, but you, that flatters her,
And out of you she sees herself more proper
Than any of her lineaments can show her.

(III.v.51–56)

Her advice is to no avail; she later dismisses Silvius with the remark
that love has made him "a tame snake" (IV.iii.71). Orlando is more
self-possessed than Silvius, not because he believes less intensely in
love's idealism, but because he consciously affirms it as his. The disguised Rosalind encourages Orlando to dramatize himself as a lover,
to submit his protestations to the discipline of a consciously contrived
performance.[11] From Orlando's point of view, the wooing game is a
trial of his love and a demonstration by which he means to prove that
his "faith" can withstand the mocks of the saucy Ganymede, who
would cure him of love (see III.ii.398–406).

If Rosalind's disguise permits Orlando much greater self-
possession than he could muster when she was undisguised, it also
dramatizes the excessive subjectivity of a passion that replaces an
actual woman with an idealized image of her. Rosalind comes to the
heart of the problem when, in pretending to disapprove of Orlando's
unconventional tidiness—a "careless desolation" (III.ii.359) being the
hallmark of a Petrarchan lover—she detects an element of narcissism
in his love: "You are rather point-device in your accoutrements, as
loving yourself than seeming the lover of any other" (III.ii.360–63).
There is some evidence in the text for what must have been quite
evident to the Elizabethan spectator, that Rosalind in her disguise
resembles Orlando. His youth and lack of a beard are repeatedly mentioned, and he is "furnished like a hunter" (III.ii.233). Rosalind—
whom Orlando describes in a poem as a "huntress" (III.ii.4)—is
"more than common tall" (I.iii.111) and augments her doublet and
hose with a hunter's gear: "a gallant curtle-axe" and a "boar-spear"
(I.iii.113,114). The resemblance between the lovers was further
marked for Elizabethan spectators by the fact that both of them, on
Shakespeare's celibate stage, were played by young men—perhaps by
the same pair who played Viola and Sebastian in *Twelfth Night*. The
wooing game of Rosalind and Orlando dramatizes the complex state
of mind suggested by Spenser's account of the poetic lover who has
turned away from his mistress to fashion her image "to his fancies
will" and to admire it in "The mirrour of his owne thought."

As Ganymede, Rosalind dramatizes for Orlando a euphuistically
satirical image of herself that counters his idealized image of "The
fair, the chaste, and unexpressive she" (III.ii.10):

> . . . I will be more jealous of thee than a
> Barbary cock-pigeon over his hen, more
> clamorous than a parrot against rain, more
> newfangled than an ape, more giddy in my
> desires than a monkey. I will weep for
> nothing, like Diana in the fountain, and I
> will do that when you are disposed to be
> merry; I will laugh like a hyen, and that
> when thou art inclined to sleep.
>
> (IV.i.136–43)

If he possesses her completely in imagination, she fools him to the top of his bent. The joyful exuberance of her role-playing should not obscure the fact that her self-dramatization as shrew projects the frustration of a woman whose independence is not respected. Her teasing implicitly criticizes the blind subjectivity of Orlando's passion by suggesting that his Rosalind has a will of her own. "She will do as I do," says Rosalind playing Ganymede playing Rosalind. If her deception of Orlando acts out his own self-deception, it also helps him to overcome it. The activity of pretending that Ganymede is Rosalind encourages in Orlando an awareness that the actual Rosalind is more real than the rarefied mistress of his Petrarchan fantasies. His "cure"—as she call it (III.ii.376–400)—is all but complete when he at last protests that he "can live no longer by thinking" (V.ii.48).

The role-playing of Rosalind and Orlando becomes a remarkably comprehensive theatrical symbol of love's complexity, but the symbol is so ingenious that it threatens to belie its referent and to entangle the lovers in the artifice of their wooing. Their saving impulse to set the game aside is signaled and partly motivated by the abrupt and utterly uncomplicated union of Celia and Oliver. "There was never anything so sudden," says Rosalind to Orlando,

> but the fight of two rams and Caesar's thrasonical
> brag of I came, saw, and overcame; for your brother
> and my sister no sooner met but they looked; no
> sooner looked but they loved; no sooner loved but
> they sighed; no sooner sighed but they asked one
> another the reason; no sooner knew the reason but
> they sought the remedy: and in these degrees have
> they made a pair of stairs to marriage, which they
> will climb incontinent, or else be incontinent before
> marriage: they are in the very wrath of love,
> and they will together; clubs cannot part them.
>
> (V.ii.28–39)

Her speech employs the scheme George Puttenham calls "the climb-

ing figure";[12] the brilliant verbal surface is entirely in the character of
the saucy and agile Ganymede, but its artifice cannot mask the real
energy of the incremental repetitions. The iterated "no sooner . . .
but" overrides the steps of love's stair distinguished by the syntax of
the *gradatio* and conveys an impression of irresistible energy ("the
very wrath of love")—betraying Rosalind's state of mind as well as
describing Celia's and Oliver's. She then promises Orlando to bring
forth the real Rosalind on the morrow:

> Therefore put you in your best array, bid
> your friends; for if you will be married
> to-morrow, you shall; and to Rosalind, if
> you will.
>
> (V.ii.59–65, 68–70)

She will have him on condition that he consciously choose the union
he instinctively desires. Her "if" reconciles idealistic aspirations to the
requirements of an enduring commitment. "Your If is the only
peacemaker," says Touchstone; "Much virtue in If" (V.iv.96–97).

Spenser's *Hymne of Beautie* proposes that while the lover's feigned
image of his mistress is more beautiful than the woman herself as
initially seen, he will find that "her fairenesse doth exceede" his
dreams when he turns to look at her again, because his idealized
image corresponds to her inner, spiritual beauty ("that inmost faire")
and enables him to perceive it "As plaine as . . . dawning day" (238). If
the lover at first desires his beloved as a physical object, and subsequently internalizes and recreates her as a mental image, he ultimately responds to her as another subject who transcends both the
object and the image. When the desires provoked by love at first sight
are tempered by love at second sight, they can sustain an enduring
relationship. The beloved's existence as a person independent of the
lover's will is no longer threatened by the unmastered importunity of
desire or ignored in the solipsism of fancy, but is cherished by a
respectful love:

> For Loue is a celestiall harmonie,
> Of likely harts composd of starres concent,
> Which ioyne together in sweete sympathie,
> To worke ech others ioy and true content.
>
> (197–200)

The courtship of Rosalind and Orlando culminates in love at second
sight when Rosalind enters undisguised, "human as she is, and without any danger":

Rosalind. [*To* Duke] To you I give myself, for I am yours.
          [*To* Orlando] To you I give myself, for I am yours.
Duke S.   If there be truth in sight, you are my daughter.
Orlando. If there be truth in sight, you are my Rosalind.

(V.iv.110–113)

Hymen's epithalamium celebrates the "celestiall harmonie" that is the crown of love in Spenser's *Hymne of Beautie:*

> Then is there mirth in heaven
> When earthly things made even
> Atone together.

(V.iv.102–4)

The final act objectifies the harmony of respectful love by combining the different modes of artifice that had distinguished the forest scenes from the opening scenes. This combination places the subjective freedom, expressed metaphorically through theatrical artifice, in the larger setting of those forces beyond the self that were established metaphorically in narrative artifice. In the last scene, Rosalind becomes a virtual stage manager as she uses the influence permitted by her disguise to ensure that all odds will be even when she discloses her true identity. Albert Cirillo observes that Hymen, who bars "confusion" and makes "conclusion / Of these most strange events" (V.iv.119, 120–21), is an objectification in music and pageantry of Rosalind's theatrical powers (p. 36).[13] But Hymen, the "god of every town" (V.iv.140), also symbolizes the claims of Nature to which Rosalind submits when she reveals her femininity and affirms her bonds to a father and a lover. The benevolence of the natural forces that guide the characters to their fourfold wedding is objectified in the overt manipulation of the narrative that makes this happy ending possible. Jaques de Boys, a second brother of Orlando, whose entrance *ex machina* is no less surprising than Hymen's, announces that Duke Frederick, miraculously converted by an old religious man, has surrendered his usurped dukedom so the exiles can go home.

The play becomes more overtly artificial when the lovers abandon the artifice of wooing games for the unfeigned commitments of marriage. By emphasizing the play's status as fiction, the conspicuous artifice of the conclusion disengages the spectators from their involvement in the inner life of the main characters. Their imaginative response, like Orlando's, is qualified and made to serve a truer perception of reality. The characters' anticipated return to court is acted out when the spectators leave the playhouse and return to their normal world, carrying with them Shakespeare's theatrical image of love.

The epilogue makes explicit this analogy of love and theatrical fiction. Rosalind reminds the spectators that her role-playing with Orlando was the mirror image of her performance for them, since both they and Orlando have accepted a boy actor as Rosalind: "If I were a woman I would kiss as many of you as had beards that pleased me, complexions that liked me, and breaths that I defied not." But she is not a woman. Just as Ganymede becomes Rosalind in the last scene, so Rosalind becomes the boy actor in the epilogue, though he continues to speak in character. Thus Rosalind does not step "out of the magic circle of the play," as Cirillo proposes (p. 38), but rather stands at, and affirms, the boundary that separates her fictive world from the reality of the audience. She speaks across that boundary, as Shakespeare's characters are often permitted to do, and "conjures" the spectators in terms that relate theatrical to erotic response: "I charge you, O women, for the love you bear to men, to like as much of this play as please you; and I charge you, O men, for the love you bear to women (as I perceive by your simp'ring none of you hates them) that between you and the women the play may please." She invites the men and women in the audience to value the play's fictive image in terms of their reality as lovers, and to value their reality in terms of the image. This reciprocity is in itself an image of love: fiction and reality, like true lovers, preserve their separate identities so that they can mutually enhance each other.[14]

As You Like It exemplifies different ramifications of withdrawal and return. Its narrative movement from court to forest and back, which emphasizes the less tangible interplay of narrative and theatrical artifice, replicates in the fiction the actual shape of the theatrical occasion as a moment of withdrawal. This extensive dimension of the narrative pattern, which subsumes the theatrical occasion, is complemented by its intensive dimension as a metaphor of the subjective development of love from desire through imagination to relationship.

Through withdrawal and return, and through numerous smaller and more intricate patterns of anticipation, repetition, and fulfillment, time is highly structured in the theater and within the fictive world of a play. This theatrical structuring of time can have two quite different consequences for the dramatist's vision of reality. First, and most obviously, the foreshortened and intensified temporality of dramatic fiction can magnify the relentless and destructive reality of time experienced by the characters. But precisely because dramatic fiction has its own beginning, middle, and end, the theatrical event as a whole is invariably experienced by spectators as a moment out of time, and this sense of liberation from the pressure of temporality can also be reflected within the fictive world. These two ways of regarding theatrical time help to distinguish comedy and tragedy, as Dame Helen Gardner suggests: "Tragedy is presided over by time, which urges the hero onward to fulfill his destiny. In Shakespeare's comedies time . . . is not so much a movement onwards as a space in which to work things out. . . . The comedies are dominated by a sense of place rather than of time."[15] As Orlando says to Rosalind, "There's no clock in the forest" (III.ii.287–88). Macbeth, on the other hand, struggles vainly to free himself from time, to "Outrun the pauser, reason" (II.iii.107) and possess "The future in the instant" (I.v.56), but Time anticipates his dread exploits and finally overwhelms him with tomorrows signifying nothing. The history play, as we might expect, falls between these extremes. Henry V has more liberty (and more success) in shaping events than Macbeth does. But Henry has only "Small time" (Epi. 5) for his heroic achievement that stands apart from the troubled times coming before and after it in the grim chronicle of English history.

Withdrawal to the theater is a movement against the current of time, "the full stream of the world" (*AYL*, III.ii.393–94). Shakespeare believed that this movement has a positive creative value that, in his Sonnets, he associates with sexual generation and poetry, both of which are "all in war with Time" (Sonnet 15). In his own career as dramatist, he often made progress by moving backwards; most of his plays are revivals. The next chapter shows how this aspect of withdrawal and return as a creative resistance to time affected his vision of history and his practice as a historical dramatist.

5

Heroism, History, and the Theater in
Henry V

Shakespearean Drama as Revision: *Edward III* and *Henry V*

Shakespeare's use of the theater as metaphor may have been prompted by the rapid development of Elizabethan drama, especially in the 1590s. Themes and techniques were invented, exploited, and discarded with astonishing speed. Plays that at first seemed highly original and lifelike soon lost their luster and were either dropped from the repertoire or retained only because their naive and extravagant theatricality turned out to have unanticipated appeal (as seems to have been the case with both *Tamburlaine* and *The Spanish Tragedy*, and possibly *Doctor Faustus* and the Ur-*Hamlet*). Shakespeare might well have written of this situation, as he did of another: "everything that grows / Holds in perfection but a little moment, / . . . this huge stage presenteth nought but shows" (Son. 15). Worn-out theatrical forms could no longer hold the mirror up to nature; but this obsolescence contributed to the Shakespearean project of disengaging theater and reality in order to exploit their metaphoric equivalence.[1] Shakespeare understood better than other dramatists that themes and techniques which were beginning to look too obviously theatrical could—for that very reason—be given greater histrionic energy and metaphoric significance than entirely novel work would have. By retaining the old forms and themes as metaphors, Shakespeare retarded the giddy pace of theatrical development and turned it back upon itself, so that he could develop his art to high levels of sophistication without forfeiting the sources of its strength in the popular tradition. In *Henry V*, Shakespeare accomplishes something of this sort and also dramatizes a political equivalent of his achievement in the figure of King Henry, who united and inspired his people by reviving the heroic conquest of his great grandfather, King Edward III.

This admittedly hypothetical view of Shakespeare's career is partly confirmed by the first extant description of him as a professional dramatist. In 1592, Robert Greene warned three "Gentlemen" who, like himself, had spent "their wits in making plaies," not to trust the common players to whom they had sold their "admired inuentions." Those "rude groomes," those "Puppets . . . that spake from our mouths, those Anticks garnisht in our colours," now presumed to write their own plays, aping the "past excellence" of their betters, whom they would now turn out of service. "Yes, trust them not," warned Greene, "for there is an vpstart Crow, beautified with our feathers, that with his *Tygers hart wrapt in a Players hyde,* supposes he is as well able to bombast out a blanke verse as the best of you: and beeing an absolute *Iohannes fac totum,* is in his owne conceit the onely Shake-scene in a countrey."[2] Shakespeare's unparalleled success resulted in large measure from the circumstances that occasioned Greene's bitterness: the growing competence and independence of the common players. As actor, playwright, and shareholder, Shakespeare was more thoroughly involved in the daily business of theatrical production than any other dramatist of his time, and he achieved the early triumphs that provoked Greene's envy just when the players were consolidating their positions as the custodians of a fully self-sustaining theatrical enterprise. Greene's diatribe is one indication that Shakespeare was the most important agent in the development of a drama emerging directly from the theatrical ambience of the playhouse and wedded to the conditions of performance established there.

Greene suggests another dimension of Shakespeare's achievement that is no less important than, and is related to, his consummate theatricality: throughout his career, he was a reviser and improver of other men's work. Most of his plays come at the end, not the beginning, of the literary and dramatic traditions they exemplify. He perfected the genres of romantic comedy and history developed by Greene and the other University Wits; *Hamlet* and *King Lear* are revisions of earlier plays; *Pericles,* "a song that old was sung," seems also a revision; and for *The Winter's Tale,* Shakespeare plucked Greene's feathers once again, dramatizing his prose romance, *Pandosto.* Shakespeare was attracted to genres and subjects that were, or were beginning to be, out of style; on occasion, as in *Hamlet,* he revised material that had apparently been worked to death.[3] Many of his plays originate not as direct representations of reality but as revisions of earlier representations, and this circumstance may partly account for the self-conscious awareness of literary conventions and theatrical artifice so often attributed to him in modern criticism. Yet Shakespeare makes this self-consciousness transcend itself, so that our attention to the play as a play enriches, instead of detracting from, our response to the reality it represents. *Henry V* provides a lucid and relatively uncomplicated instance: in no other play does Shakespeare dramatize a subject so thoroughly exploited in earlier plays; nowhere else does he show himself more acutely aware of the resources and limitations of the theatrical medium; yet nowhere else does he encourage such a complete engagement of the audience in the dramatic action he presents.

At least two plays depicting Henry V precede the one Shakespeare wrote for the Chamberlain's Men in 1599. The first was acted by Queen Elizabeth's Men in the 1580s, the second by the Admiral's Men in 1595–96. The former survives only in an imperfect text, *The Famous Victories of Henry the Fifth;* the latter is lost.[4] The theatrical tradition of the heroic English king is best exemplified in its pre-Shakespearean form by another play, the anonymous *Edward III* (ca. 1590), which was sufficiently popular to warrant two editions, the quartos of 1596 and 1599.[5] These may have been deliberately issued to coincide with the performances of *Henry V* by the Admiral's and Chamberlain's Men, performances that sustained the appeal of heroical histories. Shakespeare's play resembles *Edward III* in theme and purpose, even in plot. Their affinities may result from the indebtedness of both to *The Famous Victories;* the question is complicated by the possible influence on Shakespeare of the Admiral's *Henry V,* which may itself have derived much from both *The Famous Victories* and *Edward III.*

In his *Apology for Actors,* Thomas Heywood suggests the central importance of *Edward III* and *Henry V* to the popular tradition of the heroical history play and explains the nature of their appeal. According to Heywood, the accuracy or sophistication of these plays as dramatic representations of history was far less important than their affective power as theatrical events; he would not at all have understood the modern notion that Shakespeare's presentation of Henry is ironic. (To say this is not, of course, to refute the modern view.) Heywood writes:

What English blood seeing the person of any bold English man presented and doth not hugge his fame, and hunnye at his valor, pursuing him in his enterprise with his best wishes, and as beeing wrapt in contemplation, offers to him in his hart all prosperous performance, as if the Personater were the man Personated, so bewitching a thing is liuely and well spirited action, that it hath power to new mold the harts of the spectators and fashion them to the shape of any noble and notable attempt. What coward to see his contryman valiant would not bee ashamed of his own cowardise? What English Prince should hee behold the true portrature of that famous King *Edward* the third, foraging France, taking so great a King captiue in his owne country, quartering the English Lyons with the French Flower-delyce, and would not bee suddenly In-flam'd with so royall a spectacle, being made apt and fit for the like atchieuement. So of *Henry* the fift.[6]

This passage is preceded by one in which Heywood fancies that Her-cules undertook his twelve labors "in meere emulation of his fathers valor" after "the worthy and memorable acts of his father *Iupiter*" had been "presented vnto him by his Tutor in the fashion of a History, acted by the choyse of the nobility of Greece." To the same effect, Hercules' heroism was acted for Theseus, Theseus' for Achilles, Achilles' for Alexander, Alexander's for Julius Caesar (sig. B3[r]). The theatrical image of each hero's deeds moved his successor to emula-tion; so of Henry V when he beheld the true portraiture of Edward III and was moved to the like achievement.

Nothing in the chronicles suggests that a play about Edward in-spired Henry's famous victories; Heywood owed the suggestion to the theatrical tradition. As *Edward III* concludes, the Black Prince ex-presses the hope that the English victory will inflame "hereafter ages" with warlike resolution (see V.i.216–35). Shakespeare anticipates Heywood's notion that Henry was motivated by the example of his great predecessors; in the second scene of his play, Canterbury de-scribes Edward's conquest and offers the royal spectacle (a "tragedy") to Henry in hopes of moving him to emulation:

> Gracious lord,
> Stand for your own, unwind your bloody flag,
> Look back into your mighty ancestors;
> Go, my dread lord, to your great-grandsire's tomb,
> From whom you claim; invoke his warlike spirit,
> And your great-uncle's Edward the Black Prince,
> Who on the French ground played a tragedy,
> Making defeat on the full power of France,
> Whiles his most mighty father on a hill
> Stood smiling to behold his lion's whelp
> Forage in blood of French nobility.
>
> (I.ii.100–110)

Henry revives the heroic energies of the earlier king, just as Shakespeare revives the patriotic appeal of the earlier play.

Heywood places both plays in the tradition of heroic drama exemplified by *Tamburlaine,* while also suggesting that they modify that tradition to enhance both the didactic import and the theatrical energy of the heroic image.[7] In the familiar accents of Marlowe's hero, Edward proclaims that "Hot courage is engendred in [his] brest / Which . . . nowe doth mount with golden wings of fame" (I.i.45–47).[8] While Henry is less quickly aroused, he is even more "terrible in constant resolution" (II.iv.35)—as Exeter warns the French king:

> if you hide the crown
> Even in your hearts, there will he rake for it.
> Therefore in fierce tempest is he coming,
> In thunder and in earthquake, like a Jove.
>
> (II.iv.97–100)

But, unlike *Tamburlaine,* both plays begin by justifying heroic conquest—England has a rightful claim to France—and emphasizing the responsibilities of the hero as ruler. Edward and Henry acknowledge that they must protect their country from the troublesome Scottish raiders before seeking the greater glory of victory abroad. Moreover, they make heroic conquest express the national spirit shared by all bold Englishmen, instead of the merely personal energies of an "aspiring mind." Both plays appeal more effectively than Marlowe's could to the spectators as a group, by making them represent the nation for which the famous victories were won and by urging them to sustain the spirit of English heroism in future trials:

> O England! model to thy inward greatness,
> Like little body with a mighty heart,
> What mightst thou do that honor would thee do,
> Were all thy children kind and natural!
>
> (*H5,* II.Chor.16–19)

Edward III and *Henry V* fulfill the dual obligation assumed by Elizabethan heroic literature at its best: they arouse the auditors, urging them to exert themselves for their country through virtuous action, while they also modify the naive image of the hero as conqueror by establishing his brave deeds as the consequence, fulfillment, and symbol of inner fortitude.[9] The resistance offered to heroic aspirations in *Edward III* and *Henry V* differs from the simple opposition that in *Tamburlaine* provides a succession of progressively larger battles and greater victories; it is a resistance that tests, qualifies, and transforms the heroic impulse, without diminishing the appeal of Marlovian self-assertion. Thus Edward's "Hot courage" is made to reveal an irrational and anarchic side in his adulterous passion for the Countess of Salisbury; most of the play's images of conquest occur not in the battle scenes, but during this "lingring English seege of peeuish loue" (II.i.23).[10] The triumph of the countess's chastity brings to the play's image of heroism a capacity to act, suffer, and endure for a cause that transcends the self and can therefore restrain and guide the energies of individual will. When Edward recognizes this inner fortitude in the countess, his own valor is strengthened and purified. He awakens from his "idle dreame" (II.ii.299), and learns to conquer his base affections. Like his great predecessor, Henry deviated from the heroic norm, sharing an idle "dream" (*2H4*, V.v.52) with Falstaff; Henry's reformation and self-mastery are described in the opening scene of *Henry V* as a Herculean achievement (see I.i.33–37).

This pattern of heroic assertion, qualification, and refinement is repeated on the battlefield in both plays. At first, King Edward and the Black Prince, "his hot vnbridled sonne" (III.ii.65), triumph easily, voicing "execrations of despight" as they seize and devastate French cities with their "remorseles swordes" (see III.iii.97–108). After these initial victories, the emphasis shifts from the outer to the inner dimensions of valor. At Poitiers, the Black Prince must fight against apparently hopeless odds. He wins a miraculous victory, but the dramatist emphasizes instead what Milton would later call "the better fortitude / Of Patience and Heroic Martyrdom." Old Audley, "in the crimson brauerie of [his] bloud" (IV.viii.7), tutors the prince in this inner courage, just as the countess had earlier exemplified it for the king. Henry's army, like Edward's, wins a double victory. The first displays heroic energies in the external dimensions of military conquest. The relentless power that overwhelms both physical barriers and remorse is graphically portrayed in Henry's threatening speech to the citizens of Harfleur (III.iii.1–43). But at Agincourt, as at Poitiers, English victory over superior French forces manifests the "better fortitude" of the resolute and unconquerable spirit.

Shakespeare himself emphasizes these parallels. To this extent, the relationship of the two plays is an intrinsic feature of the later one, which subsumes its prototype. Throughout *Henry V*, Englishmen and Frenchmen alike refer to Henry's expedition as a reenactment of Edward's. The repeated association of the two monarchs adds significance to *Henry V* as the conclusion of the Lancastrian tetralogy. In the context of this series, Henry's repetition of Edward's achievement appears as a conquest of history itself, a triumph over time. By restoring Edward's heroic kingship, Henry negates the misrule of the intervening reigns and suspends the "revolution of the times" (*2H4*, III.i.46) that had subjected Richard II, Bolingbroke, and the rebels to the inexorable "necessities" of historical process, crushing them into the "monstrous form" of disorder (see *2H4*, IV.i.104–6; IV.ii.33–35). Henry's mastery of history is suggested by the fact that the pattern of his personal life—"loose behavior" followed by unlooked-for reformation—is writ large in the chronicle of his nation, when, following the disorders of Richard's and his father's reigns, he renews the feats of their heroic ancestor, "Redeeming time when men think least I will" (*1H4*, I.ii.205).

This achievement is not unqualified by the irony of history; Shakespeare's play concludes with a reminder that Henry's son would lose all that he had won. Like Edward's conquest, Henry's had no lasting consequence except to provide an example of English heroism that might encourage future ages. This fact imposed a restriction that Shakespeare found nowhere else in his sources. He was responsible for completing and validating the historical action represented in his play. Indeed, whatever exemplary value King Henry has had through the ages has depended more on Shakespeare (and, to a lesser extent, on other dramatists and chroniclers) than on the king himself. The playwright, even more than the hero, had to redeem the time. But to do so, he needed to abandon the detached, ambivalent, and ironic perspective that so impressively comprehended the complexities of the brazen world in his other history plays.

Henry V has a complexity of its own that is centered not on history itself but on the histrionic effort of king and playwright to transform the past into a heroic image. For Shakespeare, the relevant moral issue is not the nature of Henry's motives or the justice of his cause, but his own motives in appropriating this material and exploiting its affective power. It is as though Henry's admonition to the Archbishop of Canterbury (who is inciting him to emulate Edward's "tragedy" in France) were addressed to the playwright himself, urging him to make responsible use of his power to fashion the spectators by reviving the famous victories of England's hero:

> For God doth know how many now in health
> Shall drop their blood in approbation
> Of what your reverence shall incite us to.
> Therefore take heed how you impawn our person,
> How you awake our sleeping sword of war.
> We charge you in the name of God take heed.
>
> (I.ii.18–23)

Shakespeare, in turn, urges the spectator to take heed.

The overt theatricality of *Henry V* as a self-conscious revival of the heroical history play furthers the project already evident in *Edward III*: to transform the affective power of the heroic image from a superficial engagement in a fiction to a responsible assent to the moral reality of heroic commitment. The strenuous nature of such commitment is grounded in Shakespeare's unusually explicit requests for the spectators' participation in sustaining the fiction itself. He repeatedly urges his audience to do deliberately what it would do more easily and naturally without being asked:

> Piece out our imperfections with your thoughts:
> Into a thousand parts divide one man
> And make imaginary puissance.
>
> (Pro. 23–25)

The nature of the play as a revival of a heroic action that presses beyond the limits of the stage becomes the basic metaphor of the moral reality that the play fashions in its audience. The nature of that metaphor we have now to consider more closely.

Heroic and Theatrical Performance

Even if Shakespeare owed nothing to *Edward III* or the earlier plays about Henry V and relied solely on Holinshed, their mere existence would have established his *Henry V* as the latest version of a familiar theatrical subject. Partly for this reason, he displays in himself and accommodates in the spectators a greater awareness than is evident in *Edward III* that the play is an artifact of the theater distinct from the reality it presumes to represent. He dramatizes this awareness in the person of the Chorus, who repeatedly protests that heroic conquest is an action too large to be represented in the playhouse: the stage, an "unworthy scaffold," cannot contain "The vasty fields of France" (I.Chor.12), and the actors, "flat unraisèd spirits" (9), cannot represent the events of history in "their huge and proper life" (V.Chor.5). The Chorus's request for the spectators' assistance—"Work, work your thoughts, and therein see a siege" (III.Chor.25)—can only emphasize the distinction between historical reality and its dramatic image.

It is commonly assumed that Shakespeare's self-consciousness about the theatrical medium was the inevitable consequence of his decision to dramatize a theme that required the energies and scope of

epic poetry. He had little choice, so the argument runs, but to acknowledge that the epic amplitude of Henry's saga exceeded the limited mimetic capacities of the stage; accordingly, the Chorus must
apologize for the deficiencies of performance, bridge gaps in the
narrative ("Turning th' accomplishment of many years / Into an
hourglass"), and supply by rhetoric a heroic glamor that could not be
conveyed directly in action.[11] While the Chorus himself encourages
these assumptions to magnify Henry's achievement, he offers no real
grounds for supposing that the play strained the resources of the
theater. Marlowe's *Tamburlaine* had given ample demonstration, if
any were needed, that heroic conquest was not a subject too large for
the stage, and the author of *Edward III* did not hesitate to dramatize
more fighting than Shakespeare would attempt in *Henry V.*

The Chorus in Shakespeare's play is neither needed nor used to
narrate essential episodes that the actors could not perform. The
prologue, surprisingly enough, makes no effort to summarize the
king's life as presented in the preceding plays of the Lancastrian
tetralogy; this task is left to the bishops in the first scene. The Chorus
to Act Two anticipates the condemnation of the conspirators, which is
presented at length in the second scene of the act. The third Chorus
elaborately describes the voyage of Henry's army to France, although
the voyage was already accomplished in Act Two ("he is footed in this
land already" [II.iv.143]), and the siege of Harfleur, which will be
fully dramatized in the very next scene. The fourth Chorus, like those
preceding, serves no essential narrative function, but merely offers a
rhetorical description of the nocturnal setting presupposed by the
preceding and following scenes. Only the fifth Chorus supplies a
transition, by returning Henry from Agincourt to England and bringing him back to France to conclude the peace negotiations. Even this
transition, though it must bridge a five-year gap in time, could easily
have been accomplished in dialogue, as it is in *The Famous Victories*, or
made unnecessary by telescoping the events.[12]

As Dr. Johnson observed, information of the kind supplied by the
Chorus in *Henry V* is not "more necessary in this play than in many
others where it is omitted."[13] No choric apologies for the deployment
of four or five stage warriors "Right ill-disposed, in brawl ridiculous"
(IV.Chor.51) precede Shakespeare's battles at Bosworth Field,
Shrewsbury, Philippi, Troy, Alexandria, or Corioles. He was seldom
more careful than in *Henry V* to select from his sources just those
incidents that could be enacted without unduly straining the limited
scenic resources of his stage: the English deliberations about the
French campaign, and the Dauphin's mocking gift of tennis balls; the

discovery and condemnation of the conspirators; the "humors" of Pistol, Fluellen, and their respective companions, and the boasting of the French; Henry's battlefield speeches, his appearance in disguise to his soldiers, and his courtship of Katherine. Surely the spectators could have imagined the "true things" represented in these scenes without being urged to do so by the Chorus. That the playwright chooses to use a Chorus suggests less about his concern for the limits of the stage than about other challenges he poses to those spectators.

The problem that faced Shakespeare in *Henry V* lay in the fact that by 1599 heroic conquest had been successfully dramatized too often for spectators to respond with naive enthusiasm, however much they may have wished to be taken in. He personifies the tensions inherent in this situation in the comic figure of Ancient Pistol, who is entirely possessed by the old heroic plays. As Leslie Hotson writes, Pistol cherishes

> the conviction that he is essentially a Locrine, a Cambyses, a Tamburlaine. . . . His lingo is largely catchwords and misquotations of resounding bits from old plays. . . . Of course, his lofty lines and his formal inversions of verse ("My name is Pistol call'd") when absurdly pressed into scenes of realism, are taken as fustian by everyone. Yet without doubt they gave peculiar delight to an audience that at other times entered wholeheartedly into the rant of Tamburlaine.[14]

Pistol's heroics are juxtaposed throughout with the king's, and critics are still not certain whether the moldy rogue functions as parody to expose the viciousness concealed by royal bombast and archiepiscopal casuistry ("Let us to France, like horse-leeches, my boys, / To suck, to suck, the very blood to suck!" [II.iii.50–51]), or as a foil to set off the king's true heroism by contrasting it to mere braggadocio.

While the second alternative is preferable to the first,[15] neither accounts for the real value of Pistol's mock heroics. An example of that value can be seen in the juxtaposition of incidents when Henry and Pistol act defiantly toward another person. Henry serves notice on the Dauphin after receiving the mocking gift of tennis balls:

> When we have matched our rackets to these balls,
> We will in France, by God's grace, play a set
> Shall strike his father's crown into the hazard.
>
>   many a thousand widows
> Shall this his mock mock out of their dear husbands,
> Mock mothers from their sons, mock castles down.
>   (I.ii.262–64, 285–87)[16]

In the next scene, Pistol's defiance of Nym exploits the same rhetorical form:

> *Nym.*   Will you shog off? I would have you solus.
> *Pistol.* Solus, egregious dog? O viper vile!
>   The solus in thy most mervailous face!
>   The solus in thy teeth, and in thy throat,
>   And in thy hateful lungs, yea, in thy maw, perdy!
>   And, which is worse, within thy nasty mouth!
>   I do retort the solus in thy bowels.
>
> (II.i.43–49)

Either as parody or as foil, Pistol's speech would restrict the range of our responses by requiring us to reject a false heroism. But no restriction occurs. Pistol's extravagance enlarges the scope of our assent to the heroic image and increases our enjoyment. His definace of Nym indulges the instinctive posturing and the reflexive, mechanistic energies of retaliation that are suppressed in Henry's speech by his acknowledgement of the serious consequences of "wasteful vengeance" (I.ii.284). Pistol encumbers us with no such responsibilities: "For Pistol, he hath a killing tongue and a quiet sword; by the means whereof 'a breaks words and keeps whole weapons" (III.i.30–32). At Agincourt, Shakespeare omits the spectacle of Henry's personal triumph over Alençon, the French king, and the Dauphin, featured in the chronicles and the earlier plays, and gives us instead Pistol's capture of Monsieur le Fer.[17] This "brawl ridiculous" does not disgrace the name of Agincourt, but releases for comic celebration a low form of that inner conviction of heroic worth that made the English victory both possible and significant as a triumph of the human spirit. Our laughter at Pistol neutralizes the tension inherent in the play's serious assertion of heroic values and brings to our response that quickening of the spirit, the "fresh legerity" (IV.i.23), that Henry instills in his soldiers.

The Chorus serves a similar purpose. He invites the spectators to indulge and relish their "imaginary forces" (I.Chor.18) to "Play with [their] fancies" (III.Chor.7), so that the heroic image will be deliberately created and enjoyed "In the quick forge and working-house of thought" (V.Chor.23). He holds history and its theatrical image apart, even as he urges the spectators to bridge the gap in imagination. This procedure assists Shakespeare in establishing analogies between theatrical performance and heroic conquest, so that the play itself as a theatrical event becomes a metaphor of the reality it represents.

One advantage of these analogies has been well described by Michael Goldman: they make the immediate and concrete activity of performing contribute its substance and energy to the play's image of heroism.[18] If the Chorus urges us from the playhouse to the battlefield, the king addresses his soldiers as though they were actors:

> . . . imitate the action of the tiger:
> Stiffen the sinews, summon up the blood,
> Disguise fair nature with hard-favored rage;
> Then lend the eye a terrible aspect:
> . . . .
> Now set the teeth and stretch the nostril wide,
> Hold hard the breath and bend up every spirit
> To his full height!
> . . . .
> Be copy now to men of grosser blood,
> And teach them how to war!
>
> (III.i.6–9, 15–17, 24–25)

The metaphor gains validity and power in the theater, where the soldiers are in fact actors. The effect of the metaphor is not only to make us self-consciously aware that the soldiers are merely players, but also to make that awareness (which we never entirely lack) contribute to our involvement in the historical fiction.

All of Shakespeare's plays exploit the energies of performance in some fashion. In *Henry V,* the procedure not only enhances the rhetorical power of the heroic image, but also evaluates heroic deeds by defining their relation both to their past historical context and to the present moment of peformance. The relationship of heroic and theatrical endeavors is shaped by the play's structure: the movement of the action from England to France parallels the movement from history to ideal heroism and from reality to the theater.

The first scene dramatizes the world of English history in all its ambivalence by recalling the political exigencies that in the earlier plays of the tetralogy had circumscribed and perverted heroic aspirations: the Church is shown to have ulterior motives for supporting Henry's war, and we may remember Bolingbroke's advice that Henry make war for ulterior motives of his own (see *2H4,* IV.v.212–16). But the ironies of history, once acknowledged, are systematically excluded from the play: "Consideration" whips the offending Adam out of Henry; Falstaff dies; a nest of traitors is discovered and purged from the English ranks; God answers Henry's prayer at Agincourt and forgets, for a time, his father's fault in compassing the crown. As Sigurd Burckhardt has shown, when the play moves from England to France, it leaves behind the ambivalent world of English history and enters a less complicated chivalric realm where Henry's right to the crown can be tested and affirmed "without stratagem" in the "plain shock and even play of battle" (IV.viii.103, 104).[19] The play's avoidance of historical complexities is nearly complete in the final act. Victory over France is given the shape and consummation of romantic comedy, as Henry wins the French princess with his "downright oaths . . . of plain and uncoined constancy" (V.ii.143, 151–52).

The play's movement from political ambiguity in England to heroic conquest in France corresponds to the spectators' withdrawal from ordinary life to the artfully structured world offered within the playhouse. Henry's counselors make this analogy nearly explicit when they envisage France as a theater in which he should revive the famous exploits of Edward III and the Black Prince, who, as Canterbury says, "on the French ground played a tragedy, / Making defeat on the full power of France" (I.ii.106–7). Exeter insists that a royal audience awaits this reenactment of English heroism:

> Your brother kings and monarchs of the earth
> Do all expect that you should rouse yourself
> As did the former lions of your blood.
> 							(I.ii.122–24)

France will provide for Henry what it offered his ancestors: "A kingdom for a stage, princes to act / And monarchs to behold the swelling scene!" (I.Chor.3–4). Like Shakespeare and the players, he will reenact a heroic moment from England's past: "Awake remembrance of these valiant dead, / And . . . renew their feats" (I.ii.115–16).

The theatrical analogy implies that Henry's triumph owes as much to his political cunning as to his courage, although these attributes are less easily distinguished in *Henry V* than in the two parts of *Henry IV*. In *1 Henry IV*, Prince Hal consciously uses heroic deeds to dramatize himself in a politically effective manner, to "show more goodly and attract more eyes" (I.ii.202), compelling praise even from the rebels. In *2 Henry IV*, his father advises him to enlarge the drama to international proportions:

> Be it thy course to busy giddy minds
> With foreign quarrels, that action, hence borne out,
> May waste the memory of the former days.
> 							(*2H4*, IV.v.213–15)

Bolingbroke offers this stratagem as a self-serving device for keeping possession of the crown, but it will have a larger purpose for his son. In *Henry V*, the French campaign unites the people in common allegiance to a heroic ideal, so that "honor's thought / Reigns solely in the breast of every man" (II.Chor.3–4). As Samuel Daniel writes of Henry:

> He bringes abrode distracted discontent,
> Disperst ill humours into actions hie,
> And to unite them all in one consent
> Plac'd the faire marke of glorie in their eye,
> That malice had no leasure to dissent,
> Nor envie time to practise treachery,
> The present actions do divert the thought
> Of madnes past, while mindes were so well wrought.
>
> (*Civile Wars* [1595])[20]

All three of the Lancastrian plays demonstrate that the theater offered Shakespeare a kind of laboratory in which to explore the essentially rhetorical nature of Henry's actions.

The theatrical metaphor receives complex development in the battle scenes in France. The terms of the analogy—heroic conquest and theatrical performance—are at first conflated, then distinguished. This development perfects the heroic image established in *Edward III* by a movement from easy triumphs to progressively sterner tests of English courage. Shakespeare understood better than the earlier dramatist that this movement has both a narrative and an affective dimension: what it *shows* in the characters it *does* to the audience. Heroes and spectators progress, in C. L. Barber's words, "through release to clarification . . . [a] clarification about limits which comes from going beyond the limit."[21]

As Henry's army advances toward Harfleur, Shakespeare gives free reign to his "muse of fire" and allows the rhetorical power of Chorus and king to command unqualified participation in the action. English nobility and courage are confidently expressed as physical might, and stage events are identified with historical reality. At this point, not in the Agincourt scenes, the players employ their most impressive—and dangerous—sound effects, firing chambers to bring the smoke and clamor of battle into the playhouse.[22]

The soldiers' response to the challenge of war is conflated with the spectators' response to the play. In the prologue to Act Two, the Chorus proclaims that "all the youth of England are on fire"; their hearts, Westmoreland says, "have left their bodies here in England / And lie pavilioned in the fields of France" (I.ii.128–29). In his prologue to Act Three, the Chorus mobilizes such "imaginary forces" in the spectators, so that they also may fly to battle "on imagined wing." "Follow, follow," he urges:

Grapple your minds to sternage of this navy,
And leave your England as dead midnight still.
(III.Chor.18–19)

In the next scene, Henry uses the same language when he urges his troops to "Follow [their] spirit" once more unto the breach (III.i.1–43). The spectators are made to feel the spirit of heroic endeavor intimately and concretely in their own effort to press beyond the physical restrictions of the stage.

The limits of heroism and its rhetoric are reached and exceeded in the third act of *Henry V*. Qualification of the heroic impulse begins in the second scene when the British officers quarrel, and is furthered by Henry's notorious speech to the citizens of Harfleur, in which he threatens them with "heady murder, spoil, and villainy" (III.iii.1–43). Shakespeare subsequently reveals that Henry's real intention is to "Use mercy to them all" (54). The threats secure this result by prompting surrender before the battle-weary soldiers yield to anarchic impulses ("impious war") that Henry, knowing his limits and those of his men, admits he could not restrain. Yet the speech itself is remarkably excessive: its emblematic figure of the soldier, maddened with blood lust, killing old men, defiling maidens, and butchering infants like "Herod's bloody-hunting slaughtermen" (41) is described three times over (10–14, 15–27, 33–41). Some readers sense in this damnable iteration an exposure of the king's insensitivity or depravity, but its effect in the theater is to glut the appetite for violence whetted in the spectators by the preceding scenes and thereby to prepare a more thoughtful response to the presentation of heroism as "inward greatness" in subsequent scenes.

After the siege of Harfleur, Shakespeare curbs the pretensions of heroic rhetoric by dramatizing its excesses. Fluellen discovers that Pistol is no Mark Antony, despite his "prave words at the pridge" (III.vi.62–63). In the next scene, the brave words are spoken by the French. The Dauphin's absurdly vain effusions about his horse carry to excess the "imaginary puissance" that the Chorus had earlier sought from the spectators: "Think, when we talk of horses, that you see them / Printing their proud hoofs i' th' receiving earth" (I.Chor.26–27). The Dauphin's horse—a "Pegasus," he calls it, with hoofs "more musical than the pipe of Hermes" (III.vii.17–18)—is an emblem of the unbridled poetic imagination that refuses to test its mettle by engaging reality.

While the French brag of their horse and armor, Henry acknowledges the dangers that await him "in the painful field" (IV.iii.111).

His admission to the French herald that the army he must commit to battle is "weak," "sickly," and "enfeebled" (see III.vi.140–50) recalls the Chorus's initial description of the actors as

> flat unraisèd spirits that hath dared
> On this unworthy scaffold to bring forth
> So great an object.
>
> (I.Chor.9–11)

The "four or five most vile and ragged foils" (IV.Chor.50) that the Chorus fears will disgrace the battle are scarcely worse than the worn and rusty English armor scorned by Grandpré, who says that Henry's soldiers

> Ill-favoredly become the morning field.
> Their ragged curtains poorly are let loose,
>
> Big Mars seems bankrout in their beggared host,
> And faintly through a rusty beaver peeps.
>
> (IV.ii.40–41, 43–44)

If the rhetoric of Chorus and king expresses the imaginative appeal of the heroic ideal, the relative austerity of the "unworthy scaffold" and its merely human actors suggests the recalcitrant reality the ideal must confront. At Agincourt, the play's "swelling scene" (I.Chor.4) is cramped and pressed down to the straitlacing actuality of the stage.[23] The king's heroism and the play's image of heroism are simultaneously tested and made to show their foundation in the "inward greatness" (II.Chor.16) of the heroic spirit and the theatrical imagination.

This pattern of assertion and qualification gains further support from Shakespeare's use of the actor as a metaphor of the king. Henry is initially described as a Herculean actor who plays Mars in the theater of the world (I.Chor.5–8). In the first scene, Canterbury insists that Henry's royal nature is most convincingly displayed in his oratorical skills (see I.i.38–49)—the same skills that gave the actors their best claim to dignity in an age that granted to eloquence its full Circeronian value. But in harmony with the play's progressive qualification of heroic and rhetorical assertiveness, the king appears as an actor in a more somber and searching way on the eve of the battle at Agincourt. Henry's disguise in the first scene of Act Four dramatizes his ambivalent position as a man subject to human infirmities who must yet "Be like a king, and show [his] sail of greatness" (I.ii.27). The disguised king says to his soldiers: "Though I speak it to you, I think the King is but a man, as I am. . . . all his senses have but human conditions. His ceremonies laid by, in his nakedness he appears but a man" (IV.i.97–98, 100–102). Henry's disguise allows him to rehearse the lesson Richard II had been unable to learn: he distinguishes the inner sources of his strength from the delusions of outward show. Because he is unrecognized and unrespected without the trappings and the suits of kingship, he acknowledges that his royalty has no inherent or sacramental power, and that regal ceremony is merely an "idol . . . / Creating awe and fear in other men" (IV.i.226, 233). But he finds in these limitations the genuine power that outward show can have for a good performer. At Agincourt, the Chorus tells us, his "royal face" betrays "no note / How dread an army hath enrounded him"; his "cheerful semblance" comforts and encourages his troops (see IV.-Chor.35–42). He knows that even the lowest and most cowardly of his soldiers will love "from heartstring" a king who can appear as "a bawcock, and a heart of gold, / A lad of life, an imp of fame" (IV.i.44–45).

In France, as in the playhouse, the heroic role must be supported by those who seek the encouragement it offers. The disguised king emphasizes the necessity of such mutual support when he says that "no man should possess [the king] with any appearance of fear, lest he, by showing it, should dishearten his army" (IV.i.106–8). Together, king and soldiers must sustain the spirit of heroism at Agincourt, just as actors and spectators must sustain the image of heroism in the playhouse. This analogy enriches Henry's famous battlefield oration. Saint Crispin's day, he promises,

> shall ne'er go by,
> From this day to the ending of the world,
> But we in it shall be remembered—
> We few, we happy few, we band of brothers;
> For he to-day that sheds his blood with me
> Shall be my brother; be he ne'er so vile
> This day shall gentle his condition.
> (IV.iii.57–63)[24]

The method of this speech differs from that of the earlier oration, "Once more unto the breach . . ." (III.i). There the actor/king seems almost to speak over the head of the stage warriors and to exhort the audience, prescribing a warlike appearance to secure inner courage: "imitate the action of the tiger: / Stiffen the sinews. . . ." At Agincourt, "Such outward things dwell not in [Henry's] desires" (IV.iii.27), and the concomitant of noble courage is the brotherhood of the "happy few." Henry's speech at Agincourt gains its appeal not by negating but by asserting the distance of the historical event from the present moment of performance. Actors and spectators, by recreating the victory of that band of brothers, fulfill in the theater the promise of future fame that Henry offers his men in France. The fulfillment is reciprocal, since the reenactment of the French campaign "gentles" the spectators by inspiring them with the heroic spirit of the past: "so bewitching a thing is liuely and well spirited action, that it hath power to new mold the harts of the spectators and fashion them to the shape of any noble and notable attempt."

The analogy of heroic conquest and theatrical performance suggests the limit, as well as the value, of Henry's achievement in France. The play is not allowed to remain in its ideal world of heroic affirmation, any more than the spectators are allowed to remain in the playhouse. The ironies of history reassert themselves when Queen Isabel prays that the marriage of Henry and Katherine may bring peace to England and France, while the epilogue reminds us that Henry died young and left a child on the throne, "Whose state so many had the managing / That they lost France and made his England bleed." The epilogue returns the spectators from France, "the world's best garden," to England, and from ideal heroism to the burdens of history; the pattern is completed when the spectators return from the playhouse to the reality of ordinary life.

The epilogue tempers the play's affirmation of the king's heroism with an acknowledgement of both the theater's limitations and history's mutability. The complex tone of the epilogue gains support from the mixture of emotions—elation and sobering disengagement—that attends the conclusion of a theatrical performance:

> Thus far, with rough and all un-able pen,
>   Our bending author hath pursued the story,
> In little room confining mighty men,
>   Mangling by starts the full course of their glory.
> Small time; but in that small most greatly lived
>   This Star of England.

The first quatrain invites us to identify "Small time" with the brief duration of theatrical performance that has confined the great king in the little room of the playhouse and mangled the full course of his glory. But the third quatrain, with its reference to "Henry the Sixth, in infant bands crowned King," reminds us that Henry V was granted small time in the theater of the world.[25]

Shakespeare's epilogue offers a telling contrast to the ringing close of *Edward III*, with its triumphal return to England (captured kings in tow) and its chauvinistic defiance of France, Spain, Turkey, "and what

countries els / That iustly would prouoke faire Englands ire"
(V.i.233–34). Shakespeare knew that history, in its huge and proper
life, permits no lasting triumphs. He knew, with Sir Philip Sidney,
that the historian, "beeing captiued to the trueth of a foolish world,"
finds "many times" that his exemplars of virtuous action and his "best
wisedome" are overruled "by that which wee call fortune."[26] The blind
goddess, Fluellen explains, is "turning and inconstant, and mutability,
and variation; and her foot, look you, is fixed upon a spherical stone,
which rolls, and rolls, and rolls" (III.vi.33–35). Henry's famous victories were undone by civil war in the next king's reign,

> Which oft our stage hath shown; and for their sake,
> In your fair minds let this acceptance take.

If the epilogue looks forward to the subsequent course of history, it
also looks back to Shakespeare's first history plays, which had dramatized the reign of Henry VI. The final couplet modestly asks that
Henry V be accepted for the sake of those earlier plays, which had
been very popular. But since they had shown the loss of France and
the English civil wars, the reference to them has another, deeper
meaning: *Henry V* merits acceptance because in it Shakespeare and
the players have rescued Henry's achievement from the disasters that
followed it in history, and, "jumping o'er times" (I.Chor.29), have
made his heroism live again, "most greatly," in the "Small time" of
theatrical performance.

If *Henry V* is Shakespeare's most chauvinistic play, it also contains
his most evocative descriptions of the horror of war—"all those legs
and arms and heads, chopped off in a battle" (IV.i.137–38)—and his
most compelling vision of a nation desolate in the absence of peace
(see Burgundy's long speech, V.ii.23–67). This ambivalence was entirely appropriate in Elizabethan England, a nation ready to do battle
with all Europe but preferring the delicate and precarious stratagems
of diplomacy. In this spirit, Shakespeare's play concludes not with
jingoistic defiance, but with a stronger and quieter resolve, resemb-
ling that expressed by Henry at Agincourt:

> The sum of all our answer is but this:
> We would not seek a battle as we are;
> Nor, as we are, we say we will not shun it.
>
> (III.vi.158–60)

To rehearse such an answer was as much as Shakespeare and his
countrymen could do in the playhouse; what more might be required
of them rested with the Queen. Elizabethan performances of *Henry V*

probably ended with the traditional prayer for the Queen and the safety of the realm. This play could not have had a more appropriate conclusion.

Irony or Assent?

My interpretation has accounted for only some of the aspects of *Henry V* that have convinced nearly half of its critics that its affirmation of heroism is ironic, while leaving the other half convinced of the opposite. That the heroic moment of conquest is framed by the somber ironies of history—Bolingbroke's usurpation and the Wars of the Roses—nobody denies. Debate centers on whether the central achievement itself is ironic, so that the alert spectator will repudiate the hero.[27] The most recent interpretations reach the challenging conclusion that the debate is irreconcilable because Shakespeare deliberately contrived to elicit opposed and contradictory responses. Norman Rabkin puts the case in its extreme form:

> Suggesting the necessity of radically opposed responses to a historical figure about whom there would seem to have been little reason for anything but the simplest of views, Shakespeare leaves us at a loss. . . . The terrible fact about *Henry V* is that Shakespeare seems equally tempted by both its rival gestalts. And he forces us . . . to share his conflict.[28]

Rabkin proposes that this ambivalence illuminates the complexities of history. It does so, I would add, by establishing a metaphoric equivalence between the theatrical experience the play offers to spectators (and readers) and the historical experience it represents.

One way of accounting for the "incompatible and radically opposed views" of and in *Henry V* might be suggested by Rabkin's characterization of them as belonging respectively to our "private" and "public" selves. It is generally conceded that the ironic view of *Henry V* occurs more readily to the reader than to the spectator.[29] The reader is better able than the spectator to scrutinize the text and determine, for example, that Canterbury's references to the French usurpers in his long speech on the Salic Law could have an ironic bearing on Henry's own uncertain claim. Moreover, the very act of reading—private, detached, self-directed—is contrary to the intensely rhetorical nature of this play's appeal. Theatrical performance of any play—especially this one—invites our participation in an event, not our scrutiny of a text.

But these considerations do not entirely discredit the ironic view. Elizabethan spectators were not incapable of scrutiny, and some of them had read if not the play itself, at least the chronicles—as Shakespeare's Chorus acknowledges in offering to prompt "those that have not read the story" (V.Chor.1). The ironic view is based not so much on what Shakespeare presents as on what he conspicuously refuses to present. Does Henry realize that the churchmen have an ulterior motive for recommending war? If so, is he hypocritical in professing to establish the justice of his cause? If not, is he their dupe? There are no answers to these questions in the second scene of Act One, and they would not even be asked were it not for the conversation of the churchmen in the first scene—which could easily have been omitted. Henry could simply have said, as King John does in similar circumstances, "Our abbeys and our priories shall pay / This expeditious charge" (*KJ*, I.i.48–49). Nothing in the second scene of *Henry V* prompts an ironic reading so much as the dramatist's complete (and quite uncharacteristic) avoidance of irony. There is no one to whisper in Henry's ear, as Elinor whispers in John's, "Your strong possession much more than your right" (*KJ*, I.i.39). Instead, we are treated to the splendid rhetorical energies of Henry's performance: his statesmanlike deliberations and his rousing defiance of the Dauphin.

Henry's condemnation of the conspirators in the second scene of Act Two raises the same kind of question. Does Henry really think that Cambridge, Scroop, and Grey conspired against him "for the gilt of France" (II.Chor.26)? Does Shakespeare want *us* to think so? Does he hope that we will forget (if we have read the story) the real motives of the conspirators? If so, why does he allow Cambridge, in three brief lines, to jog our memory? For Cambridge will not let us rest content in the belief that he "for a few light crowns, lightly conspired" (II.ii.89):

> For me, the gold of France did not seduce,
> Although I did admit it as a motive
> The sooner to effect what I intended.
>
> (II.ii.155–57)

There is nothing in the play to explain (to those who had not read the story) what effect he did intend, an omission that is made all the more conspicuous by the Chorus's and king's elaborately expressed bewilderment that he could have acted from such a slight motive as the "gilt of France." The king professes amazement at the apparently gratuitous nature of the crime. Karl Wentersdorf argues that Henry, his court, and most of the audience knew very well what the real motives were, and understood that Henry's impassioned speech of condemnation was merely a political effort to distract attention from

"the embarrassing heart of the matter . . . that Cambridge and Scroop
are challenging Henry V's right to the English throne on grounds at
least as convincing as those justifying Henry's challenge to the French
king."[30] But it is totally unlike Shakespeare to rely completely on the
audience's prior knowledge of "the story" for even a momentary
ironic effect, let alone for an irony large enough to subvert an entire
scene. Moreover, an ironic attitude that is not shared by any character
in the play could only spoil the play itself by prompting us to resist or
deny whatever appeal it does make to our understanding and to our
sympathies.

In short, it seems perverse to adopt an ironic attitude, but willfully
narrow-minded to ignore Shakespeare's hints that such an attitude is
conceivable and would be viable if he had dramatized the story differently. I conclude from this that Shakespeare invites us to assent to his
patriotic portrait of an ideal king, but demands that we accept responsibility for doing so and for refusing to adopt the ironic attitude. He
does not wish us to surrender to the seductive rhetoric of heroic
endeavor, but more energetically to will our allegiance to it against the
counterpressure of the private self with its instinctive resistance to the
enticements of group loyalty.

The play seems to challenge its audience in much the same way that
Henry challenges his soldiers at Agincourt:

> proclaim it, Westmoreland, through my host,
> That he which hath no stomach to this fight,
> Let him depart; his passport shall be made,
> And crowns for convoy put into his purse.
> We would not die in that man's company
> That fears his fellowship to die with us.
>
> (IV.iii.34–39)

To accept the play's challenge, we must (as readers or spectators)
suppress our reservations about the ideal to which we are being asked
to assent, because the validity of the ideal depends in part on our
commitment to it. In *Henry V,* more than in any of his other plays,
Shakespeare wants us to know, and to participate directly in, the
imaginative force of such a commitment. The play is troublesome to
its critics because the response it requires seems contrary to the very
nature of the critical enterprise as dispassionate and objective inquiry.

In *Henry V,* Shakespeare asks us to imagine that commitment to a
public cause can be valid in the face of private reservations that may
also be valid. The nature of such commitment is dramatized in Henry's nocturnal meeting with his soldiers on the eve of the battle at

Agincourt. Anne Barton has shown that this episode is based on the popular dramatic convention of the disguised king's encounter with his people—a wish-fulfilling image for those distressed by the impersonality of urban life and the growing complexity of government that placed an ever-larger number of intermediaries between subjects and their sovereign. If only the king could put off his royalty and communicate directly with his people, as Henry V does in *Sir John Oldcastle* and *The Shoemaker's Holiday*, or as Prince Hal did (but we know with what reservations!) in Shakespeare's own Henry IV plays. Mrs. Barton shows that Shakespeare uses Henry's disguised encounter with his soldiers "to summon up the memory of a wistful, naive attitude toward history and the relationship of subject and king" only to reject it "as attractive but untrue: a nostalgic but false romanticism."[31] As Michael Goldman suggests, the nostalgia for personal communion belongs, in this instance, not to the commoners but to the king himself. He wants to be known and appreciated not only as king but also as a man who genuinely shares a bond of common humanity with his soldiers. But, as Goldman says, "he is asking too much."[32] Henry discovers that his soldiers do not wish to know their king intimately as he "really" is. Instead, they want (and at this hour need) him to sustain his public role. Williams is irritated not by any prior suspicion of the king's truthfulness, but by the presumption of the stranger (whom he later calls "a rascal that swaggered" [IV.vii.118–19]) to know the king's mind and to hold him accountable for his sincerity:

> *King.*   . . . Methinks I could not die anywhere so contented as
>   in the king's company, his cause being just and his
>   quarrel honorable.
> *Williams.* That's more than we know.
> *Bates.*   Ay, or more than we should seek after, for we know
>   enough if we know we are the king's subjects.
>   (IV.i.119–24)

That the king might be, in his nakedness, a man as they are is no comfort to them, since his nakedness and fear would dishearten the army. They are willing to play their parts if only he will play his.

This long nocturnal scene forbids us to identify the king either with the private self, the man with "his ceremonies laid by, in his nakedness," whose "senses have but human conditions" (IV.i.100–101), or with the public self, the regal figure dressed in the "thrice-gorgeous ceremony" (252) of his office. The real king is the man whose royalty includes both ceremony and mere humanity without subordinating either one to the other.[33] This personal equilibrium, as

Richard Sennet suggests, is the basis of effective role-playing in public life.[34] It may also be an important basis for political liberty. By respecting the differences between his "ceremony" and his mere humanity, Henry is able to understand, from within, the vital distinction between his public authority and the subject's private freedom. Both the obedience he can claim from the soldiers as subjects and the battlefield fellowship he desires with them as "brothers" depend on his respect for their personal autonomy.

Shakespeare treats both his material and his spectators with the same respect. While he exploits the naive appeal of reenactment inherent in the historical genre—"what a glorious thing it is to haue *Henrie* the fifth represented on the stage . . . our forefathers valiant acts . . . are reuiued, and they themselues raised from the Graue of Obliuion"[35]—he also acknowledges the differences between history itself and its theatrical image. This acknowledgment affirms both the independent reality of history and the spectator's critical intelligence. The paradoxical result of this theatrical self-limitation is that the spectators can respond with deeper understanding to the historical events themselves and to their significance as exemplars of heroism. They can comprehend in terms of their own experience as spectators the nature of Henry's achievement as a revival of Edward's "valiant acts," and the nature of a heroic response that requires, just as the play does, both engagement and detachment: "Every subject's duty is the king's, but every subject's soul is his own" (IV.i.166–68).

6

From Community to Society: Cultural
Transformation in *Macbeth*

Macbeth illustrates more clearly than any of Shakespeare's other plays the subjective dimension of the actor and stage as metaphors of character and world. It also illustrates the relation of this subjectivity to a myth of cultural transformation that Shakespeare often imposes on his source material. A useful summary of this transformation that enumerates several of its dimensions is provided by Alvin Kernan in his interpretation of "the passage from the England of Richard II to the England of Henry V" in the second tetralogy: a "passage from the middle ages to the Renaissance and the modern world . . . a movement from feudalism and hierarchy to the national state and individualism . . . a passage from a situation in which man knows with certainty who he is to an existential condition in which identity is only a temporary role . . . [a] passage . . . from a garden world to a fallen world."[1] In *Macbeth,* as in the history plays, this transformation is dramatized in the three-phase pattern of withdrawal and return: Duncan's communal order is destroyed by Macbeth's anarchic individualism, which in turn is supplanted by Malcolm's "national state." Malcolm's kingdom, unlike Duncan's, can accommodate (and indeed requires) the individualism and subjectivity that are imposed on all of the characters by Macbeth's tyranny.

Community, Projection, and Violence

A nostalgic image of the community as family is centered on the paternalistic figure of King Duncan.[2] The order of his realm, expressed in images of fecundity, harvest, and feasting, does not appear to be a contrivance of human will for which the king and his subjects must bear responsibility; instead; it seems dictated by the very nature of things. The king is presented not as a person discharging an office but as a personification of the one life that all his subjects share:

```
Macbeth.                          our duties
          Are to your throne and state children and servants,
          Which do but what they should by doing everything
          Safe toward your love and honor.
King.                             Welcome hither.
          I have begun to plant thee and will labor
          To make thee full of growing. Noble Banquo,
          That hast no less deserved nor must be known
          No less to have done so, let me enfold thee
          And hold thee to my heart.
Banquo.                          There if I grow,
          The harvest is your own.
```
                                              (I.iv.24–33)

The death of his king is indeed "a breach in nature" (II.iii.109) that ruins the communal order for good and thrusts each of Duncan's subjects back into himself.

The imagery of procreation and harvest expresses a concept of time as organic and cyclical rather than linear. The perpetual renewal of life in nature, the annual recurrence of planting and harvest, the assurance that the future will repeat the past and thereby confirm the stability of the present, all reflect the conservative and collectivist biases of the communal mind. For Duncan and Banquo, the future is the pregnancy of the present, an immanent energy by which the now sustains itself. This continuity of time corresponds to and helps sustain a unity of consciousness that binds thought to perception and self to world. The imagery associated with Duncan and Banquo is "natural" in two senses: (1) it attributes the source of order to nature rather than to mind; and (2) it denies the fact of attribution by making the order seem "given" or evident in appearances themselves:

```
                          This guest of summer,
          The temple-haunting martlet, does approve
          By his loved mansionry that the heaven's breath
          Smells wooingly here. No jutty, frieze,
          Buttress, nor coign of vantage, but this bird
          Hath made his pendent bed and procreant cradle.
          Where they most breed and haunt, I have observed
          The air is delicate.
```
                                              (I.vi.3–10)

The dramatic irony of this passage emphasizes for the spectator that Banquo, by projecting his own values onto the scene, has deceived himself about the real nature of Macbeth's castle. But while the imagery of procreation reflects values already associated with Banquo and Duncan, who are themselves "guests of summer," Banquo does not deliberately construct these analogies. He spontaneously describes an instinctive happiness and is too much caught up in the sensation of being at one with nature to be aware of the sensation itself as a subjective condition. For him, the moment has value as an entirely gratuitous observation; he can attend to the birds for their own sake because his mind is free, while Macbeth, who sees nothing in nature but his own guilty obsessions—and knows it—feels "cabined, cribbed, confined, bound in / To saucy doubts and fears" (III.iii.24–25).

The rapid development of Macbeth's character in the opening scenes suggests that the communal order carries the seeds of its own transformation. It is transformed not by aggression from without but by the excessive energy that it must summon to its own defense. Macbeth's heroism belies the inevitability of the communal order; the community owes its existence not to the nature of things but to the prowess of this warrior. His accomplishments so distinguish him that he can no longer be regarded as an integral part of the group. Something of this separateness is implied by Duncan's statements of gratitude, which express beneath their conventional surface an undertone of unease:

> Thou art so far before
> That swiftest wing of recompense is slow
> To overtake thee. Would thou hadst less deserved,
> That the proportion both of thanks and payment
> Might have been mine! Only I have left to say,
> More is thy due than more than all can pay.
>
> (I.iv.16–21)

Without meaning to, Macbeth confirms this statement and his own self-sufficiency by saying that his service "In doing pays itself" (23). He internalizes what should be a relationship between himself and the community based on a reciprocation of service and reward. Duncan's response, though generous, is "not really disinterested" (as Marcel Mauss would say),[3] since the community, to reintegrate its hero to itself, must give him something that is equal to his achievement in its behalf. But it cannot: "More is [his] due than more than all can pay." The threat posed by this deficiency is ironically confirmed by the recompense that is offered: Macbeth is given the title of "that most disloyal traitor / The Thane of Cawdor" (I.ii.52–53).

The fact that the community is destroyed by the recoil of its own defenses (like "cannons overcharged with double cracks") is felt at a deeper level in the opening scenes. In the account of Macbeth's victories (I.ii), the sentiments of approbation, gratitude, and relief expressed by the king do not accord with the more immediate feelings of revulsion instinctively provoked in the spectator by the "strange images of death":[4]

> *Captain.*
>
>   . . . he faced the slave;
> Which ne'er shook hands nor bade farewell to him
> Till he unseamed him from the nave to the chops
> And fixed his head upon our battlements.
>
> *King.*
>
> O valiant cousin! worthy gentleman!
>
>   (I.ii.20–24)

This dissonance between ostensible relief and underlying horror is itself projected in the imagery of dismemberment, self-canceling conflict, and repression:

>   Doubtful it stood,
> As two spent swimmers that do cling together
> And choke their art.
>
> . . . .
>
>   Bellona's bridegroom, lapped in proof,
> Confronted him with self-comparisons,
> Point against point rebellious, arm 'gainst arm,
> Curbing his lavish spirit.
>
>   (7–9, 54–57)

The commentators who have puzzled over this discrepancy reflect the unease that any spectator or audience must feel in considering how fair and foul a day is being described.

The violence of Macbeth's victory is transferred, via the spectator's uneasy awareness of glory and death, to Macbeth's psyche. There it is magnified: the fair tidings of his new title are counterpointed by a "horrid image" of murder that shakes his single state of man and smothers function in surmise. The language of his soliloquy in the third scene picks up the images of choking, drowning, and dismemberment, the figures and conceits of doubling and counterpoint ("Cannot be ill, cannot be good"), even the idea of being confronted with self-comparisons, and gives to all of these an internal, psychological reference. Because the spectator has already felt something like what Macbeth describes, he will respond to him with an unaccountable and disquieting sympathy, despite the compression of the action that obscures the sources of Macbeth's feelings.

From Macbeth's psyche, violence turns against the kingdom. His decision to kill the king, which will emerge at the end of I.iii, requires the further preparation of his encounter with the witches. That encounter is as disorienting as his violent victory. The witches alienate him from the mode of consciousness and behavior that the community (personifid by the king) requires. Their mysterious appearance and sudden vanishing shatter Macbeth's reliance on the validity of perception and negate its capacity to subordinate self to world. Neither Banquo nor Macbeth is quite certain that the witches are really there:

> Were such things here as we do speak about?
> Or have we eaten on the insane root
> That takes the reason prisoner?
>
> (83–85)

During the brief encounter, both men are unable to distinguish what is in the mind from what is outside.

The witches' prophecy undermines the stable and objective quality of Macbeth's character by exposing him to the uncertainty of the future. Prophecies were often invoked in Shakespeare's time to justify rebellion, and it was understood that they are inherently seditious because they violate the temporal order on which the cohesiveness of the community depends. As the Earl of Northampton said in his *Defensative against the Poyson of Supposed Prophecies* (1583), they "carry men from present duties into future hopes."[5] Shakespeare dramatizes the subversiveness of such hopes when Macbeth, Banquo, and (later) Lady Macbeth all assume that the witches' mere prediction that Macbeth will be "King hereafter" is an incitement to kill Duncan. The assumption is illogical, since (as Macbeth acknowledges) if chance will have him king, then chance will crown him without his stir. But "chance" destroys the continuity of time that sustained Duncan's community, so that, for Macbeth, time becomes oppressively linear ("To-morrow, and to-morrow, and to-morrow"); each moment is unique and unrepeatable ("What's done, is done"; "What's done, cannot be undone"). For him, the future is a vacancy—the crown he does not yet have, or cannot yet wear safely—a vacuum that empties the present and draws him relentlessly forward. The discontinuity of time is attended by a discontinuity of self and role, since the new roles—Thane of Cawdor and king thereafter—are what the future promises to Macbeth, who must therefore define his present identity in terms of what he lacks.[6]

The division of character into self and role, the uncertainty of the future, and the ambiguity of perception that weakens the solidity of the outer world, all come together in Macbeth's soliloquy and add up to the "suggestion" that he kill Duncan. The soliloquy, by its very form, dramatizes his self-consciousness and isolation from the group that are further emphasized by the fact that he soliloquizes in the presence of other characters who notice how he is "rapt." We have seen that his self-consciousness takes a theatrical form that confirms his divided being: he beholds himself and notes his symptoms (unfixed hair, knocking heart), as if he were standing outside of himself with the audience. Self-division, chance, and perceptual ambiguity are joined in the central statement about murder:

> My thought, whose murder yet is but fantastical,
> Shakes so my single state of man that function
> Is smothered in surmise and nothing is
> But what is not.
>
> (139–42)

His thought is now as "fantastical" as the witches' prophecy and the witches themselves. Banquo had applied that word to them, asking "Are ye fantastical, or that indeed / Which outwardly ye show?" (I.iii.53–54). Not only their prophecy but the very ambivalence of their being suggests the thought of murder and by that suggestion murders all rational thought, destroying the "single state of man."

Witches were, of course, "fantastical," and the widespread belief in them may be another instance of the community's excessive and ultimately self-destructive defenses. The belief in and persecution of witches "arose out of deep tensions in the very structure of society" that resulted from the weakening of the communal order throughout Europe in the fifteenth and sixteenth centuries.[7] The witch crazes that swept through Europe in Shakespeare's lifetime were motivated not by the delusive belief of a few deviants who thought themselves witches, but by the delusions—amounting to mass hysteria—of many persons who thought themselves potential or actual victims of witchcraft. According to H. R. Trevor-Roper, "witches were persecuted rather as types of social nonconformity than for doctrinal or other given reasons"; they were made to bear the blame for all of the obscure and unaccountable forces that were undermining traditional social arrangements.[8] By this reading the witches in *Macbeth* might be said to objectify a deep and irrational fear of disorder, a threat not so easily confronted and opposed as Macdonwald and Norway are, a threat as insidious as poison, which destroys the community from within. Lady Macbeth and Macbeth can be seen as progressively more naturalized versions of the same evil represented by the witches. She invokes the aid of "murd'ring ministers" and he gives his eternal jewel to the common enemy of man in return for unnatural powers and benefits.

But this reading does not take us very far, and it overlooks the fact that the witches' objective is not to assist but to destroy Macbeth. The researches of Alan D. Macfarlane and Keith Thomas suggest that, in England at least, the fear of nonconformity mentioned by Trevor-Roper coexisted with, or was supplanted by, its opposite: a fear of witchcraft as retribution for the *victim's* violation of the communal order. Macfarlane has demonstrated that accusations of witchcraft usually arose from just the sort of encounter that one of Shakespeare's witches describes: she is denied a small favor and seeks, by supernatural means, to take revenge:

A sailor's wife had chestnuts in her lap
And mounched and mounched and mounched. "Give me," quoth I.
"Aroint thee, witch!" the rump-fed ronyon cries.
Her husband 's to Aleppo gone, master o' th' Tiger:
But in a sieve I'll thither sail
And, like a rat without a tail,
I'll do, I'll do, and I'll do.

(I.iii.4–10)

Macfarlane offers what is, in effect, an important gloss on this passage:

Witchcraft prosecutions were usually between people who knew each other intimately—that is, between village neighbours. They almost always arose from quarrels over gifts and loans in which the victim refused the witch some small gift, heard her muttering under her breath or threatening him, and subsequently suffered some misfortune. It was usually the person who had done the first wrong under the old ideals of charity who felt himself bewitched. . . . Witchcraft beliefs provided both the justification for severing contact, and an explanation for the guilt and fear still felt by the individual when he did so: he might expect to be repaid on the spiritual plane for his lack of charity, but could be satisfied that this was witchcraft, and thus evil, rather than punishment for his own short-comings. . . . Witchcraft prosecutions, therefore, may have been principally important as a radical force which broke down the communal pattern inherited from the medieval period. . . . [They] may be seen as a means of effecting a deep social change; a change from a "neighbourly," highly integrated and mutually interdependent village society to a more individualistic one.[9]

In *Macbeth,* as in Jacobean society, belief in witches functions both as a radical force that enables the individual to break free from the community and as a retributive force that punishes him for doing so. Shakespeare focuses with relentless clarity not on the sociology of witchcraft prosecutions but on their psychological precondition: the capacity for self-deception made possible by the tendency to project onto others one's own unacknowledged ambition, guilt, or fear.

We have seen that community depends on this projective capacity to bind consciousness to the natural order created unconsciously by the mind. The action of *Macbeth,* together with the interpretation of witchcraft just cited, suggest that the projective capacity assumes pathological intensity in the individual and the community when their unity is threatened. Projections become more vivid and hallucinatory as the mind tries harder and harder to present its inmost convictions as perceptions of the outer world. When the images are diabolical witchcraft, horrible imaginings of murder, bloody daggers, and mangled ghosts, they may be interpreted as danger signals by which the mind expresses its instinctive fear of isolation from the community and self-division. Macbeth's projections become progressively more substantial as the play moves forward from the "horrid image" entirely contained within the mind (I.iii) to the "fatal vision" of the dagger that hovers in the air "before" him (II.i) to the ghost of Banquo that actually enters so the spectators share the hallucination (III.iv) to the Apparitions in the witches' cave, produced, no doubt, by elaborate theatrical machinery (IV.i). As Macbeth himself recognizes, the Apparitions harp his fears aright, presenting images of his own anxieties about Macduff and Banquo's seed while they also reflect his confidence that he is invulnerable.

The play's sequence of ever more substantial, elaborate, and delusive projections conforms to a pattern described by C. G. Jung:

It is not the conscious subject but the unconscious which does the projecting. Hence one meets with projections, one does not make them. The effect of projection is to isolate the subject from his environment, since instead of a real relation to it there is now only an illusory one. Projections change the world into the replica of one's own unknown face. In the last analysis, therefore, they lead to an autoerotic or autistic condition in which one dreams a world whose reality remains forever unattainable. The resultant *sentiment d'incomplétude* and the still worse feeling of sterility are in their turn explained by projection as the malevolence of the environment, and by means of this vicious circle the isolation is intensified. The more projections are thrust in between the subject and the environment, the harder it is for the ego to see through its illusions.[10]

These negative effects of projection come together in Macbeth's resentment of Banquo and his "seed" (III.i.48–72): the feeling of incompleteness ("To be thus is nothing, but to be safely thus—"), sterility (the "barren sceptre"), and the malevolence of the environment (Banquo's ghost, and later the moving forest). In the end, Macbeth is thoroughly isolated, shut up in his castle, where he shrivels and comes apart like the leaf fallen into the sere:

> Now does he feel his title
> Hang loose about him, like a giant's robe
> Upon a dwarfish thief.
>
> all that is within him does condemn
> Itself for being there.
>
> (V.ii.20–22, 24–25)

In Macbeth, as in the community, projection is a defensive force that eventually destroys itself through its own excessive strength. All of Macbeth's projected images are (in part, at least) admonitory or retributive, revealing to him the full horror of his anarchic impulses and deeds. But these projections become incentives to crime when their excessive strength reveals their character as projections that originate not in nature but in the unconscious mind. This revelation allows the conscious mind to repudiate the projections or else harness their force to the will that they had previously restrained. Consciousness acquires new autonomy and power when the mind recognizes and withdraws its projections; the world then appears as the objective and neutral thing that it "really" is, and the self can comprehend and shape itself independently of that world. Charles Taylor describes the seventeenth-century transition from traditional to modern notions of the self as a freeing of self "from the projection of meaning onto things." Newly able to draw back from the world and to create at least a myth of objectivity, man is free to concentrate on his own capacity to observe, manipulate, and control the world. "The old model," Taylor writes, "now looks like a dream of self-dispersal; self-presence is now to be aware of what we are and what we are doing in abstraction from the world we observe and judge."[11] This new power of self cancels and tears to pieces the "great bond" (III.ii.49) that had placed communal man within the natural order. What appears to most critics as the mere perversity of Macbeth's criminal ambition may also be seen as a clarified image of the emergence of the modern self. Yet the play may also imply a warning about the liabilities of that self, not only by presenting the attractions of a lost ideal but also by dramatizing in its most "modern" character what the new mode of being requires.

Lady Macbeth, from the first, lives within the new individualistic order and seeks its confirmation—"solely sovereign sway and masterdom"—in the murder of Duncan. She fears no witchcraft but invokes "murd'ring ministers" to lend her their power, "that no compunctious visitings of nature / Shake [her] fell purpose" (I.v.43–44). Her imagery expresses not a passive mode of perception governed by unconscious projections, but a deliberate and "witty" manipulation of appearances that makes them reflect her "fell purpose." When the breathless messenger announces the king's approach, she remarks: "The raven himself is hoarse / That croaks the fatal entrance of Duncan / Under my battlements" (36–38). She greets with scornful incomprehension Macbeth's visions of a natural order that inhibits or rebukes his actions, as though he were indeed unmanned by a dream of self-dispersal. The voice that cries "Sleep no more!", the bloody hand that will "The multitudinous seas incarnadine," the blood-boltered Banquo, are merely the "painting of [his] fear" (III.iv.61):

> You do unbend your noble strength to think
> So brainsickly of things. Go get some water
> And wash this filthy witness from your hand.
>
> A little water clears us of this deed.
> How easy is it then.
>
> (II.ii.44–46, 66–68)

She is equally scornful of Macbeth's instinctive honesty, his tendency to wear his heart on his sleeve:

> Your face, my Thane, is as a book where men
> May read strange matters.
>
>   look like th'innocent flower,
> But be the serpent under 't.
>
> (I.v.60–61, 63–64)

Under her tutelage, Macbeth discovers that the price paid for autonomy from nature and community is self-division: "False face must hide what the false heart doth know" (I.vii.82).

Macbeth differs from Lady Macbeth and from the other amoral individualists in Shakespeare, like Richard III, Iago, or Edmund, in being at first contained within the traditional world view and emerging only gradually and painfully from it. An important step in this process is taken in the dagger soliloquy of II.i; there the projective faculty operates with such force that it emerges into consciousness. Macbeth does not at this point repudiate projection as a delusion but instead appropriates it as an expression of his conscious will. When he realizes that the "fatal vision" is "A dagger of the mind, a false creation / Proceeding from the heat-oppressèd brain" (38–39) and that "the bloody business . . . informs / Thus to [his] eyes" (48–49), his speech momentarily takes on the quality of poetic wit that was evident in Lady Macbeth's and he deliberately projects a landscape that will sustain his resolution to kill:

> Now o'er the one half-world
> Nature seems dead, and wicked dreams abuse
> The curtained sleep. Withcraft celebrates
> Pale Hecate's offerings; and withered murder,
> Alarumed by his sentinel, the wolf,
> Whose howl's his watch, thus with his stealthy pace,
> With Tarquin's ravishing strides, towards his design
> Moves like a ghost.
>
> (II.i.49–56)

As Peter Ure says, Macbeth creates "an objective vision of himself in which he is assimilated to the figure of Murther playing his part in a scene which must uphold him by being appropriately set."[12] Paradoxically, he wills his own self-deception, attempting to accomplish deliberately what projection had done instinctively. This paradox of deliberate self-deception is reflected by an odd turn that his soliloquy takes immediately after the lines just quoted. Having elaborately envisaged the scene and himself (as withered murder) in it, he asks it not to notice his presence, lest it lose its power to enthrall him:

> Thou sure and firm-set earth,
> Hear not my steps which way they walk, for fear
> Thy very stones prate of my whereabout
> And take the present horror from the time,
> Which now suits with it.
>
> (56–60)

He finally disentangles himself from these imaginings, remarking that they are too weak and indirect a means of manipulating his world:

> Whiles I threat, he lives;
> Words to the heat of deeds too cold breath gives.
>
> (60–61)

What begins in the images of unconscious projection ends in the heat of deeds.

The pattern of this soliloquy is repeated in several episodes, and on a larger scale by the play as a whole. In each case, Macbeth finally recognizes that the image is a projection, denies its objective reality, and thereby frees himself for violent action. He sees that the dagger is an illusion, but then draws his own dagger, which makes the false creation real. The ghost of Banquo disappears when he dismisses it as a hallucination—"Hence, horrible shadow! / Unreal mock'ry, hence!" (III.iv.106–7)—but when he recovers his composure, he resolves to harden himself by committing further crimes: "We are yet but young in deed" (144). He dismisses the witches' apparitions—"No more sights" (IV.i.155)—but then decides to kill Macduff's family—quickly, "before this purpose cool" (154).

Bad Faith, Authenticity, and the Balanced Self

The emergence of the modern self as a subject distinct from the world as object is complicated by the same principle of replication that applies to the concept of play. When the self is distinguished from the world, it becomes internally divided in a way that corresponds to the distinction between the actor and his role. This self-division is attended by an ambivalence about human freedom. The self as subject seems, in its exercise of knowledge and will, to be entirely free, but the self as the object of its own knowledge seems entirely determined, whether by chance or fate, nature or society, the irrational or the unconscious. In our own time this ambivalence is expressed in the contrasting extremes of a psychological determinism that sees our actions as entirely governed by unconscious drives and an existential nihilism that finds us condemned to a freedom so radical that all of our actions must appear arbitrary, contingent, and empty.[13]

This ambivalence takes several forms in *Macbeth;* the one most often noticed is centered on the witches, who can be considered evil beings or mere projections of Macbeth's ambition.[14] Macbeth himself wants to have it both ways. Our confusion about the extent to which the witches limit his freedom and determine his actions is a confusion that he wills upon himself. If the witches did not exist, he would have to invent them. Lady Macbeth virtually does invent them on her first appearance in Act One, scene five. The rhetoric of her invocation to "spirits," "murd'ring ministers" and "thick night" expresses an intoxicating mixture of contradictory impulses: to yield to supernatural powers, becoming their instrument, and thereby to gain extraordinary personal power to act beyond the inhibitions that limit the behavior of others. Macbeth treats projection in the same ambivalent way, converting instinctive to deliberate self-deception, so that what had been a force of psychological determinism becomes a freely chosen stratagem that liberates the will from the "compunctious visitings of nature" (I.v.43).

The sundering of character into self and role is dramatized when Macbeth is given Cawdor's title; he reacts with discomfort: "Why do you dress me / In borrowed robes" (I.iii.108–9). Macbeth's momentary revulsion resembles the feeling that is more fully developed in Coriolanus when he objects to the necessity of appearing to the people in humble guise;

> Would you have me
> False to my nature? Rather say I play
> The man I am.
> . . . .
>   I will not do 't,
> Lest I surcease to honor mine own truth
> And by my body's action teach my mind
> A most inherent baseness.
>
> (*Cor.* III.ii.14–16, 120–23)

Macbeth's feeling is less easily accounted for, since (unlike Coriolanus) he is not being asked to humble himself; but the real objection of both warriors is to the sundering of inner unity by the self-consciousness inherent in deliberate role-playing. Macbeth's uneasiness is magnified for the spectator by the dramatic irony of the fact that the former Thane of Cawdor had been a "most disloyal traitor" (I.ii.52): Macbeth puts on his treason with his title and, by accepting the new role, ceases to honor his own truth.

Macbeth's initial uneasiness passes momentarily into its opposite when he thinks expansively of the freedom and power seemingly promised by the witches' prophecies, and even more by his new sense of separateness and independence: "Two truths are told, / As happy prologues to the swelling act / Of the imperial theme" (127–29). But his uneasiness soon returns in intensified form and crystallizes in the horrid image of murder that destroys his singleness of being. His crime is prompted by this prior sense of guilt that is connected to his sense of himself as a divided being, an actor in borrowed robes.[15] The deed itself is done in part to relieve the anguish of this dualism, to "trammel up the consequence," possess the future in an instant, close the gap "Between the acting of a dreadful thing / And the first motion" (*JC*, II.i.63–64), and so restore his unity of being—but without forfeiting the promised independence, self-determination, and sovereignty.

The association of role-playing with the treason of divided being is further rationalized when it takes the form of the hypocrisy, the "false face," needed to conceal the crime. But little is done in this play with the potentially exciting drama of deceiving others; instead, hypocrisy is internalized and transformed to objectify the original feeling of disunity. Macbeth is most concerned to deceive himself. He displays more clearly than any of Shakespeare's other characters, what Jean-Paul Sartre calls "bad faith," a deliberate lie to oneself:

> I must know in my capacity as deceiver the truth which is hidden from me in my capacity as the one deceived. Better yet I must know the truth very exactly in order to conceal it more carefully—and this not at two different moments . . . but in the unitary structure of a single project. . . . The first act of bad faith is to flee what it cannot flee, to flee what it is. The very project of flight reveals to bad faith an inner disintegration in the heart of being, and it is this disintegration which bad faith wishes to be.[16]

This is precisely Macbeth's project:

> Stars, hide your fires;
> Let not light see my black and deep desires.
> The eye wink at the hand; yet let that be
> Which the eye fears, when it is done, to see.
>
> (I.iv.50–53)

He is asking for psychic disunity, for an "inner disintegration in the heart of being," and he soon gets his wish. After he has killed the king, he notices that his hands are bloody, and they seem not to be his hands at all: "What hands are here? Ha! they pluck out mine eyes" (II.ii.58).

Macbeth's bad faith is dramatized in his willingness to let Lady Macbeth manage the first crime, in his effort to make the murderers kill Banquo out of their own hatred, in his response to the ghost ("Never shake / Thy gory locks at me" [III.iv.50–51]), in his reliance on the false assurance offered by the witches' apparitions, and in his final vision of life as a strutting player signifying nothing. The crucial question is whether Shakespeare is dramatizing a modern (but also reactionary) view that *any* division of character into self and role, and any act of deliberate role-playing, are inherently evil or (to use another existentialist term) "inauthentic." The play seems designed to provoke but then to transform this reactionary view. Subjectivity and self-division may be evil on their first appearance because they destroy the natural unity of both self and community. We recall that Hegel likened this "sundering into self-realization" to another fall of man. But this second fall, like the first, seems an inevitable part of a providential development. Thus, when Macbeth is overcome, the communal order of Duncan's reign is not restored. Malcolm's kingdom differs from his father's most of all in its capacity to assign positive social functions to the subjectivity and role-playing that otherwise subvert society and threaten the individual with the kind of degeneration shown in Macbeth and Lady Macbeth. The play is not reactionary and seeks no moral refuge in the nostalgic image of authentic selves joined in communal bonds.

As a moral ideal, authenticity is the obverse of bad faith, an extreme and uncompromising imperative to restore at the level of individual and subjective being the integrated and unself-conscious frame of mind that characterized life in the community. To be authentic, one must repudiate the division of personality into self and role by acting spontaneously, "from within." Any role that is defined by society or created by ourselves to meet the expectations of others is inauthentic. It follows that authentic behavior is often manifested (or at least described by its proponents) in perverse and violent deeds that society has not formulated as preestablished roles but has ignored or repressed.[17] Authenticity becomes violent not only because it must search out unconventional and antisocial modes of self-expression, but also (and especially) because in repudiating roles it denies the claims that others make upon the self. In extreme forms authenticity can lead to a subjective and personal equivalent of tyranny, as Lionel Trilling implies in citing the violence explicit in the Greek ancestry of *authentic:* "*Authenteo:* to have full power over; also, to commit a murder. *Authentes:* not only a master and a doer, but also a perpetrator, a murderer, even a self-murderer, a suicide."[18]

The potential violence of authenticity is acted out in *Macbeth*. The unity of communal being that authenticity tries to replace at the personal level is seen in the opening description of Macbeth. His bloody deeds are translated directly and unambiguously into names and titles: "Brave Macbeth (well he deserves that name)," "valor's minion," "Bellona's bridegroom." Even as this unity disintegrates into hypocrisy and bad faith, Lady Macbeth prescribes as its replacement a fierce unity of desire and act:

> Art thou afeared
> To be the same in thine own act and valor
> As thou art in desire?
>
> (I.vii.39–41)

which she envisages in herself as a willingness to dash her nursing infant's brains out. It reappears in Macbeth after the appearance of Banquo's ghost has made hypocrisy and self-deception unbearable:

> The very firstlings of my heart shall be
> The firstlings of my hand. And even now,
> To crown my thoughts with acts, be it thought and done.
>
> (IV.i.147–49)

The act that will crown his thoughts and confirm this integrity is the slaughter of Macduff's family, a deed which, like the infanticide imagined by Lady Macbeth, has no other value than to assert the autonomous self over against society.

When Macbeth kills Duncan, he destroys the community and forces the other characters into the same condition of isolation and divided being that is so destructive in him. This is evident at once in the oddly insensitive response of Malcolm and Donalbain to their father's murder (II.iii). They permit themselves no spontaneous expressions of grief but must "hold [their] tongues" (115), speaking only to each other and then only in brief asides. They keep themselves apart from the large group of characters on stage: Macbeth, Lady Macbeth, Banquo, Macduff, Lennox, Ross, and (perhaps) the Porter—a full stage by Shakespearean standards. At the end of the scene, these characters make their exits. Malcolm and Donalbain, left alone on the platform, resolve to seek safety in separation:

> *Malcolm.* What will you do? Let's not consort with them.
> To show an unfelt sorrow in an office
> Which the false man does easy. I'll to England.
> *Donalbain.* To Ireland I. Our separated fortune
> Shall keep us both the safer. Where we are
> There's daggers in men's smiles; the near in blood,
> The nearer bloody.
>
> (131–37)

Wilbur Sanders thinks that this scene reveals deficiencies in the princes' characters: "They are too young to feel much more than shock, and too frightened to conceal adolescent callousness and self-concern."[19] But surely the main point is not to characterize the princes but to dramatize the immediate consequences of the loss of community.

The flight of Malcolm and Donalbain "puts upon them / Suspicion of the deed" (II.iv.26–27). While they are not guilty of murder, they must adopt new and more self-centered modes of consciousness and behavior in order to respond effectively to the crisis caused by Macbeth. Macbeth's crime imposes a kind of guiltiness on other characters as well. Bradley may have overstated his case (but only a little) in describing Banquo as guilty of complicity in Macbeth's crime. Banquo does not live long enough for us (or him) to know how he would finally have acted on the suspicions he expresses at the beginning of Act Three.[20] That he expresses them in a soliloquy that he must break off—"hush, no more!"—as others approach is symptomatic of the general malady. Moreover, his indignation at suspected crime is supplanted by the hope that he will indeed "get kings" as the witches promised; one effect of Macbeth's foul play is to "enkindle" Banquo "unto the crown" (I.iii.121). Even before this moment, we find him resisting an impulse toward evil that he associates with the witches. Significantly, the evil manifests itself in the private and inward world of "curtained sleep" that is abused, as Macbeth says, by "wicked dreams" (II.i.50–51). Much as he would like to, Banquo cannot avoid falling into this nocturnal subjective realm:

> A heavy summons lies like lead upon me,
> And yet I would not sleep. Merciful powers,
> Restrain in me the cursèd thoughts that nature
> Gives way to in repose.
>
> (II.i.6–9)

Moral autonomy in the absence of a sustaining natural or social order is difficult—perhaps impossible—to maintain. As Hamlet says, "I could be bounded in a nutshell and count myself a king of infinite space, were it not that I have bad dreams" (II.ii.252–54).

Two scenes of choric commentary (II.iv and III.vi) not only describe the effects of Macbeth's tyranny but also embody them in a self-consciously indirect, understated, and devious mode of speech. The spontaneous, unmediated revelation of self to self is no longer possible; the hearer must guess the speaker's meaning:

> My former speeches have but hit your thoughts,
> Which can interpret father. Only I say
> Things have been strangely borne. The gracious Duncan
> Was pitied of Macbeth. Marry, he was dead.
> And the right valiant Banquo walked too late;
> Whom, you may say (if 't please you) Fleance killed,
> For Fleance fled. Men must not walk too late.
>
> (III.vi.1–7)

A terse exchange between Ross and Macduff at the end of II.iv parallels the dialogue of Malcolm and Donalbain in II.iii; again the interlocutors agree to go their separate ways:

> *Ross.*   Will you to Scone?
> *Macduff.* No, cousin, I'll to Fife.
> *Ross.*   Well, I will thither.
> *Macduff.* Well, may you see things well done there. Adieu,
> Lest our old robes sit easier than our new!
>
> (II.iv.35–38)

Macduff means a good deal more than he says: he will not attend the investiture of Macbeth and swear allegiance to a murderer and usurper.[21]

Macduff can kill Macbeth in the end without being guilty of regicide because he has had no king since Duncan's death and has been in effect a man without a country. His unnatural and painful autonomy, by which he gains power to defeat Macbeth, is symbolized by his violent birth: "Macduff was from his mother's womb / Untimely ripped" (V.vii.15–16). It is also symbolized by his desertion of his family, which, in his absence, is savagely slaughtered (IV.ii). To his wife, his departure seems a kind of treason. As Bradley remarks, "It does not even occur to her that he has acted from a public spirit or that there is such a thing. . . . for his country's sake he deliberately risked a danger which he fully realized."[22] In the world of the play, such "public spirit" is a radical innovation. Even Malcolm is incredulous:

> Why in that rawness left you wife and child,
> Those precious motives, those strong knots of love,
> Without leave-taking?
>
> (IV.iii.26–28)

Macduff must cancel the great bond of nature and break his instinctive ties to his family in order to serve a different entity that he calls "my country." The new loyalty seems treason to the old, and Macduff pays a terrible price for it.

The long scene between Malcolm and Macduff (IV.iii) recapitulates the earlier responses to Macbeth's tyranny and brings them to bear on a new theme, the idea of nationhood, of "Scotland." Malcolm's suspicions of Macduff and the stratagem he uses to test Macduff's loyalty recall the earlier moments of inhibited, indirect, and mistrustful speech (in II.iv and III.vi). As in II.iii, Malcolm must again preserve himself through calculated deviousness; in the process he sullies himself with "false speaking" (IV.iii.130). His falsehoods express a genuine uneasiness. Like Banquo earlier, he is implicated in the "guilt" of divided being. Malcolm's falsehoods dishearten Macduff, who is nonetheless forced to recognize that he is also guilty when, later in this scene, he learns of his family's slaughter: "Sinful Macduff, / They were all struck for thee!" (224–25).

The political implications of Malcolm's meeting with Macduff depend on both men's troubled awareness of what this new mode of being means for Scotland, and on their attempt to use it as the basis for a new society. By raising the issue of his own fitness to rule, Malcolm explores a new concept of kingship as an office distinct from its holder. He leads Macduff to affirm that a bad man could be a good ruler so long as his lust and greed were merely private vices. Macduff states—admittedly in a hypothetical and extreme form—the proposition that what matters is not the sanctity of the king's person but the effectiveness of his public services. Malcolm knows that he is not destined to be a sacramental or paternalistic embodiment of the realm, as his father had been, but its servant: "What I am truly, / Is thine and my poor country's to command" (IV.iii.131–32). Malcolm and Macduff repeatedly apostrophize "Scotland" as "my country" (7, 31, 39, 46, 53, 100, 132), and Ross joins in with "Alas, poor country, / Almost afraid to know itself" (164–65). By personifying the country, they express a new awareness of it as an entity separate from its ruler and distinct even from its people as the group to which they belong. It is as a person to be succored and freed from oppression that Scotland claims the loyalty and service of Malcolm and Macduff. The nation is not a group to be joined nor an object to be possessed; its "otherness" must be respected, even as it must respect the personal independence of its people.

This mutual respect requires both king and subjects to balance inner and outer, private and public selves. The dialogue of Malcolm and Macduff shows how awkward this balancing can be. The scene gains its peculiar intensity by dramatizing the difficulty of communication between persons only recently sundered from the unselfconscious life of the community and thus still painfully aware of the difference between the inner self and the outward character. The scene emphasizes the necessity of maintaining this difference as the source of the individual's dignity and as the model for the right relationship between the individual and his country. Malcolm must determine whether Macduff's proffered role as loyal defender of Scotland is genuine, but he proceeds in this disagreeable business by slandering himself until he provokes Macduff to repudiate him. It is as if he were atoning in advance for distrusting Macduff by forcing Macduff to distrust him. Macduff proves his own "integrity" (115) by withdrawing his allegiance from Malcolm (as he had earlier denied it to Macbeth); it is this denial of ingenuous trust that cancels Malcolm's suspicions and enables him to cancel Macduff's. Malcolm and Macduff are groping toward a new understanding of themselves and each other as separate and autonomous beings, as though they were, like Scotland, almost afraid to know themselves in this new capacity.

Malcolm offers Macduff an apology that affirms the distinction between self and role and the separate moral value of each:

> But I shall crave your pardon.
> That which you are, my thoughts cannot transpose:
> Angels are bright still though the brightest fell;
> Though all things foul would wear the brows of grace,
> Yet grace must still look so.
>
> (20–24)

Malcolm's suspicions cannot corrupt and do not invalidate ("cannot transpose") Macduff's genuine commitment, nor, if Macduff were false, would his hypocrisy discredit the "grace" he pretends to have. The virtuous person must persist in the appearance and acts of virtue, even though they can be feigned by others, even though he will himself, on occasion, be suspected of feigning, and even though he will need to suspect others whose appearance differs not from his own.

The division of self and role is more dramatically affirmed when Macduff learns that Macbeth has slaughtered his family. Malcolm urges that Macduff express his feelings lest they destroy him: "the grief that does not speak / Whispers the o'erfraught heart and bids it break" (209–10). Even here a spontaneous self-expression is denied: Macduff refuses to "let grief / Convert to anger" (229–30). He knows, as Ross says, that the main part of it "Pertains to [him] alone" (199). Scotland has no right to use this feeling, which Macduff will keep to himself.

> *Malcolm.* Dispute it like a man.
> *Macduff.*   I shall do so;
> But I must also feel it as a man.
> I cannot but remember such things were
> That were most precious to me.
>
> (220–23)

It is a mistake to assume that Macduff means to purify or authenticate his public "dispute" by linking it to his personal loss. To the contrary, his feelings of remembrance and remorse run counter to his determination to rid Scotland of Macbeth:

> Did heaven look on
> And would not take their part? Sinful Macduff,
> They were all struck for thee! Naught that I am,
> Not for their own demerits but for mine
> Fell slaughter on their souls. Heaven rest them now!
>
> (224–27)

Only by keeping his public and private selves separate can he prevent his feelings from weakening his commitment to fight or his commitment from corrupting his feelings.[23]

This separation of selves is equally evident in Macduff's great antagonist. The development of Macbeth's character culminates in the coexistence of opposed and contradictory responses: the detachment of the private, inner self, and the engagement of the self that confronts others. Macbeth is redeemed (in part, at least) because the fierce unity of his ambitious self is sundered into the unflinching spectator of his own ruin—"I have lived long enough. My way of life / Is fall'n into the sear" (V.iii.22–23)—and the yet courageous warrior who resolves to "try the last" (V.vii.32) and prefers to die "with harness on [his] back" (V.v.52), kicking an invincible foe. In the end, he lives "without appeal" (as the existentialists would say), possessed by a stubborn honesty that refuses even the solace of resignation.[24]

The ending of *Macbeth*, like the ending of *Henry V*, prompts in us as spectators a dual response that enables us to feel directly the division of engaged and detached selves and their balanced opposition. As members of the group of actors and spectators that sustain the theatrical event, we participate in, and naturally assent to, its conclusion, which is brought about by Macbeth's enemies. As separate and subjective persons—and especially as readers—we remain in sympathy with Macbeth and may feel, with many critics, that the play's ending shows the defeat of imagination by political expediency:

> Macbeth was far worse, but also far greater than any of the survivors. . . . For it is not necessary to sentimentalize Macbeth to perceive what a handful of dust we are left with after he is gone. The new world is ordered, but bare; healthy but bland. Macbeth made himself into a monster, but lived on a level to which no Malcolm or Macduff can attain.[25]

Shakespeare provokes this kind of response in us when he has Malcolm refer to the main characters as a "dead butcher and his fiend-like queen" (69). But this remark is immediately followed by lines in which the actor begins to speak through the character, addressing an implicit epilogue to the audience, as if to say "we'll strive to please you every day" (*TN*, V.i.397):

> What's more to do
> Which would be planted newly with the time—
> As calling home our exiled friends abroad
> That fled the snares of watchful tyranny,
> Producing forth the cruel ministers
> Of this dead butcher and his fiend-like queen,
> Who (as 'tis thought) by self and violent hands
> Took off her life—this, and what needful else
> That calls upon us, by the grace of Grace
> We will perform in measure, time, and place.
> So thanks to all at once and to each one,
> Whom we invite to see us crowned as Scone.
>
> (V.viii.64–75)

The actor invites our applause, even as the character repels us by failing to share our understanding of Macbeth. The play's final lines appeal to us collectively, as members of the audience, and individually, as persons who are about to disperse to our separate lives, "to all at once and to each one," giving equal scope to the assent natural to the public self and the scepticism natural to the private self. In their most comprehensive dimensions, human nature and society, like Shakespearean drama, must accommodate both.

Conclusion

Macbeth, like the other tragedies, differs from *As You Like It, Henry V,* and most comedies and histories, in that the hero is excluded from the final resolution. The development of Macbeth's character reaches a resolution of its own when he abandons false hopes and defies his fate, but this conclusion differs from and opposes the return to reality toward which the play's action leads the other characters. The pattern of withdrawal and return does not have to be completed within the experience of the main character, or any character, so long as it is in some other way established for the spectators. It is established quite emphatically in *Macbeth,* because the movement of withdrawal is focused in the hero, while the return is accomplished against him by his enemies. Macbeth's pathologically intense subjectivity is neither affirmed nor accommodated, but silenced by an antagonist who refuses to be self-expressive: "I have no words; / My voice is in my sword" (V.viii.6–7). In the end, each spectator must balance as he or she can the rival claims of Macduff's "voice" and Macbeth's. We have seen that this balancing of responses is generally required by Shakespeare's conclusions; it signals and prepares our return to reality.

The return to reality implies no single or simple judgment of the theater or of playing in its many forms. In some plays, the vision and conduct of life as theater are clearly repudiated, as when Berowne and the other lords in *Love's Labor's Lost* renounce affectation in favor of "russet yeas and honest kersey noes" (V.ii.414), or when the newly crowned Henry V turns away both his "former self" and Falstaff (see *2H4,* V.v.48–73). In other plays—the majority—the subjectivity expressed by the vision of life as theater is reconciled with the reality to which characters and spectators return. *A Midsummer Night's Dream, As You Like It,* and most of the comedies and romances conclude with a "marriage of true minds" that harmonizes reason and emotion, reality and imagination. Finally, a number of plays equate theatrical artifice

148

with reality; but their effect is to affirm the creative power of theatricality, not to reduce reality to illusion. Plays as different as *The Taming of the Shrew* and *Hamlet* display the liberating power of role-playing to "change the stamp of nature" (*Ham.*, III.iv.169). Most plays, of course, combine these alternatives to some extent. In *Twelfth Night*, for example, Olivia's happy return from love's illusions has a quality quite different from Malvolio's sour disaffection: "There was never man so notoriously abused" (IV.ii.85–86). The extent to which *Macbeth* repudiates the subjective and theatrical imagination of its hero will depend in part on how much sympathy he retains at the end—and this will vary to some degree from production to production, and from spectator to spectator.

"It is not good to stay too long in the theater."[1] The feeling that the play must end, together with the fear that it cannot, and that there is no reality to which one can return, often finds expression in the fourth or fifth act of Shakespeare's plays. Sir Toby fears that the joke on Malvolio has gone too far: "I would we were well rid of this knavery . . . for I am now so far in offense with my niece that I cannot pursue with any safety this sport to the upshot" (IV.ii.66–67, 68–70). Orlando tires of his mock courtship—"I can live no longer by thinking" (*AYL*, V.ii.48)—and wonders if Rosalind will ever appear "human as she is" (64). Prospero announces that "Our revels now are ended" (*Tmp.*, IV.i.148), only to conclude that reality is no less transient: the great globe itself shall dissolve, and our little life is rounded with a sleep. The only reality beyond theatrical magic that Prospero can imagine for himself is death: "Every third thought shall be my grave" (V.i.311); in the epilogue, the "bare island" from which he wishes to be set free seems equated with earthly life itself: "And my ending is despair / Unless I be relieved by prayer" (15–16)—or by applause. It is as though he were asking the spectators to finish the play for him, to break "with the help of [their] good hands" a spell that has grown too strong.

Macbeth's meditation on life's "sound and fury" is the most powerful Shakespearean instance of theatrical claustrophobia. Macbeth's nihilism has two closely related aspects: first, a feeling that there is no reality beyond the theater, that "Life's but . . . a poor player . . . a tale . . . Signifying nothing" (V.v.24, 26, 28); and second, an impoverishment of emotional response that results paradoxically from an overindulgence of play and spectacle. Just as Henry V is finally disgusted by "surfeit-swelled" Falstaff (*2H4*, V.v.51), Macbeth, glutted with atrocities, feels the disenchantment of satiety:

> I have supped full with horrors.
> Direness, familiar to my slaughterous thoughts,
> Cannot once start me.
>
> (V.v.13–15)

When speech, gesture, and action (on stage or off) no longer refer beyond themselves, they lose their emotional value and affective power as well. What remains is either an empty shell, mere strutting and fretting, or a fullness that chokes itself on "sound and fury." The reduction of life to theater reduces both life and theater to "nothing."

Yet from and through that "nothing" grows affirmation. Two ways of explaining this affirmation correspond to the basic critical stances—the oral, performance-oriented, and the literary—described in the Introduction to this book. A critic who reads a play as a literary text might emphasize the dramatist's visionary power as poet, and might say of Macbeth's soliloquy what Una Ellis-Fermor says of *Troilus and Cressida:*

> The idea of chaos, of disjunction, of ultimate formlessness and negation, has by a supreme act of artistic mastery been given form. . . . [The] vision of evil has been brought under the governance of those artistic laws which are themselves the image of the ultimate law of an ordered universe. Thus in Shakespeare's *Troilus and Cressida* we meet a paradoxical dualism. The content of this thought is an implacable assertion of chaos as the ultimate fact of being; the presence of artistic form is a deeper, unconscious testimony to an order which is actually ultimate and against which the gates of hell shall not prevail.[2]

This formulation places the entire burden of affirmation on the solitary struggle of writing and revising; the fruits of such labor are "mastery," "comprehension," and "vision . . . brought under governance."

Shall we say that the ordering power of the playwright's imagination opposes and contains the nihilistic vision of the character? Only if we add that Shakespeare also appropriated the very different powers of theatrical performance. That difference is suggested by Stephen Gosson's opinion that the theater violated the ultimate law of an ordered universe and swung wide the gates of hell. "Play is the disruption of presence":[3] the playhouse opens in the universe a place, a heterocosm, where playing can occur. Theatrical performance does not master, order, and comprehend—it evokes and brings to life. Its energies are called forth by just such a gap in nature as Macbeth's nihilism discloses. The obverse of the nihilism that reduces life to theater is the imaginative response that brings the theater to life.

Imagination confers value on the bare stage of the world and thereby discloses its underlying reality:

> Nothing is good, I see, without respect;
> . . . .
> The crow doth sing as sweetly as the lark
> When neither is attended.
>
> (MV, V.i.99, 102–3)

Shakespearean theater as metaphor gives cognitive and moral functions to our willing participation in make-believe. "The king's a beggar when the play is done" (*AWW*, V.iii.331), and he owes his temporary royalty as much to our imaginative responses as to the actor's skill in impersonation: "The best in this kind are but shadows; and the worst are no worse, if imagination amend them. . . . If we imagine no worse of them than they of themselves, they may pass for excellent men" (*MND*, V.i.209–10, 213–14). Shakespeare makes our human capacity to pretend correspond to and illuminate whatever faith—whether self-confidence or trust in others—sustains or deludes the characters. This correspondence of our imagination to the reality of other selves is grounded in the social occasion of performance, where the subjective activity of make-believe (which is private for the reader) is shared by actors and spectators. The generosity of Shakespearean imagination flows from the vitality of the theatrical event. To recover this value in and for the act of reading is the best reason for studying the plays in their original theatrical context.

Notes

Introduction

1. I quote Shakespeare throughout from *The Complete Works*, general ed. Alfred Harbage (Baltimore, Md.: Penguin Books, 1969).

2. See Maynard Mack, "Engagement and Detachment in Shakespeare's Plays," in *Essays on Shakespeare and Elizabethan Drama in Honor of Hardin Craig*, ed. Richard Hosley (Columbia, Mo.: University of Missouri Press, 1962), p. 281.

3. Giovanni Pico della Mirandola, *Oration on the Dignity of Man*, trans. Elizabeth Livermore Forbes, in *The Renaissance Philosophy of Man*, ed. Ernst Cassirer, Paul Oskar Kristeller, and John Herman Randall, Jr. (Chicago: University of Chicago Press, 1948), p. 225.

4. Philip Sidney, *An Apologie for Poetrie, Elizabethan Critical Essays*, ed. G. Gregory Smith, 2 vols. (London: Oxford University Press, 1904), 1:157.

5. Ibid., 1:157.

6. Walter J. Ong, *Interfaces of the Word* (Ithaca, N.Y. and London: Cornell University Press, 1977), p. 18; see also, by the same author, *The Presence of the Word* (New Haven, Conn. and London: Yale University Press, 1967), pp. 22–35.

7. G. W. F. Hegel, *Hegel's Logic, Being Part One of the Encyclopaedia. . .* , trans. William Wallace (1873); Oxford: Clarendon Press, 1975), p. 44. See Geoffrey H. Hartman, "Romanticism and Anti-Self-Consciousness" (1962), *Beyond Formalism* (New Haven, Conn. and London: Yale University Press, 1970), pp. 298–310. The passage from Hegel's *Logic* is quoted on p. 301.

8. See Ong, *The Presence of the Word*, p. 45; also pp. 8–9, 136.

9. Sidney, *An Apologie for Poetrie*, 1:158.

10. William Wordsworth, *The Prelude* [1850], Book 2, line 77, quoted from *The Prelude*, ed. Ernest De Selincourt, 2d ed. rev. by Helen Darbishire (Oxford: Clarendon Press, 1959), p. 47.

11. See G. E. Bentley, *Shakespeare and His Theatre* (Lincoln, Neb.: University of Nebraska Press, 1964), pp. 1–26; and J. R. Brown, "The Theatrical Element of Shakespeare Criticism," in *Reinterpretations of Elizabethan Drama*, ed. Norman Rabkin (New York and London: Columbia University Press, 1969), pp. ‹77–95. Both Bentley and Brown urge that readers attempt to "create a theatrical context" (Bentley, p. 26) as they read, and thereby "to read Shakespeare with greater consciousness of theatrical potentialities" (Brown, p. 190). This is sensible advice, of course, but it should not lead us to ignore the profoundly literary values of Shakespearean performance.

12. See the prefatory letter "To the great Variety of Readers," in *Mr. William Shakespeares Comedies, Histories, & Tragedies* (London: Jaggard and Blount, 1623), sig. A3^r. I

quote from *The Norton Facsimile: The First Folio of Shakespeare,* ed. Charlton Hinman (New York: Norton, 1968), p. 7.

13. Richard Fly, *Shakespeare's Mediated World* (Amherst, Mass.: University of Massachusetts Press, 1976), p. 32.

14. Ibid., p. x.

15. Howard Felperin, in a Review of Jackson Cope, *The Theater and the Dream,* in *Modern Philology* 74 (1976–77): 97.

16. See, for example, Anne Righter, *Shakespeare and the Idea of the Play* (London: Chatto & Windus; New York: Barnes & Noble, 1962), p. 192: "In his final romances, particularly *The Winter's Tale* and *The Tempest,* Shakespeare turns the world itself into a theatre, blurring the distinctions between art and life. . . . He creates a world in which illusion and reality are indistinguishable and the same." James L. Calderwood, *Shakespearean Metadrama* (Minneapolis, Minn.: University of Minnesota Press, 1971), p. 127: "The internal fiction of the drama not only mirrors but actually merges with the theatrical occasion, and the division between art and actuality vanishes." Jackson I. Cope, *The Theater and the Dream: From Metaphor to Form in Renaissance Drama* (Baltimore, Md.: Johns Hopkins University Press, 1973), pp. 13, 8: "The Renaissance play . . . is a little world which both boasts and mocks aesthetic objectivity as it incorporates the *theatrum mundi* into itself upon its own terms. . . . Life is a dream, but dreams are more real than life. The world is a theater, but the theater is more real than this world." My own view is closer to that expressed long ago by Samuel L. Bethell in *Shakespeare and the Popular Dramatic Tradition* (London and New York: Staples Press, 1944). Bethell supposed that Shakespeare's self-conscious theatricality enabled him to maintain the distinctions of play and reality that are collapsed in metacriticism and to enhance, instead of precluding, drama's mimetic power. As Bethell has it, Shakespeare deliberately emphasized "the essential artificiality of the play-world" in order to hold "play-world and real world before the mind simultaneously yet without confusion" (p. 33). This "multi-consciousness" enabled Shakespeare to establish the play-world as a theatrical equivalent of the real: "If Shakespeare put the whole of life into his plays, he reciprocally interpreted life in terms of the theatre" (p. 41). This view of Shakespearean drama anticipates Ernst Gombrich's theory of mimesis cited later in this Introduction and W. K. Wimsatt's theory of metaphor cited in Chapter 3.

17. Johan Huizinga, *Homo Ludens: A Study of the Play-Element in Culture* (1950; Boston: Beacon Press, 1964), p. 8. The play concept and modern game theory are sensibly assessed in the opening paragraphs of W. K. Wimsatt's "Belinda Ludens" [1973], in *Day of the Leopards: Essays in Defense of Poems* (New Haven, Conn. and London: Yale University Press, 1976), pp. 99–103. See also Robert Anchor, "History and Play: Johan Huizinga and His Critics," *History and Theory* 17 (1978): 63–93.

18. Jacques Ehrmann, "Homo Ludens Revisited," in *Games, Play, Literature,* ed. Jacques Ehrmann, vol. 41 of *Yale French Studies* (New Haven, Conn.: Yale University Press, 1968), 33, 56.

19. Jonas A. Barish, "The Antitheatrical Prejudice," *Critical Quarterly* 8 (1966): 333.

20. Ehrmann, "Homo Ludens Revisited," p. 33.

21. Huizinga, *Homo Ludens,* pp. 13–15.

22. Ernst H. Gombrich, *Art and Illusion,* 2d ed. rev. (New York: Pantheon, 1961), p. 345.

23. For "complementarity," see Norman Rabkin, *Shakespeare and the Common Understanding* (New York: The Free Press; London Collier-Macmillan, 1967). That Shakespearean drama moves away from singleness of vision toward balanced opposition or *concordia discors* is argued by Margaret Beckman: "Opposition need not be overcome to

be resolved. If comedy celebrates life, it may regard the rich contrariety of life as its particular vision . . . [and present] a reconciliation of opposites in which both members of the opposition are retained in the face of all temptation to choose one or the other," "The Figure of Rosalind In *As You Like It*," *Shakespeare Quarterly* 29 (1978): 46. An exemplary interpretation of Shakespearean "complementarity" is Janet Adelman's *The Common Liar: An Essay on "Antony and Cleopatra,"* (New Haven, Conn. and London: Yale University Press, 1973).

Chapter 1. Playhouse Architecture and the Poetics of Theatrical Space

1. Rudolf Arnheim, *The Dynamics of Architectural Form* (Berkeley and Los Angeles: University of California Press, 1977), pp. 272, 274.

2. Alvin B. Kernan, "This Goodly Frame, The Stage: The Interior Theater of Imagination in English Drama," *Shakespeare Quarterly* 25 (1974): 2.

3. See Glynne Wickham, *Early English Stages, 1300 to 1660*, vol. 2, *1576 to 1660*, Pt. 2 (London: Routledge & Kegan Paul; New York: Columbia University Press, 1972), pp. 30–31, 67, 71, 160–61, 173. See also John Orrell, *The Quest for Shakespeare's Globe* (Cambridge: Cambridge University Press, 1983), pp. 103–26. Orrell indicates that there may have been a standard plan for the playhouse auditorium, and he describes the standardized methods that builders probably used to lay out the stage within the auditorium.

4. Frances A. Yates, *Theatre of the World* (Chicago: University of Chicago Press, 1969), p. 101. The panoramas are closely examined by John Orrell in *The Quest for Shakespeare's Globe*.

5. See below, pp. 24–25, and the authorities cited there.

6. John Cranford Adams, *The Globe Playhouse: Its Design and Equipment* (Cambridge: Harvard University Press, 1942), p. 35.

7. C. L. Barber, *Shakespeare's Festive Comedy: A Study of Dramatic Form and its Relation to Social Custom* (Princeton, N.J.: Princeton University Press, 1959), p. 15.

8. G. K. Hunter, *John Lyly: The Humanist as Courtier* (Cambridge: Harvard University Press, 1962), pp. 306, 307, 308.

9. David Burrows, "Interiors: Ritual, Art, and Games in the Field of Symbolic Action," *Centennial Review* 15 (1971): 338, 330–31.

10. Jaspers' remark is quoted from *Von der Wahrheit* by Gaston Bachelard, *The Poetics of Space*, trans. Maria Jolas (Boston: Beacon Press, 1969), p. 232. See also Christian Norberg-Schulz, *Existence, Space and Architecture* (New York: Praeger, 1971), pp. 18–24.

11. "On a Drop of Dew," lines 2–3, 6–8, in *Andrew Marvell: Complete Poetry*, ed. George deF. Lord (New York: Random House, 1968), p. 6.

12. Bachelard, *Poetics of Space*, pp. 239, 234.

13. Arnheim, *Dynamics of Architectural Form*, pp. 93, 94, 96.

14. Quoted from the description *Of an Excellent Actor* (1615) as given by E. K. Chambers, *The Elizabethan Stage* (Oxford: Clarendon Press, 1923), 4:257–58. Chambers attributes the description to Webster and suggests that the actor may have been Richard Burbage, in which case the "full Theater" may have been the Globe.

15. José Ortega y Gasset, "The Self and the Other," trans. Willard R. Trask, in *The Dehumanization of Art* (New York: Doubleday, 1956), p. 167.

16. For the dimensions of the playhouse, see Richard Hosley, "The Playhouses," in *The Revels History of Drama in English, Volume 3: 1576–1613*, ed. Clifford Leech and

T. W. Craik (London: Methuen; New York: Harper & Row, 1975), pp. 142–43, 174–81; and Orrell, *The Quest for Shakespeare's Globe*, pp. 101–3.

17. William Ringler, "The First Phase of the Elizabethan Attack on the Stage, 1558–1579," *Huntington Library Quarterly* 5 (1942): 412.

18. See M. C. Bradbrook, *The Rise of the Common Player: A Study of Actor and Society in Shakespeare's England* (Cambridge: Harvard University Press, 1962), pp. 40–41, 62–63, 98–100.

19. Thomas Heywood, *An Apology for Actors* (London, 1612), sigs. D1^r–E1^r. I quote Heywood throughout from the facsimile prepared by Richard H. Perkinson (New York: Scholars' Facsimiles and Reprints, 1941).

20. See Wickham, *Early English Stages* 2, ii, p. 116:

The first Globe was the first playhouse built in England exclusively by professional actors and for their own exclusive use: to that extent we are right to credit it as being a major advance on any of its predecessors, and indeed Ben Jonson tells us as much when describing it as "the glory of the Bank." For all that, its basic shape was still that of the traditional gamehouse.

21. Ringler, "The First Phase," pp. 406, 411. See also Jonas A. Barish, "The Anti-theatrical Prejudice," *Critical Quarterly* 8 (1966): 329–48, and "Exhibitionism and the Antitheatrical Prejudice," *ELH* 36 (1969): 1–29.

22. John Stockwood, *A Sermon Preached at Paules Crosse* (London, 1578), p. 134, quoted by Yates in *Theatre of the World*, p. 94.

23. Stephen Gosson, *Playes Confuted in fiue Actions* . . . (London, [1582]), in *Markets of Bawdrie: The Dramatic Criticism of Stephen Gosson*, ed. Arthur F. Kinney, Salzburg Studies in English Literature, no. 4 (Salzburg: Institut für Englische Sprache und Literatur, 1974), p. 151. I quote the works of Stephen Gosson throughout from this edition.

24. See E. K. Chambers, *The Elizabethan Stage* (Oxford: Clarendon Press, 1923), 2:298; 3:423–24.

25. C. S. Lewis, *English Literature in the Sixteenth Century, Excluding Drama*, Oxford History of English Literature 3 (Oxford: Clarendon Press, 1954), p. 319.

26. Gosson, *Playes Confuted*, p. 177.

27. *Two Other, very commendable Letters of the same mens writing*, printed with *Three Proper, and wittie, familiar Letters* (London, 1580), G3^v. Quoted from *Elizabethan Critical Essays*, ed. G. Gregory Smith, 2 vols. (Oxford: Oxford University Press, 1904), 1:89. See William Ringler, *Stephen Gosson: A Biographical and Critical Study* (Princeton, N.J.: Princeton University Press, 1942), pp. 35–37.

28. *An Apologie for Poetrie, Elizabethan Critical Essays* 1:150–51. (Smith reprints the Henry Olney text published in 1595.) Subsequent references to Sidney's *Apologie* are in the text. Most scholars believe that Sidney's *Apologie* was "in part at least, a reply to Gosson" (Ringler, *Stephen Gosson*, p. 122, see pp. 117–24). If Sidney took any interest in Gosson, it is likely that he read *Playes Confuted* as well as the *Schoole of Abuse;* Ringler remarks that *Playes Confuted* is "the most carefully considered and acutely argued essay against the drama produced by any Elizabethan or Jacobean critic" (*Stephen Gosson*, p. 73). See also Kinney's Introduction to *Markets of Bawdrie*, pp. 43–51.

29. Meyer H. Abrams, *The Mirror and the Lamp* (New York: Oxford University Press, 1953), p. 272.

30. Saint Augustine, *De Trinitate*, 3:9, quoted from Erwin Panofsky, "Artist, Scientist, Genius: Notes on the 'Renaissance-Dämmerung'," *The Renaissance: Six Essays* (1953; New York and Evanston: Harper & Row, 1962), p. 171.

31. [George Puttenham], *The Arte of English Poesie* (1582), ed. Gladys Doidge Willcock

and Alice Walker (Cambridge: Cambridge University Press, 1936), p. 3. For a similar metaphoric equivalence of God and the human artist in the writings of Nicholas of Cusa, see Jackson I. Cope, *The Theater and the Dream: From Metaphor to Form in Renaissance Drama* (Baltimore, Md. and London: Johns Hopkins University Press, 1973), pp. 14–22.

32. Heywood, *Apology for Actors*, sigs. [A4ʳ]–[A4ᵛ].

33. Thomas Dekker, *The Guls Horne Booke* (1609), facsimile ed. (Menston, England: The Scolar Press, 1969), p. 7.

34. See the Introduction by R. A. Skelton to *The Theatre of the Whole World* (London, 1606; rpt. Amsterdam: Theatrum Orbis Terrarum; Chicago: Rand McNally, 1968). Walter Ong suggests a close and deep connection between the *theatrum mundi* commonplace and cartography. Zwinger's collection, and other "theaters" of knowledge, presuppose that "the mind is its own place" with a geography of its own, so that the collection is a kind of atlas: "Over and over again [Zwinger] compares his work to that of geographers and cartographers," *Interfaces of the Word* (Ithaca, N.Y.: Cornell University Press, 1977), p. 174, see pp. 171–81.

35. See Jonas A. Barish, "The Uniqueness of Elizabethan Drama," *Comparative Drama* 11 (1977): 103–12.

36. On Molyneux and his globes, see: Clements R. Markham's Introduction to his edition of Robert Hues, *Tractatus de Globis . . .* (London: The Hakluyt Society, 1889), pp. xxv–xxxiv; and Edward Luther Stevenson, *Terrestrial and Celestial Globes: Their History and Construction,* 2 vols. (New Haven, Conn.: Yale University Press, 1921), 1:190–96. Stevenson provides a photograph of Molyneux's terrestrial globe, fig. 79, opposite 1:192. See also Oswald Muris and Gert Saarmann, *Der Globus im Wandel der Zeiten: Eine Geschichte der Globen* (Berlin: Columbus Verlag Paul Oestergaard, 1961), pp. 123, 178.

37. Stevenson, *Terrestrial and Celestial Globes,* 1:191.

38. See the edition of Hues cited above in note 36; Thomas Hood, *The Vse of Both the Globes Celestiall and Terrestriall* (London, 1594); and Thomas Blundeville, *M. Blundevile His Exercises, containing sixe Treatises . . .* (London, 1594), fols, 242–45. Of these works Hues's was the most important, having thirteen editions in four languages between 1594 and 1663.

39. "A Valediction: of Weeping," lines 10, 13, in *John Donne: The Elegies and The Songs and Sonnets,* ed. Helen Gardner (Oxford: Clarendon Press, 1965), p. 69. The first edition of Mercator's *Atlas* was published in Dusseldorf in 1595; see the facsimile, Brussels: Culture and Civilization, 1963.

40. See Georges Poulet, *The Metamorphoses of the Circle,* trans. Carley Dawson and Elliott Coleman (Baltimore, Md.: Johns Hopkins University Press, 1966), pp. xi–xxvii, 1–14.

41. *Atlas or A Geographicke description of . . . the world,* trans. Henry Hexham, 2 vols. (Amsterdam: Henry Hondius and Iohn Iohnson, 1636), 1:n.p.

42. Hues, *Tractatus de Globis,* pp. 6, 16.

43. See Ernst Cassirer, *The Individual and the Cosmos in Renaissance Philosophy,* trans. Mario Domandi (Oxford: Basil Blackwell, 1963), pp. 123–191.

44. Paul Oskar Kristeller, "Ficino and Pomponazzi on the Place of Man in the Universe" [1944], in *Renaissance Thought II: Papers on Humanism and the Arts* (New York and Evanston, Ill.: Harper & Row, 1965), pp. 109–10.

45. Cassirer, *The Individual and the Cosmos,* p. 84.

46. Sir Thomas Browne, *Selected Writings,* ed. Sir Geoffrey Keynes (London: Faber & Faber; Chicago: University of Chicago Press, 1968), p. 83.

47. Ernest Schanzer, "Hercules and His Load," *Review of English Studies,* NS 19 (1968), 52.

48. Geffrey Whitney, *A Choice of Emblemes,* ed. Henry Green (1866; rpt. New York: Benjamin Blom, 1967), p. 223.

49. Ovid, *Metamorphoses,* 3:466; ed. and trans. Frank Justus Miller, Loeb Classical Library, 2 vols. (1916; Cambridge: Harvard University Press; London, Heinemann, 1971), p. 156.

50. *The Faerie Queene,* I.iv.29, in *The Poetical Works of Edmund Spenser,* ed. J. C. Smith and E. De. Selincourt (London: Oxford University Press, 1912), p. 21. See also the "embleme" and "glosse" to the "September" Eclogue in *The Shepheardes Calender.*

51. See Mercator, "The Preface Vpon Atlas," *Atlas or A Geographicke description,* 1:n.p.; and Hues, *Tractatus de Globis,* p. 5.

52. See Sir Walter Ralegh, *The History of the World,* ed. C. A. Patrides (Philadelphia, Penn.: Temple University Press, 1971), pp. xv–xvi ["A Note on the Frontispiece"].

53. Schanzer, "Hercules and his Load," p. 52.

54. Ejner J. Jensen, "A New Allusion to the Sign of the Globe Theater," *Shakespeare Quarterly* 21 (1970): 95–97. I have quoted Marston as given by Jensen.

55. As given by Jensen, "A New Allusion," p. 95.

56. Fernand Braudel, *Capitalism and Material Life: 1400–1800,* trans. Miriam Kochan (New York: Harper & Row, 1974), pp. 396, 397–98.

57. See Michael Walzer, *The Revolution of the Saints: A Study in the Origins of Radical Politics* (Cambridge: Harvard University Press, 1965), pp. 171–83.

58. Richard Sennett, *The Fall of Public Man* (New York: Alfred A. Knopf, 1977), pp. 47–63.

59. Ibid., pp. 50–51.

60. Gale Stokes, "Cognition and the Function of Nationalism," *Journal of Interdisciplinary History* 4 (1973–74): 532. See also Harry Berger, Jr., "Naive Consciousness and Culture Change: An Essay in Historical Structuralism," *Bulletin of the Midwest Modern Language Association* 6 (1973): 1–44.

61. Stokes, "Cognition and the Function of Nationalism," p. 533.

62. Ibid., p. 534.

63. Sennett, *The Fall of Public Man,* pp. 28–29, 38, 40, 39.

Chapter 2. Reality in Play: Playhouse as Emblem, Performance as Metaphor

1. Frances A. Yates, *Theatre of the World* (Chicago: University of Chicago Press, 1969), p. 189.

2. Rudolf Wittkower, *Architectural Principles in the Age of Humanism* (New York: Random House, 1965), p. 7.

3. Ibid., p. 16. John Orrell in *The Quest for Shakespeare's Globe,* pp. 108–26, finds no evidence of Vitruvian architectural symbolism in playhouse design but does indicate that standardized methods of setting out a building or courtyard *ad quadratum* involved inscribing squares within circles.

4. I allude to Robert Venturi, *Complexity and Contradiction in Architecture,* 2d ed. (1966; New York: The Museum of Modern Art, 1977).

5. Licisco Magagnato, "The Genesis of the *Teatro Olimpico,*" *Journal of the Warburg and Courtauld Institutes* 14 (1951): 214.

6. Glynne Wickham, *Shakespeare's Dramatic Heritage* (New York: Barnes & Noble, 1969), p. 137; and *Early English Stages, 1300–1600*, vol. 2, *1576 to 1660*, pt. 1 (London: Routledge & Kegan Paul; New York: Columbia University Press, 1963), p. 300. See also, in the same volume, pp. 161–63, 186. See *Early English Stages, 1300 to 1600*, vol. 2, *1576 to 1660*, pt. 2 (London: Routledge & Kegan Paul; New York: Columbia University Press, 1972), 115, 160, 185–91.

7. *Early English Stages*, 2, i (1963): 204. On the Tudor hall stage as a model for the playhouse stage, see also the works cited above in note 6, and the following: Fletcher Collins, "The Relation of Tudor Halls to Elizabethan Public Theaters," *Philological Quarterly* 10 (1931): 313–16; Charles Prouty, "An Early Elizabethan Playhouse," *Shakespeare Survey* 6 (1953): 64–74; Richard Hosley, "The Origins of the Shakespearean Playhouse," *Shakespeare Quarterly* 15, 2 (Spring 1964): 29–39; Glynne Wickham, *Early English Stages*, 2, ii (1972): 9–29.

8. C. Walter Hodges, *The Globe Restored: A Study of the Elizabethan Theatre*, 2d ed. (1953; New York: Coward-McCann, 1968), p. 25.

9. On the "multiple unity" of Elizabethan drama, see Madeleine Doran, *Endeavors of Art: A Study of Form in Elizabethan Drama* (Madison, Wis.: University of Wisconsin Press, 1954), pp. 3–23; David M. Bevington, *From Mankind to Marlowe: Growth of Structure in the Popular Drama of Tudor England* (Cambridge: Harvard University Press, 1962), pp. 1–5; Robert Weimann, *Shakespeare and the Popular Tradition in the Theater*, trans. Robert Schwartz (German ed., 1967; Baltimore, Md. and London: Johns Hopkins University Press, 1978), pp. 174–77, 251–52; and Albert Cook, *Shakespeare's Enactment: The Dynamics of Renaissance Theatre* (Chicago: Swallow Press, 1976), chap. 1 *et passim*.

10. Yates, *Theater of the World*, pp. 189 and xiii. On the iconography of the amphitheater as a cosmic emblem, see Yates, pp. 162–68; Richard Bernheimer, "Theatrum Mundi," *The Art Bulletin* 38 (1956): 225–47; Harriett Bloker Hawkins, "'All the World's a Stage': Some Illustrations of the *Theatrum Mundi*," *Shakespeare Quarterly* 17 (1966): 174–78; Albert R. Cirillo, "Guilio Camillo's *Idea of the Theater:* The Enigma of the Renaissance," *Comparative Drama* 1 (1967): 19–27. Charlotte Spivack offers an interpretation of the playhouse as a cosmic emblem similar to but even more boldly speculative than Miss Yates's in "The Elizabethan Theatre: Circle and Center," *The Centennial Review* 13 (1969): 424–43. For further evidence that the playhouse was thought of as a revival of the Roman amphitheater, see (in addition to Miss Yates's study) Donald C. Mullin, "An Observation on the Origin of the Elizabethan Theatre," *Educational Theatre Journal* 19 (1967): 322–26.

11. Alvin B. Kernan, "This Goodly Frame, the Stage: the Interior Theater of Imagination in English Renaissance Drama," *Shakespeare Quarterly* 25 (1974): 2. See also Glynne Wickham, *Early English Stages, 1300–1660*, vol. 1, *1300 to 1576* (London: Routledge & Kegan Paul; New York: Columbia University Press, 1959), 156–57; and Thomas Stroup, *Microcosmos: The Shape of the Elizabethan Play* (Lexington, Ky.: University of Kentucky Press, 1965), pp. 32–36. Stroup argues that "the basic structure of the Elizabethan play of whatever kind lies in . . . the concept of the world as stage" (p. vii), but his argument requires a loose definition of "structure." His thesis is anticipated, and more sensibly put, by Maynard Mack in "Engagement and Detachment in Shakespeare's Plays," *Essays on Shakespeare and Elizabethan Drama in Honor of Hardin Craig*, ed. Richard Hosley (Columbia, Mo.: University of Missouri Press, 1962): "Perhaps the efficacy of the architectural symbolism of the Elizabethan theater had weakened by Shakespeare's time; but [his plays retain] the sense of the player as universal man, suffering and acting as epitome of the race . . . on his little space of earth, working out

his destiny between the painted Heavens of the canopy and the Hell opened into by the trap" (p. 282).

12. Christian Norberg-Schulz, *Existence, Space and Architecture* (New York: Praeger, 1971), pp. 21, 20. For a brief but suggestive interpretation of the playhouse as a three-level "shamanic cosmos," see David Cole, *The Theatrical Event* (Middletown, Conn.: Wesleyan University Press, 1975), pp. 104–5.

13.. Francis Berry, "Shakespeare's Stage Geometry," *Deutsche Shakespeare-Gesellschaft West*, Jahrbuch, 1974, pp. 160–71. For the structuring properties and symbolic coordinates of rectangular spaces see Rudolf Arnheim, *The Dynamics of Architectural Form* (Berkeley and Los Angeles: University of California Press, 1977), pp. 32–39, and Kent C. Bloomer and Charles W. Moore, *Body, Memory, and Architecture* (New Haven, Conn. and London: Yale University Press, 1977), pp. 40–44.

14. For the Roman ancestry of Burbage's Theater and Heywood's view of the playhouse as amphitheater, see chapter 1. De Witt's comment on his drawing of the Swan reads, in part: "Amphitheatra Londinij sunt IV visendae pulcritudinis. . . . Theatrorum autem omnium prestantissimum est et amphlissimum id cuius intersignium est cygnus. . . . Cuius quidem forma[m] quod Romani operis vmbram videatur exprimere supra adpinxi," quoted from the transcript prepared by John Dover Wilson in *Shakespeare Survey* 1 (1948): 24.

15. Arnheim, *Dynamics of Architectural Form*, pp. 96–97.

16. Juan Luis Vives, *A Fable About Man*, trans. Nancy Lenkeith, in *The Renaissance Philosophy of Man*, ed. Ernst Cassirer, Paul Oskar Kristeller, and John Herman Randall, Jr. (Chicago: University of Chicago Press, 1948), pp. 387.

17. See Richard Southern, "The Contribution of the Interludes to Elizabethan Staging," *Essays on Shakespeare and Elizabethan Drama in Honor of Hardin Craig*, ed. Richard Hosley (Columbia, Mo.: University of Missouri Press, 1962), pp. 3–14. Southern indicates that, in the first half of the sixteenth century, actors and spectators shared the same rectangular space defined by the hall, which was appropriate to interludes that did not consistently locate their action in an independent fictive world. When, midway through the century, authors of interludes turned from topical themes and debates to more self-contained forms of action—adaptations of medieval narrative like Phillips's *Patient Grissell* (1559), or redactions of classical drama like Pickering's *Horestes* (1567)—the players required architectural modifications to the hall that would define, in spatial terms, a fictive locale distinct from the reality of the audience. Accordingly, the action was confined to a platform built up from the floor, and features of the hall screen—the two doors and gallery—were appropriated as parts of the play's fictive setting. In the playhouse, the acting area had even greater independence, while the presence of spectators was made more prominent by the unusually large size of the audience (over two thousands persons in a full house) accommodated in the yard and galleries.

18. Stanislavsky relates the naturalistic style of acting to a clearly defined acting area, distinct from the auditorium. He describes an ideal performance as follows: "I felt that all [the actor's] attention was concentrated on his side of the footlights and not on ours, that he was occupied with what was happening on the stage and not in the auditorium, and that it was precisely this attention of his, concentrated on one point, that forced me to take an interest in his life on the stage and aroused my curiosity to find out what it was that interested him so much there" (*Stanislavsky on the Art of the Stage*, ed. and trans. David Magarshack [New York: Hill & Wang, 1961], p. 20).

19. Quoted from the description "Of an Excellent Actor" (1615) in E. K. Chambers, *The Elizabethan Stage* (Oxford: Clarendon Press, 1923), 4:258.

20. Lionel Abel, *Metatheatre: A New View of Dramatic Form* (New York: Hill & Wang, 1963), quoted from Jackson I. Cope, *The Theater and the Dream: From Metaphor to Form in Renaissance Drama* (Baltimore, Md.: Johns Hopkins University Press, 1973), p. 2.

21. See Muriel C. Bradbrook, *Themes and Conventions of Elizabethan Tragedy* (Cambridge: Cambridge University Press, 1935), p. 8.

22. Francis Berry, *The Shakespeare Inset: Word and Picture* (London and Amsterdam: Feffer & Simons; Carbondale and Edwardsville, Ill.: Southern Illinois University Press, 1965), pp. 3, 20.

23. Ibid., pp. 1–2.

24. Jonas A. Barish, "The Antitheatrical Prejudice," *Critical Quarterly* 8 (1966): 333. On Cleopatra as an embodiment of the poet's creative power, see Phyllis Rackin, "Shakespeare's Boy Cleopatra, the Decorum of Nature, and the Golden World of Poetry," *PMLA* 87 (1972): 201–12.

25. Sir Philip Sidney, *An Apologie for Poetrie, Elizabethan Critical Essays*, ed. G. Gregory Smith, 2 vols. (London: Oxford University Press, 1904), 1:156. Subsequent references to Sidney are in the text.

26. Francis Bacon, *The Advancement of Learning*, in *The Works of Francis Bacon*, 14 vols., ed. James Spedding, R. L. Ellis, D. D. Heath (London: Longmans, 1870–74), 3 (1870): 343.

27. See Hal H. Smith, "Some Principles of Elizabethan Stage Costume," *Journal of the Warburg and Courtauld Institutes* 25 (1962): 240–57.

28. Kernan, "This Goodly Frame," p. 2.

29. Ibid., p. 5.

30. *The New Organon*, book I, aphorism 44, in *The Works of Francis Bacon*, 8 (1874): 78.

31. E. N. Tigerstedt, "The Poet as Creator: Origins of a Metaphor," *Comparative Literature Studies* 5 (1968): 455–88. On the theme of self transformation in Renaissance thought see Thomas Greene, "The Flexibility of the Self in Renaissance Literature," in *The Disciplines of Criticism*, ed. Peter Demetz, Thomas Greene, and Lowry Nelson, Jr. (New Haven, Conn. and London: Yale University Press, 1968), pp. 241–64, and, in the same volume, A. Bartlett Giamatti, "Proteus Unbound: Some Versions of the Sea God in the Renaissance," pp. 437–75.

32. Giovanni Pico della Mirandola, *Oration on the Dignity of Man*, trans. Elizabeth Livermore Forbes, in *The Renaissance Philosophy of Man*, pp. 224–25.

33. Sidney qualifies his enthusiasm for self-transformation with a sobering insistence on the value of stability. In effect, he combines Pico's enthusiasm with Montaigne's scepticism. Montaigne laments the protean instability of human nature and believes that we must achieve integrity by striving to remain constant to an appropriate role: "The glorious masterpiece of man is to live to the purpose. . . . There is nothing so goodly, so fair, and so lawful as to play the man well and duly" ("Of Experience" [*Essais*, III.13], *Selected Essays of Montaigne in the Translation of John Florio*, ed. Walter Kaiser (Boston: Houghton Mifflin, 1964), pp. 384, 387. See, in the same volume, "Of the Inconstancy of Our Actions" [*Essais*, II.i], especially pp. 25, 28. For an analysis of the expression "to play the—" in Shakespeare, see Thomas F. Van Laan, *Role Playing in Shakespeare* (Toronto: University of Toronto Press, 1978), pp. 4–5. Van Laan concludes that Shakespeare's use of expressions like "play the man," "play the tyrant," "play the flouting Jack," etc., help "to establish a world in which *action* equals *acting*, in which to do something is to take on a particular role with fixed attributes" (pp. 4–5).

34. Stephen Gosson, *The Schoole of Abuse*, in *Markets of Bawdrie: The Dramatic Criticism of Stephen Gosson*, ed. Arthur F. Kinney, Salzburg Studies in English Literature, no. 4 (Salzburg: Institut für Englische Sprache und Literatur, 1974), p. 100.

35. F. Clement, *The Petie Schole with an English Orthographie* (London, 1587), p. 40, quoted in William Ringler, *Stephen Gosson: A Biographical and Critical Study* (Princeton, N.J.: Princeton University Press, 1942), p. 70.

36. *Playes Confuted,* ed. Kinney, p. 196. I have added the parentheses to clarify the syntax.

37. *Schoole of Abuse,* ed. Kinney, p. 77. The concept of imagination in Elizabethan popular psychology supports Gosson's argument; see William Rosskey, "Imagination in the English Renaissance: Psychology and Poetic," *Studies in the Renaissance* 5 (1958): 49–73.

38. See Peter Ure, "Character and Role from *Richard III* to *Hamlet*" [1963], *Elizabethan and Jacobean Drama: Critical Essays by Peter Ure,* ed. J. C. Maxwell (Liverpool: Liverpool University Press; New York: Harper & Row, 1974), pp. 22–43.

39. That Herod was in some sense a source or model for Macbeth is argued by: Glynne Wickham, "Macbeth: Out-heroding Herod," *Shakespeare's Dramatic Heritage,* pp. 224–31; Howard Felperin, *Shakespearean Representation: Mimesis and Modernity in Elizabethan Tragedy* (Princeton, N.J.: Princeton University Press, 1977), pp. 118–44; Emrys Jones, *The Origins of Shakespeare* (Oxford: Clarendon Press, 1977), pp. 79–83. None of these critics anticipates the specific comparison I am making here.

40. *The Magi, Herod, and the Slaughter of the Innocents,* in *Chief Pre-Shakespearean Dramas,* ed. Joseph Quincey Adams (Boston: Houghton Mifflin, 1924), p. 163.

41. See Robert Weimann, *Shakespeare and the Popular Tradition in the Theater,* trans. Robert Schwartz (German ed. 1967; Baltimore, Md. and London: Johns Hopkins University Press, 1978), p. 72.

42. *Everyman,* ed. A. C. Cawley (Manchester: Manchester University Press, 1961), p. 13.

43. See Lionel Trilling, *Sincerity and Authenticity* (Cambridge: Harvard University Press, 1972), pp. 14–16.

44. On the size and composition of the playhouse audience, see Alfred Harbage, *Shakespeare's Audience* (New York: Columbia University Press, 1941), pp. 19–91. Ann Jennalie Cook challenges Harbage's interpretation in *The Privileged Playgoers of Shakespeare's London, 1576–1642* (Princeton, N.J.: Princeton University Press, 1981). See also Trilling, *Sincerity and Authenticity,* p. 21 n.

45. See Stanley Cavell, *Must We Mean What We Say?* (New York: Scribners; Cambridge: Cambridge University Press, 1969), pp. 338–39. See also Helene Keyssar, "I Love You. Who Are You? The Strategy of Drama in Recognition Scenes," *PMLA* 92 (1977): 297–306.

46. Keyssar, "I Love You," p. 303.

Chapter 3. Reality and Play in Dramatic Fiction

1. Northrop Frye, "The Argument of Comedy," *English Institute Essays, 1948,* ed. D. A. Robertson, Jr. (New York: Columbia University Press, 1949), p. 68.

2. Don Cameron Allen, *Image and Meaning: Metaphoric Traditions in Renaissance Poetry,* 2d ed. (Baltimore, Md.: Johns Hopkins University Press, 1968), p. 82.

3. Walter R. Davis, *Idea and Act in Elizabethan Fiction* (Princeton, N.J.: Princeton University Press, 1969), pp. 60–61. For similar accounts of the pastoral sojourn in Renaissance fiction, see David Young, *The Heart's Forest: A Study of Shakespeare's Pastoral Plays* (New Haven, Conn. and London: Yale University Press, 1972), pp. 18–21; and Charles W. Hieatt, "The Quality of Pastoral in *As You Like It,*" *Genre* 7 (1974): 166–69.

See also, Harry Berger, Jr., "The Renaissance Imagination: Second World and Green World," *Centennial Review* 9 (1965): 36–78. I am indebted to this essay for the key concept of the "green world" as a replication within Renaissance fiction of the fiction itself as a second world.

4. For Hegel, see below, note 6; for developmental psychology, see above, chapter 1. Arnold Toynbee's description of the pattern of withdrawal and return in individuals and "creative minorities" is in vol. 3 of *A Study of History;* I have consulted the abridgement by D. C. Somervell, 2 vols. (1946, 1957; New York: Dell, 1965), 1 : 256–82.

5. José Ortega y Gasset, "The Self and the Other" [1939], trans. Willard R. Trask, in *The Dehumanization of Art* (New York: Doubleday, 1956), p. 172. See also Harry Berger, Jr., "The Ecology of the Mind," *The Review of Metaphysics* 17 (1963): 109–34; Berger quotes the passage from Ortega's essay on p. 120.

6. G. W. F. Hegel, *Hegel's Logic, Being Part One of the Encyclopaedia . . .* (1830), trans. William Wallace (1873; Oxford: Clarendon Press, 1975), pp. 43–44. See above, Introduction, p. 13.

7. For "the naivete inherent in perception," see Harry Berger, Jr., "Naive Consciousness and Culture Change: An Essay in Historical Structuralism," *Bulletin of the Midwest Modern Language Association* 6 (1973): 1–44, especially pp. 4–15.

8. Ernst H. Gombrich, *Art and Illusion,* 2d ed. rev. (New York: Pantheon, 1961), p. 345. See above, Introduction, pp. 7–8, where this statement is quoted more fully in connection with the principle of replication.

9. W. K. Wimsatt, Jr., "Verbal Style: Logical and Counterlogical" [1947] in *The Verbal Icon* (Lexington, Ky.: University of Kentucky Press, 1954), p. 217. Paul Ricoeur oversimplifies Wimsatt's theory in describing the verbal icon as "closed in on itself and non-referential." In fact, Wimsatt's description of metaphor's "relation to reality" anticipates and clarifies Ricoeur's study of "Metaphor and Reference"; see *The Rule of Metaphor,* trans. Robert Czerny (1975; Toronto: University of Toronto Press, 1977), pp. 210, 216–56. See also, Paul Ricoeur, "The Metaphoric Process as Cognition, Imagination, and Feeling," *Critical Inquiry* 5 (1978–79): 143–59, especially p. 153. What Ricoeur calls "the metaphoric process" corresponds to the pattern of withdrawal and return: a suspension of ordinary reference that is the condition of a second-order reference that reveals the deep structures of reality.

10. Robert Frost, "The Figure a Poem Makes," *Complete Poems of Robert Frost* (New York: Holt, Rinehart and Winston, 1949), p. vi.

11. See Charles Taylor, *Hegel* (Cambridge: Cambridge University Press, 1975), pp. 563–71.

12. The following plays seem to begin in unlocalized, open settings: *Richard III, Titus Andronicus, The Two Gentlemen of Verona, Romeo and Juliet, The Merchant of Venice, Much Ado About Nothing, Julius Caesar, Troilus and Cressida, Othello, Macbeth, Coriolanus.* The opening scenes in the following plays seem to require, or at least to suggest, interiors of great halls or throne rooms: *2* and *3 Henry VI, A Midsummer Night's Dream, King John, 1* and *2 Henry IV, Henry V, Twelfth Night, All's Well that Ends Well, Measure for Measure, King Lear, Antony and Cleopatra, Timon of Athens, Cymbeline, The Winter's Tale, Henry VIII.*

13. Stephen Booth has shown how elaborately the first two scenes of *Hamlet* exploit the audience's expectation of an expository opening: "Scene one is set in the dark, and it leaves the audience in the dark. . . . Unlike the first scene, the second gives the audience all the information it could desire, and gives it neatly"—too neatly, so that the audience is made uneasy by an excessive ordering. See "On the Value of *Hamlet,*" *Reinterpretations of Elizabethan Drama,* ed. Norman Rabkin [Selected Papers from the

English Institute] (New York and London: Columbia University Press, 1969), pp. 137–76. (The passage quoted is from p. 147.)

14. See David P. Young, *Something of Great Constancy: The Art of "A Midsummer Night's Dream"* (New Haven, Conn. and London: Yale University Press, 1966), pp. 74–84. I am generally indebted to interpretations of the play in C. L. Barber, *Shakespeare's Festive Comedy: A Study of Dramatic Form and Its Relation to Social Custom* (Princeton, N.J.: Princeton University Press, 1959), pp. 119–62; and James L. Calderwood, *Shakespearean Metadrama* (Minneapolis, Minn.: University of Minnesota Press, 1971), pp. 120–48.

15. John Russell Brown, *Shakespeare and His Comedies*, 2d ed. rev. (London: Methuen, 1962), p. 90.

16. I. A. Richards, *The Philosophy of Rhetoric* (1936; New York: Oxford University Press, 1965), p. 127.

17. See John Bayley, *The Characters of Love: A Study in the Literature of Personality* (London: Constable, 1960), pp. 3–47.

18. See Barber, pp. 157–62, and Judith Scherer Herz, "Play World and Real World: Dramatic Illusion and the Dream Metaphor," *English Studies in Canada* 3 (1977), 386–400, especially pp. 391–92.

19. See Sherman Hawkins, "The Two Worlds of Shakespearean Comedy," *Shakespeare Studies* 3 (1967): 62–80. Hawkins distinguishes "closed-world comedies" (e.g. *The Comedy of Errors, Twelfth Night*) from Northrop Frye's "green-world comedies" (e.g. *A Midsummer Night's Dream, As You Like It*). Both types of comedy conform to the pattern of withdrawal and return, but only the "green-world comedies" define this pattern by means of contrasted settings.

20. Bernard Beckerman, *Shakespeare at the Globe: 1599–1609* (New York: Macmillan, 1962), pp. 56, 35.

21. *Menaechmi*, trans. William Warner (1595), in *Narrative and Dramatic Sources of Shakespeare*, ed. Geoffrey Bullough 1 (New York: Columbia University Press; London: Routledge & Kegan Paul, 1957), 12–39.

22. I am indebted to John Arthos, "Shakespeare's Transformation of Plautus," *Comparative Drama*, 1 (1967–68), 239–42.

23. See *The Comedy of Errors*, ed. R. A. Foakes, The New Arden Shakespeare (London: Methuen; Cambridge: Harvard University Press, 1962), pp. xxix, 113–15. See also Rolf Soellner, *Shakespeare's Patterns of Self-Knowledge* (Columbus, Ohio: Ohio State University Press, 1972), p. 71: "Self-knowledge is achieved only when the positioning of each self toward the other selves has taken place."

24. I am partly anticipated by Maynard Mack, Northrop Frye, and Alvin Kernan, each of whom discerns a three-phase pattern of character development. Maynard Mack has shown that the Shakespearean tragic hero is developed through "a cycle of change": the first phase delineates the hero; in the second, he "tends to become his own antithesis"; finally, he "exhibits one or more aspects of his original, or—since these may not coincide—his better self" ("The Jacobean Shakespeare: Some Observations on the Construction of the Tragedies," *Jacobean Theatre*, ed. John Russell Brown and Bernard Harris, Stratford-upon-Avon Studies [London: Arnold, 1960], 1:33, 34, 37). Northrop Frye discerns a similar three-phase pattern in the development of comic characters, who undergo "a phase of temporarily lost identity . . . normally portrayed by the stock device of inpenetrable disguise" (*A Natural Perspective: The Development of Shakespearean Comedy and Romance* [New York: Columbia University Press, 1965], p. 76). Rosalind and Viola become their own antitheses by playing the part of boys, but recover their feminine selves as the action concludes. Alvin Kernan detects something like this pat-

tern in the history plays of the second tetralogy. In Richard's England, "the individual is submerged within the role imposed upon him by prescribed ways of thinking, acting, and speaking." As Bolingbroke asserts his power, the old order breaks up, "and reality becomes theatrical, a playing of many roles." Finally, Henry V must circumscribe his personal and histrionic self within the compass of his public and official character as king—though Kernan and others question whether he thereby recovers "his better self." (See Alvin B. Kernan, "From Ritual to History: The English History Play," in *The Revels History of Drama in English, Volume 3, 1576–1613*, [London: Methuen, 1975], pp. 271, 276). Since the three-phase pattern is common to tragedy, comedy, and history, its source can hardly be the specific requirements of any one of these genres. It derives in fact from the replication in dramatic fiction of the pattern of withdrawal and return that structures the theatrical occasion.

25. See Maynard Mack, "Engagement and Detachment in Shakespeare's Plays," *Essays on Shakespeare and Elizabethan Drama in Honor of Hardin Craig*, ed. Richard Hosley (Columbia, Mo.: University of Missouri Press, 1962), pp. 275–96.

26. John Donne, "The Exstasie," line 68, *The Elegies and The Songs and Sonnets*, ed. Helen Gardner (Oxford: Clarendon Press, 1965), p. 61.

Chapter 4. Theatrical Fiction and the Reality of Love in *As You Like It*

1. David P. Young, *The Heart's Forest: A Study of Shakespeare's Pastoral Plays* (New Haven, Conn. and London: Yale University Press, 1972), pp. 42, 32.

2. Albert R. Cirillo, "*As You Like It*: Pastoralism Gone Awry," *ELH* 38 (1971): 38.

3. *Narrative and Dramatic Sources of Shakespeare*, ed. Geoffrey Bullough, II (New York: Columbia University Press; London: Routledge & Kegan Paul, 1958), pp. 182–83.

4. Walter R. Davis, *Idea and Act in Elizabethan Fiction* (Princeton, N.J.: Princeton University Press, 1969), p. 81.

5. That "the forest mirrors one's mind" is demonstrated by John Russell Brown, *Shakespeare and His Comedies* (1957; 2d ed. rev., London: Methuen, 1962), pp. 147–49; see also, Young, *The Heart's Forest*, pp. 50–51.

6. Werner Habicht, "Tree Properties and Tree Scenes in Elizabethan Theater," *Renaissance Drama*, NS 4 (1971): 75.

7. This hypothesis is supported by George F. Reynolds in "'Trees' on the Stage of Shakespeare," *Modern Philology* 5 (1907): 153–68, and *The Staging of Elizabethan Plays at The Red Bull Theater, 1605–1625* (New York: Modern Language Association, 1940), pp. 70–75. See also Glynne Wickham, *Early English Stages: 1300–1660*, 2, pt. i (London: Routledge & Kegan Paul; New York: Columbia University Press, 1963), pp. 314–20; and Habicht, "Tree Properties and Tree Scenes," p. 91. Edmund K. Chambers, to the contrary, believed that "at need, trees ascended and descended through traps" (*The Elizabethan Stage* [Oxford: Clarendon Press, 1923], 3:89).

8. Such relationships are explored at length by D. J. Palmer in "Art and Nature in *As You Like It*," *Philological Quarterly* 49 (1970): 30–40. Palmer notes the relation of the internal reflections to the play itself as a mirror of love held up to the audience (p. 30). See also Young, *The Heart's Forest*, pp. 51–55, and Brown, *Shakespeare and His Comedies*, pp. 149–51.

9. Spenser's *Fowre Hymnes* are quoted throughout from *The Poetical Works of Edmund Spenser*, eds. J. C. Smith and E. De Selincourt (London: Oxford University Press, 1912). I owe some valuable suggestions about the Hymnes to Harry Berger, Jr., "A Secret

Discipline: *The Faerie Queene,* Book VI," in *Form and Convention in the Poetry of Edmund Spenser.* [Selected Papers from the English Institute] ed. William Nelson (New York: Columbia University Press, 1961), pp 52–53.

10. The Folio spelling may suggest the pun in Touchstone's speech: "the truest poetrie is the most faining, and Louers . . . do feigne." But, given the imprecision of the Folio's orthography, the suggestion is probably accidental. In II.vii, the Folio renders a line from Amiens's song, "Most friendship, is fayning; most Louing, meere folly," where *feigning* is clearly meant: the song contrasts winter's harshness with man's unkindness. Shakespeare, writing for spectators, not readers, had to rely on the context of Touchstone's speech to support the pun: "lovers" suggests *fain,* while "poetry" and "not honest" suggest *feign.*

11. See Thomas Kelly, "Shakespeare's Romantic Heroes: Orlando Reconsidered," *Shakespeare Quarterly* 24 (1973): 12–24.

12. "The *marching figure* . . . may as well be called the *clyming* figure, for *Climax* is as much to say as a ladder" (*The Arte of English Poesie,* ed. Gladys D. Willcock and Alice Walker [Cambridge: Cambridge University Press, 1936], p. 208).

13. See also George K. Hunter's interpretation of the final scene in *John Lyly: The Humanist as Courtier* (Cambridge: Harvard University Press, 1962), pp. 344–45.

14. The importance of reciprocity, of *concordia discors,* in this play is also affirmed by Margaret Boerner Beckman in "The Figure of Rosalind in *As You Like It,*" *Shakespeare Quarterly* 29 (1978): 44–51.

15. Helen Gardner, "*As You Like It,*" in *More Talking of Shakespeare,* ed. John Garrett (London: Longmans, Green & Company; New York: Theatre Arts Books, 1959), p. 22.

Chapter 5. Heroism, History, and the Theater in *Henry V*

1. See Howard Felperin, *Shakespearean Representation: Mimesis and Modernity in Elizabethan Tragedy* (Princeton, N.J.: Princeton University Press, 1977). Felperin argues that "mimesis . . . arises not from the direct imitation of 'nature' or 'life' or 'experience' but . . . from the *re-presentation,* with a difference, of inherited models or constructs of 'nature,' 'life,' and 'experience'" (p. 8). Shakespeare "invalidates older models even as he includes them, supersedes them in the very act of subsuming them" (p. 60) and uses this sublation as a technique of mimesis "by subsuming within his work a recognizably conventional model of life, repudiating that model, and thereby creating the illusion that he uses no art at all, that he is presenting life directly" (p. 66). My own view is similar to this, but I find that Shakespeare does not always invalidate or repudiate the older model, but instead gives it a metaphoric reference to reality. Felperin finds most of Shakespeare's models in the morality tradition, but important models may have been closer to hand in the drama of Shakespeare's contemporaries and immediate predecessors.

2. *Greenes Groats-worth of Wit* (1592), as given by E. K. Chambers, *William Shakespeare* (Oxford: Clarendon Press, 1930), 2:188.

3. See William Empson, "*Hamlet* When New," *Sewanee Review* 61 (1953): 15–42, 185–205, and Felperin, *Shakespearean Representation,* pp. 44–67.

4. See W. W. Greg, ed., *Henslowe's Diary* (London: A. H. Bullen, 1908), 2:177–78; E. K. Chambers, *The Elizabethan Stage* (Oxford: Clarendon Press, 1923), 3:191; and *William Shakespeare,* 1:383–84, 393–95.

5. See MacD. P. Jackson, "'Edward III,' Shakespeare, and Pembroke's Men," *Notes and Queries,* n.s., 12 (1965): 329–31; and Karl P. Wentersdorf, "The Date of *Edward III,*"

Shakespeare Quarterly 16 (1965): 227–31. My interpretation does not rest on the speculation that Shakespeare wrote part (or all) of *Edward III;* the whole question is well treated by Kenneth Muir in his *Shakespeare as Collaborator* (London: Methuen, 1960), pp. 10–55.

6. *An Apology for Actors* (London, 1612), sig. [B4ʳ], quoted from the facsimile prepared by Richard H. Perkinson (New York: Scholars Facsimiles and Reprints, 1941).

7. See Robert Egan, "A Muse of Fire: *Henry V* in the Light of *Tamburlaine*," *Modern Langauge Quarterly* 29 (1968): 15–28; and David Riggs, *Shakespeare's Heroical Histories: Henry VI and Its Literary Tradition* (Cambridge: Harvard University Press, 1971). Riggs shows that the heroical history play establishes the ethical dimensions of heroism by placing the hero's personal aspirations to power and glory in a historical context where they must confront the constraints of social order and the requirements of a nation's collective destiny. Riggs proposes that Shakespeare's initial response to this genre was to dramatize the incompatibility of heroism and order; in the historical world of the first tetralogy, the Marlovian "aspiring mind" is corrupted by baser motives and provokes deadly rivalries, violence, anarchy, and despotism (see especially, chapters 1 and 4). When Shakespeare concluded his second tetralogy with the celebration of a heroic king, he found his own earlier history plays less useful as models than *Edward III*, which is a straightforward affirmation of heroism in a historical context.

8. Quotations of *Edward III* are from *The Shakespeare Apocrypha*, ed. C. F. Tucker Brooke (Oxford: Clarendon Press, 1908).

9. See Herbert Howarth, *The Tiger's Heart* (New York: Oxford University Press, 1970), pp. 27–30.

10. See Muir, *Shakespeare as Collaborator*, pp. 14–15, 18–19.

11. This traditional argument is best stated by Geoffrey Bullough in *Narrative and Dramatic Source of Shakespeare*, (London: Routledge; New York: Columbia University Press, 1962), 4:351.

12. On the basis of these and other considerations, Warren D. Smith argues that the Choruses were added to the play after 1599 for a court performance; see his "The *Henry V* Choruses in the First Folio," *Journal of English and Germanic Philology* 53 (1954): 38–57. The argument is refuted by Robert Adger Law ("The Choruses in Henry the Fifth," *University of Texas Studies in English* 35 [1956]: 11–21), but revived in modified form by G. P. Jones in "'Henry V': The Chorus and the Audience," *Shakespeare Survey* 31 (1978): 93–104. Jones argues that the Chorus's deferential appeals for audience participation are "not generally characteristic of the Elizabethan public playhouse" (p. 98), but surely they are appropriate to this play's unusually direct patriotic appeal. Jones seems to overestimate the difference between public and private theater audiences; see above Chapter 2, note 44.

13. *Samuel Johnson on Shakespeare*, ed. W. K. Wimsatt, Jr., (New York: Hill & Wang, 1960), p. 92.

14. Leslie Hotson, *Shakespeare's Sonnets Dated and Other Essays* (New York: Oxford University Press, 1949), pp. 61, 72, 74.

15. See Richard Levin, *The Multiple Plot in English Renaissance Drama* (Chicago and London: University of Chicago Press, 1971), pp. 116–19.

16. Both Henry's speech and Pistol's parody of it at II.i.44–51 were probably suggested by the Black Prince in *Edward III:* "Defiance, French man? we rebound it back / Euen to the bottom of thy master's throat" (I.i.89–90). "Rebound" may also have reminded Shakespeare of Puttenham's description of "*Antanaclasis* or the Rebounde" in *The Arte of English Poesie:* "Ye haue [a] . . . figure which by his nature we may call the Rebound, alluding to the tennis ball which being smitten with the racket reboundes backe againe. . . . This [figure] playeth with one word written all alike but carrying

diuers sences as thus: . . . 'To pray for you euer I cannot refuse, / To pray vpon you I should you much abuse'" (ed. Gladys Doidge Willcock and Alice Walker [Cambridge: Cambridge University Press, 1936], p. 207). Puttenham is cited in connection with Henry's speech by Bertram Joseph, *Acting Shakespeare* (1960; New York: Theatre Arts Books, 1969), pp. 3–5.

17. Holinshed describes Henry's fight with the Duke of Alençon; see Bullough, *Narrative and Dramatic Sources,* 4:396. Nashe is probably describing an episode in the original *Famous Victories* not preserved in the extant text when he writes, in *Pierce Penilesse* (1592): "what a glorious thing it is to haue *Henrie* the fifth represented on the Stage, leading the French King prisoner, and forcing both him and the Dolfin to sweare fealty," *The Works of Thomas Nashe,* ed. Ronald B. McKerrow, with corrections by F. P. Wilson (Oxford: Basil Blackwell, 1958), 1:213.

18. Michael Goldman, *Shakespeare and the Energies of Drama* (Princeton, N.J.: Princeton University Press, 1972), pp. 58–73. See also Harry Berger, Jr., *"Troilus and Cressida:* The Observer as Basilisk," *Comparative Drama* 2 (1968): 122–24, and Eugene M. Waith, *Ideas of Greatness: Heroic Drama in England* (New York: Barnes & Noble, 1971), p. 98.

19. Sigurd Burckhardt, *Shakespearean Meanings* (Princeton, N.J.: Princeton University Press, 1968), p. 189.

20. Bullough, *Narrative and Dramatic Sources,* 4:425. See Joan Webber, "The Renewal of the King's Symbolic Role: From *Richard II* to *Henry V," Texas Studies in Language and Literature* 4 (1963): 536, 537:

> Henry gives his people a common aim, toward which they can direct all the energy that in the previous plays [of the Lancastrian tetralogy] is so often set against the kingdom. . . . Henry's battle speeches show, not a desire for personal glory, but a wish to elevate his soldiers to share with him, to create a larger symbol of courage and greatness, for posterity. . . . Working upon their imaginary forces, he gives them a reality impressive enough to capture their loyalty.

21. C. L. Barber, *Shakespeare's Festive Comedy* (Princeton, N.J.: Princeton University Press, 1959), pp. 4, 13.

22. Years later (on 29 June 1613), the Globe was set on fire and burned to the ground "by negligent discharging of a peal of Ordinance" during a production of *Henry VIII.* See *The Elizabethan Stage,* 2:419.

23. I allude here to Charles Lamb's complaint that theatrical performance limits the imaginative scope of Shakespeare's poetry: "How cruelly this operates upon the mind, to have its free conceptions thus crampt and pressed down to the measure of a strait-lacing actuality. . . ." While the complaint may have been prompted by the scenic excesses of nineteenth-century productions, it points to a tension between the verbal and the visual dimensions of a play inherent in any production. See Charles Lamb, "On the Tragedies of Shakespeare," *Works,* ed. William Macdonald (London, 1903–8), 3:17–22.

24. A similar relationship between a historical event and its theatrical representation is established in *Julius Caesar,* though to ironic effect, when Brutus and Cassius enthusiastically predict that the assassination of Caesar will often be acted as a triumph of liberty (see III.i.111–18).

25. Holinshed records Henry's prophecy upon the birth of his son: "I, Henry born at Monmouth, shall *small time* reign and much get; and Henry born at Windsor shall long reign and all lose—but, as God will, so be it" (*Shakespeare's Holinshed,* ed. Richard Hosley [New York: Capricorn Books, 1968], p. 143—my italics. Berger notes the ambivalence of "Small time" in the epilogue of *Henry V* (p. 123).

26. *An Apologie for Poetrie, Elizabethan Critical Essays,* ed. G. Gregory Smith (Oxford: Oxford University Press, 1904), 1:170, 186.

27. The major critical statements on both sides of the question are enumerated by Karl P. Wentersdorf, "The Conspiracy of Silence in *Henry V,*" *Shakespeare Quarterly* 18 (1976): 266.

28. Norman Rabkin, *Shakespeare and the Problem of Meaning* (Chicago and London: University of Chicago Press, 1981), pp. 61–62. See also Anne Barton, "The King Disguised: Shakespeare's *Henry V* and the Comical History," *The Triple Bond: Plays, Mainly Shakespearean, in Performance,* ed. Joseph G. Price (University Park, Penn. and London: Pennsylvania State University Press, 1975), p. 102: "Among Shakespeare's other histories, only *Henry VIII* is so deliberately ambiguous, so overtly a puzzle in which the audience is left to forge its own interpretation of action and characters with only minimal guidance from a dramatist apparently determined to stress the equivalence of mutually exclusive views of a particular complex of historical event."

29. See, for example, Harold C. Goddard, *The Meaning of Shakespeare* (Chicago: University of Chicago Press, 1951), pp. 224, 229.

30. Wentersdorf, "The Conspiracy of Silence," p. 283.

31. Barton, "The King Disguised," p. 99.

32. Michael Goldman, *Shakespeare and the Energies of Drama* (Princeton, N.J.: Princeton University Press, 1982), p. 69.

33. Ibid., p. 70: "A king is not simply his role; his power and authority do not flow directly from his person, as Richard [II], tragically, tried to insist. Neither, however, is a king simply a man like other men, no matter how attractive and at times politically useful the pretence may be. The demands of office change a man. A king is not a man like other men—but he is a man, and his humanity consists in this: he must pay the price of his role."

34. See above, chapter 1, pp. 39–40.

35. *The Works of Thomas Nashe,* ed. McKerrow, 1:212, 213.

Chapter 6. From Community to Society: Cultural Transformation in *Macbeth*

1. Alvin B. Kernan, "From Ritual to History: The English History Play," *The Revels History of Drama in English, Volume 3: 1576–1613,* p. 270.

2. See Maynard Mack, Jr., *Killing the King: Three Studies in Shakespeare's Tragic Structure* (New Haven, Conn. and London: Yale University Press, 1973), pp. 149–50: "Duncan fulfills what seems to be a common Shakespearean need (expressed throughout his career in figures as different as the Henry of the *Henry VI* plays and Gonzalo in *The Tempest*) for a character representing an essentially nostalgic idealizing view of the world." I am generally indebted to Mack's interpretation of *Macbeth* (pp. 138–85) and to Wilbur Sanders, *The Dramatist and the Received Idea: Studies in the Plays of Marlowe and Shakespeare* (Cambridge: Cambridge University Press, 1968), pp. 253–307.

3. Marcel Mauss, *The Gift: Forms and Functions of Exchange in Archaic Societies,* trans. Ian Cunnison (1925; New York: Norton, 1967), p. 71. That gift giving can no longer hold the community together is confirmed by Duncan's last act, which is to send a diamond to Lady Macbeth in gratitude for her hospitality. Banquo delivers the diamond to Macbeth just before the murder (see II.i.12–17). On Duncan and gift giving,

see Harry Berger, Jr., "The Early Scenes of *Macbeth:* Preface to a New Interpretation," *ELH* 47 (1980): 19–22.

4. See J. I. M. Stewart, *Character and Motive in Shakespeare* (London: Longmans, 1949), pp. 92–93; and Bernard McElroy, *Shakespeare's Mature Tragedies* (Princeton, N.J.: Princeton University Press, 1973), pp. 218–19.

5. See Keith Thomas, *Religion and the Decline of Magic* (New York: Scribners, 1971), p. 405.

6. See Sanders, *The Dramatist and the Received Idea,* pp. 280–81. See also Jean-Paul Sartre's remarks about "anguish in the face of the future" in *Being and Nothingness,* trans. Hazel Barnes (New York: Philosophical Library, 1956), pp. 29–32.

7. H. R. Trevor-Roper, *The European Witch-Craze of the Sixteenth and Seventeenth Centuries* (1967; Harmondsworth, England: Penguin Books, 1969), p. 7.

8. Trevor-Roper, *The European Witch-Craze,* p. 35; see also, pp. 52–53.

9. Alan Macfarlane, *Witchcraft in Tudor and Stuart England* (London: Routledge & Kegan Paul, 1970), pp. 196–97. See also Thomas, *Religion and the Decline of Magic,* pp. 535–69.

10. C. G. Jung, *Aion: Researches into the Phenomenology of the Self* [1951], in *The Collected Works of C. G. Jung,* ed. Sir Herbert Read, *et al.* (Princeton, N.J.: Princeton University Press, 1968), 9, part ii, pp. 9–10.

11. Charles Taylor, *Hegel* (Cambridge: Cambridge University Press, 1975), pp. 6, 7, 8.

12. Peter Ure, *Elizabethan and Jacobean Drama,* ed. J. C. Maxwell (Liverpool: Liverpool University Press; New York: Harper & Row, 1974), p. 54.

13. See Taylor, *Hegel,* pp. 9–10, 559–63.

14. Allardyce Nicoll, *Studies in Shakespeare* (London, 1927), p. 119, quoted by Sanders, *The Dramatist and the Received Idea,* p. 278.

15. See Matthew N. Proser, *The Heroic Image in Five Shakespearean Tragedies* (Princeton, N.J.: Princeton University Press, 1965), pp. 67–68.

16. Sartre, *Being and Nothingness,* pp. 49, 70.

17. See Michael Polanyi, *The Tacit Dimension* (Garden City, N.Y.: Doubleday, 1966), pp. 58–59; Lionel Trilling, *Sincerity and Authenticity* (Cambridge: Harvard University Press, 1972), p. 11; and Marjorie Grene, "Authenticity: An Existential Virtue" [1952], in *Philosophy In and Out of Europe* (Berkeley and Los Angeles: University of California Press, 1976), pp. 50–60.

18. Trilling, *Sincerity and Authenticity,* p. 131.

19. Sanders, *The Dramatist and the Received Idea,* p. 131.

20. A. C. Bradley, *Shakespearean Tragedy,* 2d ed. (London: Macmillan, 1905), pp. 382–87.

21. See Henry N. Paul, *The Royal Play of Macbeth* (New York: Macmillan, 1950), pp. 195–96.

22. Bradley, *Shakespearean Tragedy,* pp. 392, 393.

23. Some corruption of Macduff's grief might be evident in his later statement, uttered in the heat of battle, that seems to convert his patriotic motive to personal revenge: "If [Macbeth] be slain and with no stroke of mine, / My wife and children's ghosts will haunt me still" (V.vii.15–16). But, even here, he thinks of revenge more as an obligation to others than as an expression of merely personal hatred.

24. See Wilbur Sanders, "Macbeth: What's Done, Is Done," in Wilbur Sanders and Howard Jacobson, *Shakespeare's Magnanimity: Four Tragic Heroes, Their Friends and Families* (New York: Oxford University Press, 1978), pp. 78–94.

25. Mack, *Killing the King,* pp. 183, 184.

Conclusion

1. Francis Bacon, *The Advancement of Learning,* in *The Works of Francis Bacon,* 3:346.

2. Una Ellis-Fermor, *The Frontiers of Drama* (1945; London: Methuen, 1967), pp. 72, 73.

3. Jacques Derrida, "Structure, Sign and Play in the Discourse of the Human Sciences" [1966], rpt. in *Writing and Difference,* trans. Alan Bass (Chicago: University of Chicago Press, 1978), p. 292.

Works Cited

Abel, Lionel. *Metatheatre: A New View of Dramatic Form.* New York: Hill & Wang, 1963.

Abrams, Meyer H. *The Mirror and the Lamp.* New York: Oxford University Press, 1953.

Adams, John Cranford. *The Globe Playhouse: Its Design and Equipment.* Cambridge: Harvard University Press, 1942.

Adams, Joseph Quincey, ed. *The Magi, Herod, and the Slaughter of the Innocents.* In *Chief Pre-Shakespearean Dramas.* Boston: Houghton Mifflin, 1924.

Adelman, Janet. *The Common Liar: An Essay on* Antony and Cleopatra. New Haven: Yale University Press, 1973.

Allen, Don Cameron. *Image and Meaning: Metaphoric Traditions in Renaissance Poetry.* 2d ed. Baltimore: Johns Hopkins University Press, 1968.

Anchor, Robert. "History and Play: Johan Huizinga and His Critics." *History and Theory* 17 (1978): 63–93.

Arnheim, Rudolf. *The Dynamics of Architectural Form.* Berkeley and Los Angeles: University of California Press, 1977.

Arthos, John. "Shakespeare's Transformation of Plautus." *Comparative Drama* 1 (1967–68): 239–53.

Bachelard, Gaston. *The Poetics of Space.* Translated by Maria Jolas. Boston: Beacon Press, 1969.

Bacon, Francis. *The Works of Francis Bacon.* 14 vols. Edited by James Spedding, R. L. Ellis, and D. D. Heath. London: Longmans, 1870–74.

Barber, C. L. *Shakespeare's Festive Comedy: A Study of Dramatic Form and Its Relation to Social Custom.* Princeton: Princeton University Press, 1959.

171

Barish, Jonas A. "The Antitheatrical Prejudice." *Critical Quarterly* 8 (1966): 329–48.

———. "Exhibitionism and the Antitheatrical Prejudice." *ELH: A Journal of English Literary History* 36 (1969): 1–29.

———. "The Uniqueness of Elizabethan Drama." *Comparative Drama* 11 (1977): 103–12.

———. *The Antitheatrical Prejudice.* Berkeley and Los Angeles: University of California Press, 1981.

Barton, Anne. "The King Disguised: Shakespeare's *Henry V* and the Comical History." In *The Triple Bond: Plays, Mainly Shakespearean, in Performance,* edited by Joseph G. Price, pp. 92–117, 290–91. University Park: The Pennsylvania State University Press, 1975.

Bayley, John. *The Characters of Love: A Study in the Literature of Personality.* London: Constable, 1960.

Beckerman, Bernard. *Shakespeare at the Globe: 1599–1609.* New York: Macmillan, 1962.

Beckman, Margaret. "The Figure of Rosalind in *As You Like It.*" *Shakespeare Quarterly* 29 (1978): 44–51.

Bentley, Gerald Eades. *Shakespeare and His Theater.* Lincoln: University of Nebraska Press, 1964.

Berger, Harry, Jr. "A Secret Discipline: *The Faerie Queene,* Book VI." In *Form and Convention in the Poetry of Edmund Spenser,* edited by William Nelson, pp. 35–75, 171–74. Selected Papers from the English Institute. New York: Columbia University Press, 1961.

———. "The Ecology of the Mind." *The Review of Metaphysics* 17 (1963): 109–34.

———. "The Renaissance Imagination: Second World and Green World." *Centennial Review* 9 (1965): 36–78.

———. "*Troilus and Cressida:* The Observer as Basilisk." *Comparative Drama* 2 (1968): 122–36.

———. "Naive Consciousness and Culture Change: An Essay in Historical Structuralism." *Bulletin of the Midwest Modern Language Association* 6 (1973): 1–44.

———. "The Early Scenes of *Macbeth:* Preface to a New Interpretation." *ELH* 47 (1980): 1–31.

Bernheimer, Richard. "Theatrum Mundi." *The Art Bulletin* 38 (1956): 225–47.

Berry, Francis. "Shakespeare's Stage Geometry." *Deutsche Shakespeare-Gesellschaft West* (1974): 160–71.

————. *The Shakespeare Inset: Word and Picture*. London: Feffer & Simons; Carbondale: Southern Illinois University Press, 1965.

Bethell, Samuel L. *Shakespeare and the Popular Dramatic Tradition*. London: Staples Press, 1944.

Bevington, David. *From* Mankind *to* Marlowe: *Growth of Structure in the Popular Drama of Tudor England*. Cambridge: Harvard University Press, 1962.

Bloomer, Kent C., and Charles W. Moore, *Body, Memory, and Architecture*. New Haven: Yale University Press, 1977.

Blundeville, Thomas. *M. Blundevile His Exercises, containing sixe Treatises*. London, 1594.

Booth, Stephen. "On the Value of *Hamlet*." In *Reinterpretations of Elizabethan Drama*, edited by Norman Rabkin, pp. 137–76. New York: Columbia University Press, 1969.

Bradbrook, Muriel C. *Themes and Conventions of Elizabethan Tragedy*. Cambridge: Cambridge University Press, 1935.

————. *The Rise of the Common Player: A Study of Actor and Society in Shakespeare's England*. Cambridge: Harvard University Press, 1962.

Bradley, A. C. *Shakespearean Tragedy*. 2d ed. London: Macmillan, 1905.

Braudel, Fernand. *Capitalism and Material Life: 1400–1800*. Translated by Miriam Kochan. New York: Harper & Row, 1974.

Brooke, C. F. Tucker, ed. *Edward III*. In *The Shakespeare Apocrypha*. Oxford: Clarendon Press, 1908.

Brown, John Russell. *Shakespeare and His Comedies*. 2d ed., rev. London: Methuen, 1962.

————. "The Theatrical Element of Shakespeare Criticism." In *Reinterpretations of Elizabethan Drama*, edited by Norman Rabkin, pp. 177–95. New York: Columbia University Press, 1969.

Browne, Sir Thomas. *Selected Writings*. Edited by Sir Geoffrey Keynes. London: Faber & Faber; Chicago: University of Chicago Press, 1968.

Burckhardt, Sigurd. *Shakespearean Meanings*. Princeton: Princeton University Press, 1968.

Burrows, David. "Interiors: Ritual, Art, and Games in the Field of Symbolic Action." *Centennial Review* 15 (1971): 330–46.

Calderwood, James L. *Shakespearean Metadrama*. Minneapolis: University of Minnesota Press, 1971.

Cassirer, Ernst. *The Individual and the Cosmos in Renaissance Philosophy.* Translated by Mario Domandi. Oxford: Basil Blackwell, 1963.

Cavell, Stanley. *Must We Mean What We Say?* New York: Scribners; Cambridge: Cambridge University Press, 1969.

Cawley, A. C., ed. *Everyman.* Manchester: Manchester University Press, 1961.

Chambers, E. K. *The Elizabethan Stage.* 4 vols. Oxford: Clarendon Press, 1923.

———. *William Shakespeare.* 2 vols. Oxford: Clarendon Press, 1930.

Cirillo, Albert R. "Guilio Camillo's *Idea of the Theater:* The Enigma of the Renaissance." *Comparative Drama* 1 (1967): 19–27.

———. "*As You Like It:* Pastoralism Gone Awry." ELH 38 (1971): 19–39.

Clement, Francis. *The Petie Schole with an English Orthographie.* London, 1587.

Cole, David. *The Theatrical Event.* Middletown: Wesleyan University Press, 1975.

Collins, Fletcher. "The Relation of Tudor Halls to Elizabethan Public Theaters." *Philological Quarterly* 10 (1931): 313–16.

Cook, Albert. *Shakespeare's Enactment: The Dynamics of Renaissance Theatre.* Chicago: Swallow Press, 1976.

Cook, Ann Jennalie. *The Privileged Playgoers of Shakespeare's London, 1576–1642.* Princeton: Princeton University Press, 1981.

Cope, Jackson I. *The Theater and the Dream: From Metaphor to Form in Renaissance Drama.* Baltimore: Johns Hopkins University Press, 1973.

Davis, Walter R. *Idea and Act in Elizabethan Fiction.* Princeton: Princeton University Press, 1969.

Dekker, Thomas. *The Guls Horne Booke.* [1609.] Facsimile ed. Menston, England: The Scolar Press, 1969.

Derrida, Jacques. *Writing and Difference.* Translated by Alan Bass. Chicago: University of Chicago Press, 1978. Originally published as *L'écriture et la différence.* Paris: Editions du Seuil, 1967.

Donne, John. *John Donne: The Elegies and The Songs and Sonnets.* Edited by Helen Gardner. Oxford: Clarendon Press: 1965.

Doran, Madeleine. *Endeavors of Art: A Study of Form in Elizabethan Drama.* Madison: University of Wisconsin Press, 1954.

Egan, Robert. "A Muse of Fire: *Henry V* in the Light of *Tamburlaine.*" *Modern Language Quarterly* 29 (1968): 15–28.

Ehrmann, Jacques. "Homo Ludens revisited." In *Games, Play, Literature,* edited by Jacques Ehrmann. *Yale French Studies* 41 (1968): 31–57.

Ellis-Fermor, Una. *The Frontiers of Drama.* 1945. Reprint. London: Methuen, 1967.

Empson, William. "*Hamlet* When New." *Sewanee Review* 61 (1953): 15–42, 185–205.

Felperin, Howard. Review of *The Theater and the Dream,* by Jackson Cope. *Modern Philology* 74 (1976–77): 94–97.

———. *Shakespearean Representation: Mimesis and Modernity in Elizabethan Tragedy.* Princeton: Princeton University Press, 1977.

Fly, Richard. *Shakespeare's Mediated World.* Amherst: University of Massachusetts Press, 1976.

Frost, Robert. *Complete Poems of Robert Frost.* New York: Holt, Rinehart and Winston, 1949.

Frye, Northrop. "The Argument of Comedy." In *English Institute Essays, 1948,* edited by D. A. Robertson, Jr., pp. 58–73. New York: Columbia University Press, 1949.

———. *A Natural Perspective: The Development of Shakespearean Comedy and Romance.* New York: Columbia University Press, 1965.

Gardner, Helen. "*As You Like It.*" In *More Talking of Shakespeare,* edited by John Garrett, pp. 17–32. London: Longmans; New York: Theatre Arts Books, 1959.

Giamatti, A. Bartlett. "Proteus Unbound: Some Versions of the Sea God in the Renaissance." In *The Disciplines of Criticism,* edited by Peter Demetz, Thomas Greene, and Lowry Nelson, Jr., pp. 437–75. New Haven: Yale University Press, 1968.

Goddard, Harold C. *The Meaning of Shakespeare.* Chicago: University of Chicago Press, 1951.

Goldman, Michael. *Shakespeare and the Energies of Drama.* Princeton: Princeton University Press, 1972.

Gombrich, Ernst H. *Art and Illusion.* 2d ed., rev. New York: Pantheon, 1961.

Gosson, Stephen. *The Schoole of Abuse.* [1579]. In *Markets of Bawdrie: The Dramatic Criticism of Stephen Gosson,* edited by Arthur F. Kinney, pp. 69–120. Salzburg Studies in English Literature, No. 4. Salzburg: Institut fur Englische Sprache und Literatur, 1974.

———. *Plays Confuted in fiue Actions.* [1582]. In *Markets of Bawdrie: The Dramatic Criticism of Stephen Gosson,* edited by Arthur F. Kinney, pp. 138–200. Salzburg Studies in English Literature, No. 4. Salzburg: Institut fur Englische Sprache und Literatur, 1974.

Greene, Robert. *Greenes Groats-worth of Wit.* London, 1592.

Greene, Thomas. "The Flexibility of the Self in Renaissance Literature." In *The Disciplines of Criticism,* edited by Peter Demetz, Thomas Greene, and Lowry Nelson, Jr., pp. 241–64. New Haven: Yale University Press, 1968.

Greg, Walter W., ed. *Henslowe's Diary.* 2 vols. London: A. H. Bullen, 1908.

Grene, Marjorie. *Philosophy In and Out of Europe.* Berkeley and Los Angeles: University of California Press, 1976.

Habicht, Werner. "Tree Properties and Tree Scenes in Elizabethan Theater." *Renaissance Drama,* n.s., 4 (1971): 69–92.

Harbage, Alfred. *Shakespeare's Audience.* New York: Columbia University Press, 1941.

Hartman, Geoffrey. *Beyond Formalism. Literary Essays: 1958–1970.* New Haven: Yale University Press, 1970.

Harvey, Gabriel, and Edmund Spenser. *Two Other, very commendable Letters of the same mens writing,* printed with *Three Proper, and wittie, familiar Letters.* 1580. Reprint. In *Elizabethan Critical Essays,* edited by G. Gregory Smith, 1:87–126. Oxford: Oxford University Press, 1904.

Hawkins, Harriett Bloker. "'All the World's a Stage': Some Illustrations of the *Theatrum Mundi.*" *Shakespeare Quarterly* 17 (1966): 174–78.

Hawkins, Sherman. "The Two Worlds of Shakespearean Comedy." *Shakespeare Studies* 3 (1967): 62–80.

Hegel, George W. F. *Hegel's Logic, being Part One of the Encyclopaedia.* 1st ed., 1873. Translated by William Wallace. Oxford: Clarendon Press, 1975.

Herz, Judith Scherer. "Play World and Real World: Dramatic Illusion and the Dream Metaphor." *English Studies in Canada* 3 (1977): 386–400.

Heywood, Thomas. *An Apology for Actors.* Facsimile ed., prepared by Richard H. Perkinson. 1612. New York: Scholars' Facsimiles and Reprints, 1941.

Hieatt, Charles W. "The Quality of Pastoral in *As You Like It.*" *Genre* 7 (1974): 164–82.

Hodges, C. Walter. *The Globe Restored: A Study of the Elizabethan Theatre.* 2d ed. New York: Coward-McCann, 1968.

Hood, Thomas. *The Vse of Both the Globes Celestiall and Terrestriall.* London, 1594.

Hosley, Richard. "The Origins of the Shakespearean Playhouse." *Shakespeare Quarterly* 15, no. 2 (Spring 1964): 29–39.

———. "The Playhouses." In *The Revels History of Drama in English.* Edited by Clifford Leech and T. W. Craik. Vol. 3, *1576–1613,* edited by J. Leeds Barroll, Alexander Leggatt, Richard Hosley, and Alvin B. Kernan, pp. 119–235. London: Methuen, 1975.

———. ed. *Shakespeare's Holinshed.* New York: Capricorn Books, 1968.

Hotson, Leslie. *Shakespeare's Sonnets Dated and Other Essays.* New York: Oxford University Press, 1949.

Howarth, Herbert. *The Tiger's Heart.* New York: Oxford University Press, 1970.

Hues, Robert. *Tractatus de Globis.* 1594. Reprint. London: The Hakluyt Society, 1889.

Huizinga, Johan. *Homo Ludens: A Study of the Play-Element in Culture.* Boston: Beacon Press, 1964.

Hunter, George K. *John Lyly: The Humanist as Courtier.* Cambridge: Harvard University Press, 1962.

Jackson, MacD. P. "'Edward III,' Shakespeare, and Pembroke's Men." *Notes and Queries,* n.s. 12 (1965): 329–31.

Jensen, Ejner J. "A New Allusion to the Sign of the Globe Theater." *Shakespeare Quarterly* 21 (1970): 95–97.

Jones, Emrys. *The Origins of Shakespeare.* Oxford: Clarendon Press, 1977.

Jones, G. P. "'Henry V': The Chorus and the Audience." *Shakespeare Survey* 31 (1978): 93–104.

Joseph, Bertram. *Acting Shakespeare.* 1960. Reprint. New York: Theatre Arts Books, 1969.

Jung, Carl Gustav. *The Collected Works of C. G. Jung.* 20 vols. Edited by Sir Herbert Read, Michael Fordham, and Gerhard Holden. London: Routledge & Kegan Paul; Princeton: Princeton University Press, 1953–79.

Kelly, Thomas. "Shakespeare's Romantic Heroes: Orlando Reconsidered." *Shakespeare Quarterly* 24 (1973): 12–24.

Kernan, Alvin B. "This Goodly Frame, The Stage: The Interior Theater of Imagination in English Renaissance Drama." *Shakespeare Quarterly* 25 (1974): 1–5.

———. "From Ritual to History: The English History Play." In *The Revels History of Drama in English.* Edited by Clifford Leech and

T. W. Craik. Vol. 3, *1576–1613*, edited by J. Leeds Barroll, Alexander Leggatt, Richard Hosley, and Alvin B. Kernan, pp. 262–99. London: Methuen, 1975.

Keyssar, Helene. "I Love You. Who Are You? The Strategy of Drama in Recognition Scenes." *Publications of the Modern Language Association of America* 92 (1977): 297–306.

Kristeller, Paul Oskar. *Renaissance Thought II: Papers on Humanism and the Arts.* New York: Harper & Row, 1965.

Lamb, Charles. *Works.* Edited by E. V. Lucas. London: Methuen, 1905.

Law, Robert Adger. "The Choruses in *Henry the Fifth.*" *University of Texas Studies in English* 35 (1956): 11–21.

Levin, Richard. *The Multiple Plot in English Renaissance Drama.* Chicago: University of Chicago Press, 1971.

Lewis, C. S. *English Literature in the Sixteenth Century, Excluding Drama.* Vol. 3 of *Oxford History of English Literature.* Oxford: Clarendon Press, 1954.

Lodge, Thomas. *Rosalynde.* 1590. Reprint. In *Narrative and Dramatic Sources of Shakespeare,* 8 vols., edited by Geoffrey Bullough, 2:158–266. New York: Columbia University Press; London: Routledge & Kegan Paul, 1957–75.

McElroy, Bernard. *Shakespeare's Mature Tragedies.* Princeton: Princeton University Press, 1973.

Macfarlane, Alan. *Witchcraft in Tudor and Stuart England.* London: Routledge & Kegan Paul, 1970.

Mack, Maynard. "The Jacobean Shakespeare: Some Observations on the Construction of the Tragedies." In *Jacobean Theatre,* edited by John Russell Brown and Bernard Harris, pp. 11–41. Stratford-upon-Avon Studies, No. 1. London: Arnold, 1960.

———. "Engagement and Detachment in Shakespeare's Plays." In *Essays on Shakespeare and Elizabethan Drama in Honor of Hardin Craig,* edited by Richard Hosley, pp. 275–96. Columbia: University of Missouri Press, 1962.

Mack, Maynard, Jr. *Killing the King: Three Studies in Shakespeare's Tragic Structure.* New Haven: Yale University Press, 1973.

Magagnato, Licisco. "The Genesis of the Teatro Olimpico." *Journal of the Warburg and Courtauld Institutes* 14 (1951): 209–20.

Marvell, Andrew. *Complete Poetry.* Edited by George deF. Lord. New York: Random House, 1968.

Mauss, Marcel. *The Gift: Forms and Functions of Exchange in Archaic Societies.* 1925. Translated by Ian Cunnison. New York: Norton, 1967.

Mercator, Gerardus. *Atlas sive cosmographicae meditationes de fabrica mundi et fabricati figura.* 1595. 2 vols. Facsimile ed. Translated by Henry Hexam. Amsterdam: Henry Hondius and Iohn Iohnson, 1636; Brussels: Culture and Civilization, 1963.

Montaigne, Michel de. *Selected Essays of Montaigne in the Translation of John Florio.* Edited by Walter Kaiser. Boston: Houghton Mifflin, 1964.

Muir, Kenneth. *Shakespeare as Collaborator.* London: Methuen, 1960.

Mullin, Donald C. "An Observation on the Origin of the Elizabethan Theatre." *Educational Theatre Journal* 19 (1967): 322–26.

Muris, Oswald, and Gert Saarmann. *Der Globus im Wandel der Zeiten: Eine Geschichte der Globen.* Berlin: Columbus Verlag Paul Oestergaard, 1961.

Nashe, Thomas. *The Works of Thomas Nashe.* 5 vols. Edited by Ronald B. McKerrow with corrections by F. P. Wilson. Oxford: Basil Blackwell, 1958.

Nicoll, Allardyce. *Studies in Shakespeare.* London: L. & V. Woolf, at the Hogarth Press, 1931.

Norberg-Schulz, Christian. *Existence, Space and Architecture.* New York: Praeger, 1971.

Ong, Walter J. *The Presence of the Word.* New Haven: Yale University Press, 1967.

———. *Interfaces of the Word.* Ithaca: Cornell University Press, 1977.

Orrell, John. *The Quest for Shakespeare's Globe.* Cambridge: Cambridge University Press, 1983.

Ortega y Gasset, José. "The Self and the Other." In *The Dehumanization of Art and Other Writings on Art and Culture.* Translated by Willard R. Trask. Garden City, N.Y.: 1956.

Ortelius, Abraham. *The Theatre of the Whole World.* 1606. Reprint. Amsterdam: Theatrum Orbis Terrarum; Chicago: Rand McNally, 1968.

Ovidius Naso, Publius. *Metamorphoses.* 2 vols. 3d ed., rev. Edited and translated by Frank Justus Miller. Loeb Classical Library. Cambridge: Harvard University Press; London: Heinemann, 1977.

Palmer, D. J. "Art and Nature in *As You Like It.*" *Philological Quarterly* 49 (1970): 30–40.

Panofsky, Erwin. "Artist, Scientist, Genius: Notes on the 'Renaissance—Dämmerung.'" In *The Renaissance: Six Essays,* pp. 121–82. New York: Harper & Row, 1962.

Paul, Henry N. *The Royal Play of* Macbeth. New York: Macmillan, 1950.

Pico della Mirandola, Giovanni. "Oration on the Dignity of Man." Translated by Elizabeth Livermore Forbes. In *The Renaissance Philosophy of Man,* edited by Ernst Cassirer, Paul Oskar Kristeller, and John Herman Randall, Jr., pp. 223–54. Chicago: University of Chicago Press, 1948.

Plautus. *Menaechmi.* Translated by William Warner. 1595. Reprint. In *Narrative and Dramatic Sources of Shakespeare,* 8 vols., edited by Geoffrey Bullough, 1:12–39. New York: Columbia University Press; London: Routledge & Kegan Paul, 1957–75.

Polanyi, Michael. *The Tacit Dimension.* Garden City, N.Y.: Doubleday, 1966.

Poulet, Georges. *The Metamorphosis of the Circle.* Translated by Carley Dawson and Elliott Coleman. Baltimore: Johns Hopkins University Press, 1966.

Proser, Matthew N. *The Heroic Image in Five Shakespearean Tragedies.* Princeton: Princeton University Press, 1965.

Prouty, Charles T. "An Early Elizabethan Playhouse." *Shakespeare Survey* 6 (1953): 64–74.

Puttenham, George. *The Arte of English Poesie.* [1582]. Edited by Gladys Doidge Willcock and Alice Walker. Cambridge: Cambridge University Press, 1936.

Rabkin, Norman. *Shakespeare and the Common Understanding.* New York: The Free Press; London: Collier-Macmillan, 1967.

———. *Shakespeare and the Problem of Meaning.* Chicago: University of Chicago Press, 1981.

Rackin, Phyllis. "Shakespeare's Boy Cleopatra, the Decorum of Nature, and the Golden World of Poetry." *Publications of the Modern Language Association of America* 87 (1972): 201–12.

Ralegh, Sir Walter. *The History of the World.* Edited by C. A. Patrides. Philadelphia: Temple University Press, 1971.

Reynolds, George F. "'Trees' on the Stage of Shakespeare." *Modern Philology* 5 (1907): 153–68.

———. *The Staging of Elizabethan Plays at the Red Bull Theater, 1605–1625.* New York: Modern Language Association, 1940.

Richards, I.A. *The Philosophy of Rhetoric.* 1936. Reprint. New York: Oxford University Press, 1965.

Ricoeur, Paul. *The Rule of Metaphor.* Translated by Robert Czerny. Toronto: University of Toronto Press, 1977.

———. "The Metaphoric Process as Cognition, Imagination, and Feeling." *Critical Inquiry* 5 (1978–79): 143–59.

Riggs, David. *Shakespeare's Heroical Histories:* Henry VI *and Its Literary Tradition.* Cambridge: Harvard University Press, 1971.

Righter, Anne. *Shakespeare and the Idea of the Play.* London: Chatto & Windus; New York: Barnes & Noble, 1962.

Ringler, William. "The First Phase of the Elizabethan Attack on the Stage, 1558–1579." *Huntington Library Quarterly* 5 (1942): 391–418.

———. *Stephen Gosson: A Biographical and Critical Study.* Princeton: Princeton University Press, 1942.

Rosskey, William. "Imagination in the English Renaissance: Psychology and Poetic." *Studies in the Renaisasnce* 5 (1958): 49–73.

Sanders, Wilbur. *The Dramatist and the Received Idea: Studies in the Plays of Marlowe and Shakespeare.* Cambridge: Cambridge University Press, 1968.

———. "Macbeth: What's Done, Is Done." In *Shakespeare's Magnanimity: Four Tragic Heroes, Their Friends and Families,* edited by Wilbur Sanders and Howard Jacobson, pp. 78–94. New York: Oxford University Press, 1978.

Sartre, Jean-Paul. *Being and Nothingness.* Translated by Hazel Barnes. New York: Philosophical Library, 1956.

Schanzer, Ernest. "Hercules and His Load." *Review of English Studies,* n.s., 19 (1968): 51–53.

Sennett, Richard. *The Fall of Public Man.* New York: Alfred A. Knopf, 1977.

Shakespeare, William. *Mr. William Shakespeares Comedies Histories, & Tragedies.* 1623. *The Norton Facsimile: The First Folio of Shakespeare.* Edited by Charlton Hinman. New York: Norton, 1968.

———. *The Comedy of Errors.* Edited by R. A. Foakes. The New Arden Shakespeare. London: Methuen; Cambridge: Harvard University Press, 1962.

———. *The Complete Works.* General Editor Alfred Harbage. Baltimore: Penguin Books, 1969.

Sidney, Sir Philip. *An Apologie for Poetrie.* In *Elizabethan Critical Essays,* 2 vols., edited by G. Gregory Smith, 1:150–207. London: Oxford University Prses, 1904.

Smith, Hal H. "Some Principles of Elizabethan Stage Costume." *Journal of the Warburg and Courtauld Institutes* 25 (1962): 240–57.

Smith, Warren D. "The *Henry V* Choruses in the First Folio." *Journal of English and Germanic Philology* 53 (1954): 38–57.

Soellner, Rolf. *Shakespeare's Patterns of Self-Knowledge.* Columbus: Ohio State University Press, 1972.

Southern, Richard. "The Contribution of the Interludes to Elizabethan Staging." In *Essays on Shakespeare and Elizabethan Drama in Honor of Hardin Craig,* edited by Richard Hosley, pp. 3–14. Columbia: University of Missouri Press, 1962.

Spenser, Edmund. *The Poetical Works of Edmund Spenser.* Edited by J. C. Smith and E. de Selincourt. London: Oxford University Press, 1912.

Spivack, Charlotte. "The Elizabethan Theatre: Circle and Center." *Centennial Review* 13 (1969): 424–43.

Stanislavski, Konstantin. *Stanislavsky on the Art of the Stage.* Edited and translated by David Magarshack. New York: Hill & Wang, 1961.

Stevenson, Edward Luther. *Terrestrial and Celestial Globes: Their History and Construction.* 2 vols. New Haven: Yale University Press, 1921.

Stewart, J. I. M. *Character and Motive in Shakespeare.* London: Longmans, 1949.

Stokes, Gale. "Cognition and the Function of Nationalism." *Journal of Interdisciplinary History* 4 (1973–74): 525–42.

Stroup, Thomas. *Microcosmos: The Shape of the Elizabethan Play.* Lexington: University of Kentucky Press, 1965.

Taylor, Charles. *Hegel.* Cambridge: Cambridge University Press, 1975.

Thomas, Keith. *Religion and the Decline of Magic.* New York: Scribners, 1971.

Tigerstedt, E. N. "The Poet as Creator: Origins of a Metaphor." *Comparative Literature Studies* 5 (1968): 455–88.

Toynbee, Arnold. *A Study of History.* 2 vols., abridged ed. Edited by D. C. Somervell. 1946, 1957. Reprint. New York: Dell, 1965.

Trevor-Roper, H. R. *The European Witch-Craze of the Sixteenth and Seventeenth Centuries.* 1967. Reprint. Harmondsworth: Penguin Books, 1969.

Trilling, Lionel. *Sincerity and Authenticity.* Cambridge: Harvard University Press, 1972.

Ure, Peter. "Character and Role from *Richard III* to *Hamlet.*" 1963. In

Elizabethan and Jacobean Drama: Critical Essays by Peter Ure; edited by J. C. Maxwell, pp. 22–43. Liverpool: Liverpool University Press; New York: Harper & Row, 1974.

Van Laan, Thomas F. *Role Playing in Shakespeare.* Toronto: University of Toronto Press, 1978.

Venturi, Robert. *Complexity and Contradiction in Architecture.* 2d ed. New York: The Museum of Modern Art, 1977.

Vives, Juan Luis. *A Fable About Man.* Translated by Nancy Lenkeith. In *The Renaissance Philosophy of Man,* edited by Ernst Cassirer, Paul Oskar Kristeller, and John Herman Randall, Jr., pp. 87–93. Chicago: University of Chicago Press, 1948.

Waith, Eugene M. *Ideas of Greatness: Heroic Drama in England.* New York: Barnes & Noble, 1971.

Walzer, Michael. *The Revolution of the Saints: A Study in the Origins of Radical Politics.* Cambridge: Harvard University Press, 1965.

Webber, Joan. "The Renewal of the King's Symbolic Role: From *Richard III* to *Henry V.*" *Texas Studies in Language and Literature* 4 (1962–63): 530–38.

Weimann, Robert. *Shakespeare and the Popular Tradition in the Theater.* Translated by Robert Schwartz. Baltimore: Johns Hopkins University Press, 1978.

Wentersdorf, Karl P. "The Date of *Edward III.*" *Shakespeare Quarterly* 16 (1965): 227–31.

———. "The Conspiracy of Silence in *Henry V.*" *Shakespeare Quarterly* 18 (1976): 264–87.

Whitney, Geffrey. *A Choice of Emblems.* 1866 ed. Reprint. Edited by Henry Green. New York: Benjamin Blom, 1967.

Wickham, Glynne. *Early English Stages, 1300 to 1660.* 3 vols. London: Routledge & Kegan Paul; New York: Columbia University Press, 1959–.

———. *Shakespeare's Dramatic Heritage.* New York: Barnes & Noble, 1969.

Wimsatt, William K. *The Verbal Icon: Studies in the Meaning of Poetry.* Lexington: University of Kentucky Press, 1954.

———. *Day of the Leopards: Essays in Defense of Poems.* New Haven: Yale University Press, 1976.

———, ed. *Samuel Johnson on Shakespeare.* New York: Hill & Wang, 1960.

Wittkower, Rudolf. *Architectural Principles in the Age of Humanism.* New York: Random House, 1965.

Wordsworth, William. *The Prelude*. 2d ed., rev. Edited by Ernest de Selincourt. Oxford: Clarendon Press, 1959.

Yates, Frances A. *Theatre of the World*. Chicago: University of Chicago Press, 1969.

Young, David P. *Something of Great Constancy: The Art of "A Midsummer Night's Dream."* New Haven: Yale University Press, 1966.

———. *The Heart's Forest: A Study of Shakespeare's Pastoral Plays*. New Haven: Yale University Press, 1972.

Index